A HISTORICAL GUIDE TO ROMAN YORK

In the earliest records of English History, Ebor, Eboracum or York, is represented as a place of great importance; and, in the zenith of meridian splendour, it was the residence of Imperial Power, and the legislative seat of the Roman Empire. Hence we may readily suppose, especially when the ancient historic accounts of this city are contrasted with those of London, that York far exceeded in dignity and consequence, if not in population and extent, the present capital of the British Empire, at that period.

William Hargrove, *History of York*, 1818

To the memory of Frank Norman (1913–2000), my classics professor at the University of Hull 1973–1976

A HISTORICAL GUIDE TO ROMAN YORK

PAUL CHRYSTAL

PEN & SWORD
HISTORY
AN IMPRINT OF PEN & SWORD BOOKS LTD.
YORKSHIRE - PHILADELPHIA

First published in Great Britain in 2021 by
PEN AND SWORD HISTORY
An imprint of
Pen & Sword Books Ltd
Yorkshire – Philadelphia

ISBN 978 1 52678 128 4

A CIP catalogue record for this book is available from the British Library.

Typeset in Times New Roman 11.5/14 by
SJmagic DESIGN SERVICES, India.
Printed and bound by CPI Group (UK) Ltd, Croydon, CR0 4YY

Pen & Sword Books Limited incorporates the imprints of Atlas, Archaeology,
Aviation, Discovery, Family History, Fiction, History, Maritime, Military, Military
Classics, Politics, Select, Transport, True Crime, Air World, Frontline Publishing,
Leo Cooper, Remember When, Seaforth Publishing, The Praetorian Press,
Wharncliffe Local History, Wharncliffe Transport, Wharncliffe True Crime and
White Owl.

For a complete list of Pen & Sword titles please contact
PEN & SWORD BOOKS LIMITED
47 Church Street, Barnsley, South Yorkshire, S70 2AS, England
E-mail: enquiries@pen-and-sword.co.uk
Website: www.pen-and-sword.co.uk

Or
PEN AND SWORD BOOKS
1950 Lawrence Rd, Havertown, PA 19083, USA
E-mail: Uspen-and-sword@casematepublishers.com
Website: www.penandswordbooks.com

Contents

Acknowledgements

No book is the work of one man or woman. This one certainly is not. Thanks are due to a number of people and associations who have helped me make this book a lot better than it would have been without their generous interventions. They are, in no particular order: Martin Drake for map 001; York Archaeological Trust for the photos relating to the 'Headless gladiators' excavations; Richard Saward, Head of Visitor Experience and Commercial and Andrew Woods, Senior Curator (Yorkshire Museum) at the Yorkshire Museum in York, as well as Rebecca Vickers who painstakingly sourced all the photos for us; Geoff Cook, Rheolwr Cynadleddau a Digwyddiadau (Conference and Events Manager), Neuadd Y Ddinas (City Hall) Caerdydd (Cardiff) for the image of the wonderful statue of Boudica; The Schiller Inc, Washington DC, for the Thomas Cole *Destruction* image; Professor Paul Readman, Department of History, King's College London for permission to use material from the Historic Pageants website relating to the York Pageant: www.historicalpageants.ac.uk/pageants/.

As always we have tried our hardest to obtain permission for anything which is or may be in copyright; if anything has slipped through the net please accept our apologies and do advise us so that we can ensure that due credit is given in any reprint or new edition.

About the Author

Paul Chrystal was educated at the universities of Hull and Southampton where he took degrees in Classics. For the past thirty-five years he has worked in medical publishing, much of the time as an international sales director for one market or another while latterly creating medical educational programmes for the pharmaceutical industry.

He has since been history advisor to local visitor attractions such as the National Trust in York and 'York's Chocolate Story', writing features for national newspapers, and broadcasting on BBC Radio York, BBC Radio Manchester, BBC Radio Tees, on the Radio 4 PM programme and on the BBC World Service.

He is a contributor to a number of newspapers, history and archaeology magazines and the author of over 120 books published since 2010 on a wide range of subjects including classical social and military history, pandemics and epidemics, social histories of chocolate, coffee, sweets and tea, the British Army of the Rhine, the 'Troubles', transport and local history of many towns and cities in Yorkshire, Durham and Greater Manchester.

He is a regular reviewer for and contributor to 'Classics for All', editorial advisor for Yale University Press and a contributor to the classics section of 'Bibliographies Online' published by Oxford University Press.

In 2020, he took over the history editorship of the *Yorkshire Archaeological Journal*, the journal of the Yorkshire Archaeological Society. In 2019, he was guest speaker for Vassar College New York's London Programme in association with Goldsmith University. In 2021 he assisted in the research for an episode of the BBC's *Who Do You Think You Are?*

paul.chrystal@btinternet.com
www.paulchrystal.com

By the same author

The History of the World in 100 Pandemics, Epidemics, Plagues & Poxes: from the Plague of Athens to COVID-19 (in press 2021*)*
Women at War in the Ancient World (2020)
War in Greek Myth (2020)
War in Roman Myth and Legend (2020)
The Romans in the North of England (2019)
Republic into Empire: the 1st Century BCE Civil Wars in Ancient Rome (2019)
Wars and Battles of Ancient Greece (2018)
Emperors of Rome: The Monsters – from Tiberius to Elagabalus (2018)
Roman Record Keeping & Communications (2018)
How to be a Roman: A Day in the Life of a Roman Family (2017)
Women in Ancient Greece: Seclusion, Exclusion, or Illusion? (2017)
When in Rome: A Social History of Rome (2017)
In Bed with the Ancient Greeks (2016)
Roman Military Disasters (2016)
The Ancient Greeks in 100 Facts (2016)
Wars and Battles of the Roman Republic (2015)
In Bed with the Romans (2015)
Roman Women: The Women Who Influenced Roman History (2015)
Women in Ancient Rome (2015)

Maps

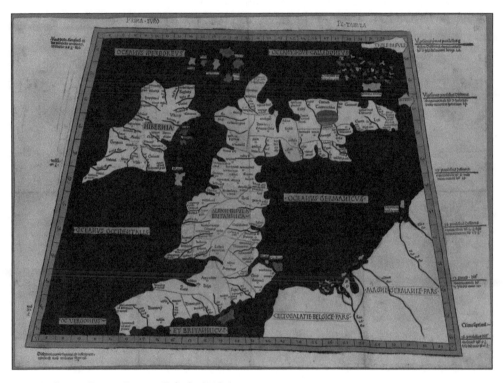

Ptolemy: *Prima Europe Tabula* (1486)
One of the earliest surviving copies of Ptolemy's second-century map of the British
Isles. Originally published in Ptolemy's *Geographia*. This is the second issue of the
1482 map, printed at Ulm, which was the first woodcut map of the British Isles and
the first to be printed outside Italy. (*National Library of Wales*)

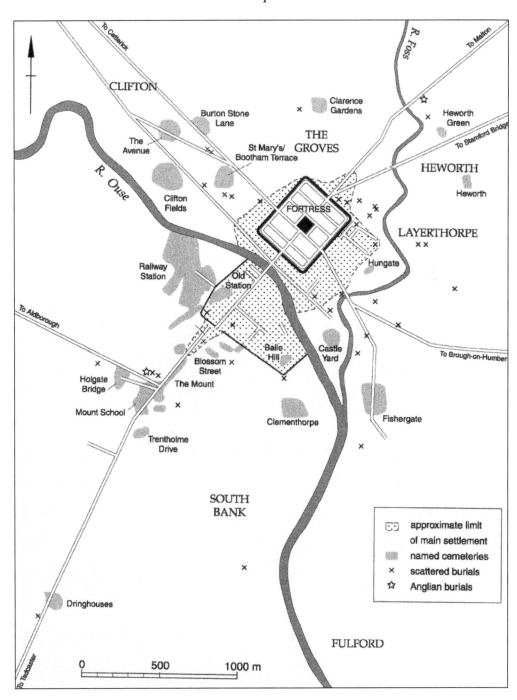

Roman York

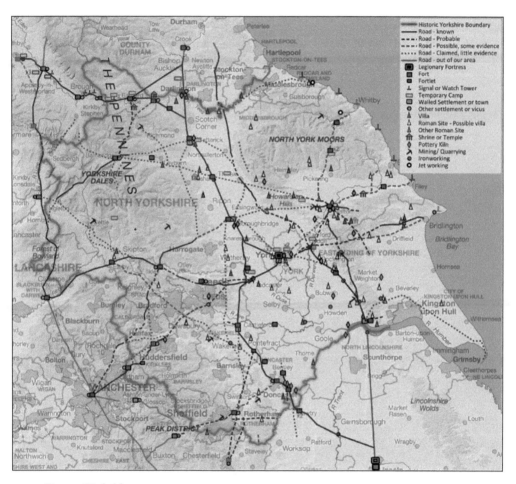

Roman Yorkshire

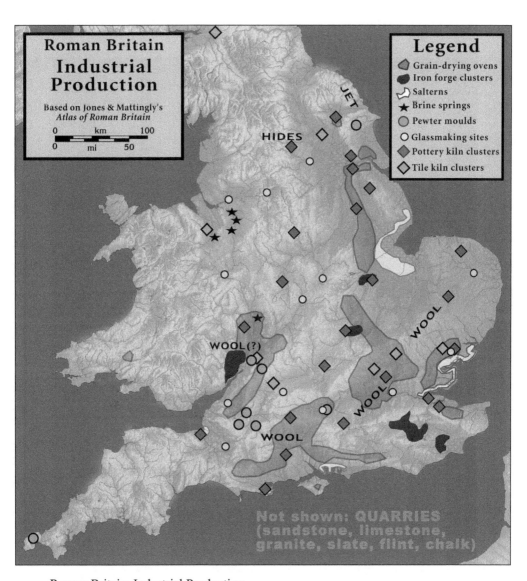

Roman Britain: Industrial Production

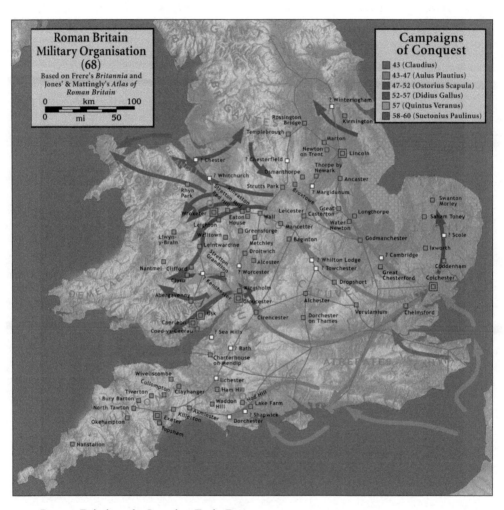

**Roman Britain
Military Organisation
(68)**

Based on Frere's *Britannia* and
Jones' & Mattingly's *Atlas of
Roman Britain*

0   km   100
0   mi   50

**Campaigns
of Conquest**

43 (Claudius)
43-47 (Aulus Plautius)
47-52 (Ostorius Scapula)
52-57 (Didius Gallus)
57 (Quintus Veranus)
58-60 (Suetonius Paulinus)

Roman Britain – the Invasion Early Days

xiv

Roman Britain: the Military Situation in the North

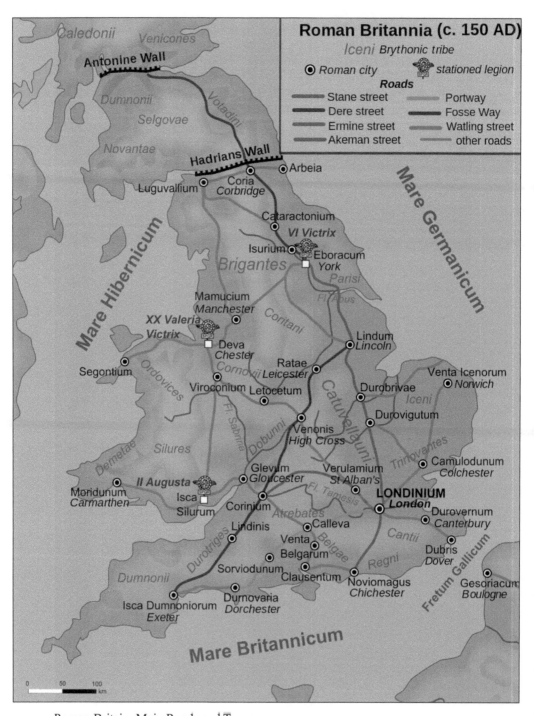

Roman Britannia (c. 150 AD)

Iceni Brythonic tribe

◉ Roman city   🛡 stationed legion

Roads

Stane street			Portway
Dere street			Fosse Way
Ermine street			Watling street
Akeman street			other roads

Caledonii   *Venicones*

Antonine Wall

Dumnonii

Selgovae

Novantae

Votadini

Hadrians Wall

◉ Arbeia

Luguvallium

Coria
Corbridge

Mare Germanicum

Cataractonium

VI Victrix

Isurium ◉   Eboracum
York

Brigantes

Parisi

Fl. Abus

Mamucium
Manchester

Coritani

Mare Hibernicum

XX Valeria
Victrix

Deva
Chester

Ordovices

Segontium

Cornovii

Ratae
Leicester

Lindum
Lincoln

Venta Icenorum
◉ Norwich

Viroconium   Letocetum

Durobrivae

Iceni

Durovigutum

Fl. Sabrina

Dobunni

Venonis
High Cross

Catuvellauni

Trinovantes

Demetae   *Silures*

II Augusta

Isca
Silurum

Glevum
Gloucester

Verulamium
St Alban's

Camulodunum
Colchester

Moridunum
Carmarthen

Corinium

Calleva

LONDINIUM
London

Fl. Tamesis

Atrebates

Durovernum
Canterbury

Lindinis

Venta
Belgarum

Belgae

Cantii

Dubris
Dover

Durotriges

Sorviodunum

Clausentum

Noviomagus
Chichester

Regni

Gesoriacum
Boulogne

Dumnonii

Isca Dumnoniorum
Exeter

Durnovaria
Dorchester

Fretum Gallicum

Mare Britannicum

0   50   100 km

Roman Britain: Main Roads and Towns

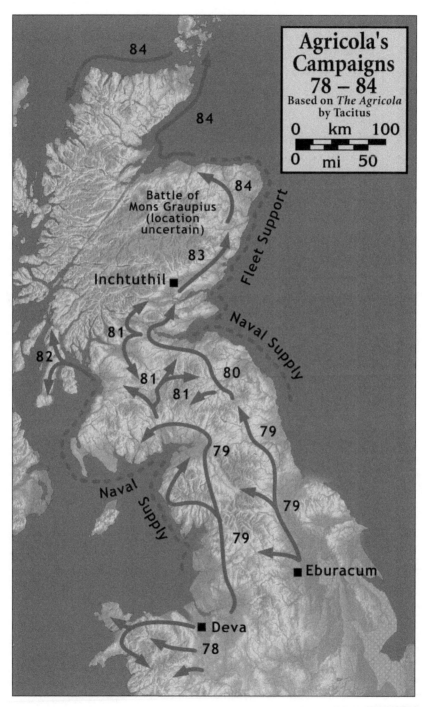

Agricola's Campaigns

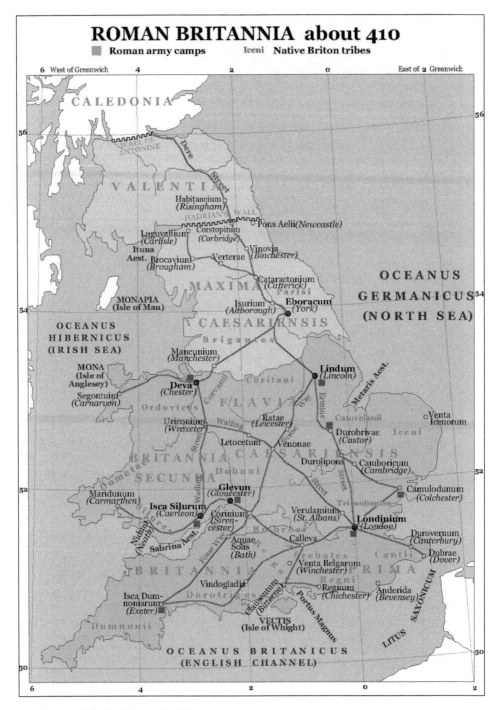

Roman Britain About AD 410

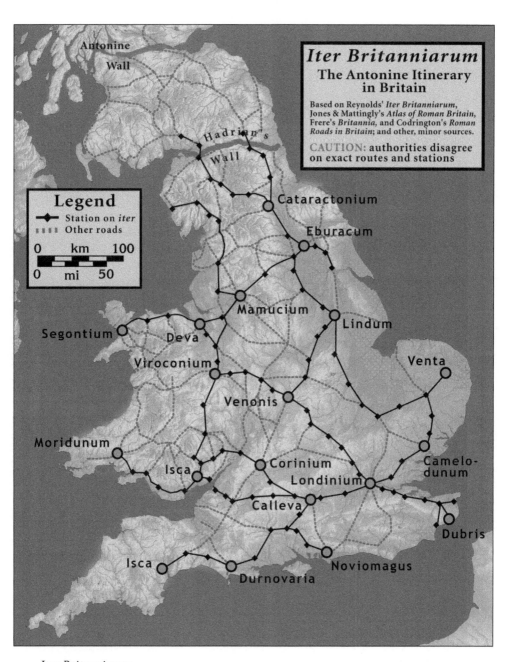

Iter Britanniarum

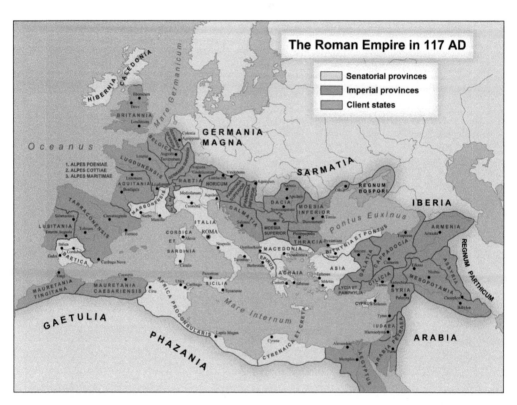

The Roman Empire AD 117

Introduction

A Historical Guide to Roman York is published to coincide with the 1950th anniversary of the founding of the city by the Romans in AD 71. There have been numerous books published on the Roman city of York over the years. The majority deal with Eboracum (to give York its Roman name) in a thorough and interesting way, basing their accounts, in the absence of much real literary evidence, on the epigraphical and archaeological evidence which is being dug up here all the time. The sites and finds are described in intriguing detail – but often in a one-dimensional way; there is very little *context* to be found, context explaining why such and such a thing happened, what a tombstone tells us beyond its notice of death, why an artefact was found here and what it signifies, or why this person or that did this or that. In other words, the tendency has often been to view Roman York in isolation from the empire that was going on all around it informing, engaging and dictating life in York. Many of the existing descriptions of Roman York do not give the circumstances that form the wider context for, or a more precise perspective on, a particular building, tombstone or find – be it exposing an historical event, military strategy, imperial policy or fashion trend. Only with this background detail can we fully understand what we are digging up and what we are looking at. If we are to understand York properly, it is vital to know and understand the norms, practices and events prevalent in Rome and in other parts of the Roman Empire and how they impinged on this northernmost fortress.

The Roman world in and after AD 43 for some 300 years – from the Roman invasion by Claudius and the establishment of York twenty-eight years later, to the Roman exodus around AD 410 – was a huge, diverse and multi-faceted world: York had a significant role to play in its development and progress, exemplifying or reflecting many of the political, societal and military concepts, factors and events that were going on from Egypt to north Germany, from Iberia to Persia. This book describes Roman York, but in the context of the wider empire.

So, for example, we will examine, empire wide, what really attracted the Romans to Britannia; the military and political motives behind Julius Caesar's invasions; what was going on in Rome to make Claudius feel the need to annex Britannia; we ask the intriguing question, why York for a fortress and as second city of the province? We follow the progress of the invasion under Agricola and others before and after him and ask what drove Hadrian and Antoninus to build their walls? We expatiate on Roman religion in York and on Christianity and its eventual acceptance; we describe 'Romanisation', army life and what triggered the Severan reform of Britannia's imperial status and why Severus made Eboracum the political and administrative centre of the known world. We describe York's communications, we meet empresses Julia Domna and Helena and Alaric the Hun; we ask what actually triggered that history-changing Roman withdrawal.

We examine funerary epigraphical evidence; we discuss the significance of Serapis and Mithras; and we cover the importance of local jet deposits. We pay the ferryman and discuss other funerary conundrums and burial rituals. We elaborate on fortress, *castrum*, *vicus*, *canaba* and *colonia*. We pursue gladiators, imperial visits and imperial deaths here, and the social function fulfilled by the bath house and putative and sought-after amphitheatre. And we look at the evidence for the existence of an imperial palace and much, much, more . . .

PART ONE
Eboracum and Empire

Britain Before the Romans

What did the ancients know about Britain and what was it they saw here which attracted them?

In the beginning, the islands we know as Britain were populated by peoples involved in a series of migrations westwards across Europe in the early Stone Age when there was no Channel to impede them. In time, melting glaciers and sinking land marooned these itinerants when Britain was cut adrift, and they became islanders. They had brought with them the religious beliefs and skills to construct the megalithic stone burial chambers we see at Avebury and Stonehenge; they also introduced a facility for metallurgy which was to shape prehistoric life and our history, for it was bronze and iron which they fashioned into weaponry and agricultural tools, replacing the crude stone and flint of earlier civilisations. This not only ushered in armed conflict and agronomy, it also developed a trade in luxurious and desirable objects exchanged with visitors from or visits to tribes on the European mainland and further east. Inevitably, their more sophisticated weapons enabled subsequent waves of invaders and the more powerful indigenous tribes to muscle in on the weaker, less developed natives, and establish themselves on the productive, most fertile lands, relegating their previous occupants to the less forgiving moors, marshes and weather-beaten uplands, mainly in Wales and the north. It did not take long before an obvious division emerged between the more workable and productive regions of much of the south and east and the comparatively barren northern and western areas. By the time the Romans arrived, this geographical dichotomy naturally created an economic and social divide which was to manifest itself in relative affluence for one and discontent and relative poverty for the other. This latter population was more inclined to foment opposition against the Roman way and against Roman rule which was to bedevil the Romans for many years of their occupation. It was also to account for the establishment of a fortress at York.

Pytheas of Massalia

The earliest name of the archipelago which we now know as the British Isles was first used some 2,000 years ago when classical geographers described our island group, from about the fourth century to around 50 BC, using variations of the word 'Prettanikē'.

Indeed, our first record comes from the fourth century BC Greek explorer and geographer Pytheas of Massalia (Marseilles), who vaguely referred to Prettanikē or Brettaniai as a group of islands off the coast of Northwestern Europe. This was an ancient Greek transliteration of the original Brittonic term in a non-extant work by Pytheas on his travels and discoveries. Other early records of the word are in the *peripli* by later authors, such as those in Strabo's *Geographica*, Pliny's *Natural History* and Diodorus Siculus' *Bibliotheca Historica*. Pliny the Elder (AD 23–79) says of Britain: 'Its former name was Albion; but at a later period, all the islands . . . were included under the name of "Britanniæ".' He mentions a multitude of things related to Britain including the long days, the tides recorded by Pytheas, local magic, the daubing with warlike woad, the wild geese, oysters, coracles, pearls, the cherry tree, amber, tin and lead.

A *periplus* is a manuscript document that lists the ports and coastal landmarks, in order and with approximate intervening distances, that the captain of a vessel could expect to find along a shore – in short, a type of coastal gazetteer or log.

In 325 BC, Pytheas journeyed from his home in the Greek colony of Massalia in southern Gaul to Britain. On this voyage, he circumnavigated and visited much of modern-day Great Britain and Ireland. He was the first known scientist to see and describe the Arctic, polar ice, Thule (Iceland or Orkney or Norway?) and the Celtic and Germanic tribes. He is also the first on record to describe the midnight sun. According to Strabo (63 BC–c. AD 24), the Greek geographer, philosopher, and historian, Pytheas referred to Britain as Bretannikē, which is treated as a feminine noun. Bretannikē may derive from a Celtic word meaning 'the painted ones' or 'the tattooed people' in a reference to local body art and the use of woad. He tells us that Pytheas 'travelled over the whole of Britain that was accessible' (*Geographica* 2, 4, 1). Ptolemy (c. AD 100–c. 170) the Greek-Egyptian mathematician, astronomer, geographer and astrologer later gives more information between AD 127 and 141 based on the work of Marinus of Tyre from around AD 100.

Marcian of Heraclea (fl. c. fourth century AD), in his *Periplus Maris Exteri*, described the island group as αἱ Πρεττανικαὶ νῆσοι (the Prettanic Isles). Marcian was a minor Greek geographer; his known works include *A Periplus of the Outer Sea* which mentions places from the Atlantic Ocean to China.

Diodorus Siculus (fl. first century BC)

In the first century BC, Diodorus Siculus in his *Bibliotheca Historica* of 36 BC mentioned Pretannia, a version of the indigenous name for the Pretani people whom the Greeks believed to inhabit the British Isles. This is his description:

> Britain is triangular in shape, very much like Sicily, but its sides are not equal. This island stretches obliquely along the coast of Europe, and the point where it is least distant from the mainland, we are told, is the promontory which men call Cantium [Kent] and this is about one hundred stades [eleven miles] from the land, at the place where the sea has its outlet, whereas the second promontory, known as Belerium [Cornwall] is said to be a voyage of four days from the mainland, and the last, writers tell us, extends out into the open sea and is named Orca [Orkney] ... . And Britain, we are told, is inhabited by native tribes and preserve in their ways of living the ancient manner of life ... . Their way of living is modest, since they are far from the luxury which comes with wealth. The island is also heavily populated . . . . It is controlled by many kings and potentates, who for the most part live at peace among themselves.
>
> (*Bibliotheca Historica* 21, 3-6)

Diodorus goes on to tell us about a cold and frosty place where the people live in thatched cottages, store their grain underground and bake bread. When they fight they do so from chariots, just like the Greeks did in the Trojan War. It was, however, a place shrouded in mystery and dread, with some writers (anticipating the Flat Earth Society and those who insist that the moon doesn't exist) denying its existence completely, according to Plutarch (*Life of Caesar* 23, 2): 'The island was incredibly big, and caused so much controversy amongst many a writer, some of whom swore that its name and story had been made up, since it had never existed and did not exist then.' Or that it was just a fantasy according to Strabo, *Geography* 2,4, 1, written soon after Caesar; Polybius' *Histories* 34.5 is less than convinced although his rubbishing of Pytheas may have been to amplify his own more modest Atlantic expedition.

The Romans referred to the Insulae Britannicae in the plural, a place consisting of Albion (Great Britain), Hibernia (Ireland), Thule and many smaller islands. However, when the Romans wanted to describe the place later they used the Latin name 'Britannia'. Britannia is a Latinisation of the native Brittonic word for the island, Pretanī, which also gave that Greek form Prettanike or Brettaniai. Brittonic was an ancient Celtic language spoken in Britain.

The earliest reference we have for Great Britain, Albion (Ἀλβιών) or insula Albionum, is either from the Latin *albus* meaning 'white' – possibly a reference to the white cliffs of Dover, the first thing you see of us from the continent, or the 'island of the Albiones'. Pseudo-Aristotle gives us our oldest mention of Great Britain:

> ... ἐν τούτῳ γε μὴν νῆσοι μέγιστοι τυγχάνουσιν οὖσαι δύο, Βρεττανικαὶ λεγόμεναι, Ἀλβίων καὶ Ἰέρνη, ...

There are two very large islands in it, called the British Isles, Albion and Ierne.

(Aristotle: *On the Cosmos,* 393)

Ptolemy referred to the larger island as great Britain (μεγάλη Βρεττανία) and to Ireland as little Britain (μικρὰ Βρεττανία) in his *Almagest* (AD 147–148). In his later work, *Geography* (c. AD 150), he gave the islands the names Alwion, Iwernia, and Mona (the Isle of Man), suggesting these may have been the names of the individual islands not known to him at the time of writing *Almagest*. The name Albion appears to have fallen out of use sometime after the Roman conquest of Britain, after which Britannia became the more usual name.

Tin Islands

Britain first attracted serious attention from outsiders when the Greeks, Phoenicians and Carthaginians – inveterate travellers and traders all – began commerce in Cornish tin. The Greeks called Britain (specifically Cornwall and the Scillies), amongst other north Atlantic places, the *Cassiterides*, or 'tin islands'. A rather sceptical Herodotus in fifth century BC (*Histories* 3, 115) vaguely located these somewhere off the west coast of Europe. He declares no real evidence for this, though, but concedes that they must exist if only because the Greeks have to get their tin from somewhere, probably from 'the ends of the earth'. He prefers this explanation to the story that tin comes from the Arimaspians who steal it from the griffins who guard it. The Arimaspians were a legendary tribe of one-eyed people of northern Scythia.

The Cassiterides were reputedly known first to the Phoenicians or Carthaginians from Gades (Cadiz). Pliny reports that a Greek named Midacritus (c. 600 BC) imported tin from Cassiteris island (*Natural History* 7, 197). The Carthaginians kept their tin routes secret; hence Herodotus' doubts about the existence of the Cassiterides. Pytheas visited the miners of Belerium (Land's End) and their tin depot at Ictis; but it was a Roman, probably Publius Licinius Crassus, governor in Spain around 95 BC, who revealed the tin routes: Strabo refers to a (non-extant) treatise on the Cassiterides written by Publius Crassus, grandson of the above. Several scholars of the nineteenth and early twentieth centuries, including Mommsen and Rice Holmes, believed this to be based on an expedition during Publius' occupation of Armorica (Brittany). More recently, scholars assign authorship to the elder Publius, during his proconsulship in Spain in the 90s BC, in which case the grandson's Armorican foray may have been prompted in part by commercial interests to capitalise on the survey of resources established earlier.

Diodorus, (5, 38, 4) tells how 'tin is brought in large quantities also from the island of Britain to Gaul opposite, where it is taken by merchants on horses through the interior of Celtica both to the Massalians and to the city of Narbo [Narbonne], as it is called.'

Himilco

Himilco was a Carthaginian navigator and explorer of the late sixth or early fifth century BC, at a time when Carthage dominated the region. He is the first known explorer from the Mediterranean to reach the northwestern shores of Europe. The oldest reference to Himilco's account of his voyage is a brief mention in Pliny's *Natural History* (2, 169a); he was referenced three times by Rufus Festus Avienus, who wrote *Ora Maritima* (*The Sea Shore*), a poetical geographical account in the fourth century AD.

Himilco sailed along the Atlantic coast from the Iberian Peninsula to the British Isles. He traveled to northwestern France to trade for tin (to be used for making bronze) and other metals. Records of the voyages of Himilco also mention the islands of Albion and Ierne.

Himilco embroidered his journeys with tales of sea monsters and seaweed, no doubt a stunt to deter Greek rivals from crowding in on his trade routes.

Avienus also tells us that the Tartessians – native Iron Age Andalusians – visited the Oestrumnidan isles to trade with the inhabitants; later, Carthaginian tradesmen travelled along the same route. But where were the Oestrumnidan isles? Avienus says they were two days' sailing distance from Ireland, and they 'were rich in the mining of tin and lead. A vigorous tribe lives here, proud spirited, energetic and skilful. On all the ridges trade is carried on.' All things considered it seems that Avienus meant ore-rich Brittany and the small islands off the coast rather than Cornwall or the Scilly Isles – the other two possibilities – although the Tartessians traded not just with the inhabitants of Brittany, but beyond to Cornwall, Wales and Ireland.

So, Britain was well known to the Greeks, Carthaginians and Phoenicians from at least the sixth century BC. Apart from its initial fascination as an uncharted, undiscovered and unconquered archipelago, it had long-term lucrative commercial possibilities well worth the perilous, monster-ridden journeys required to exploit them. Around the time of Julius Caesar and Claudius 100 years later, Britain would have been very much on the Romans' radar, so to speak, with references in libraries from a number of extant and non-extant historians, geographers and encyclopedists. These sources would have been readily available for those with a mind to look.

Britannia

By the first century BC, Britannia was synonymous with, and came to be used for, Great Britain specifically. After the Roman conquest in AD 43, Britannia *was* Roman Britain, a province covering the island south of Caledonia (roughly today's mid to southern Scotland). Indigenous people living in Britannia were called *Britanni*, or Britons.

We know that Britannia was well enough known amongst the learned and literate classes in Rome before that, even during the turbulent years of the first century BC before Caesar's invasions. The Epicurean poet Lucretius (99 BC–55 BC) uses the adjective *Britannus* as a metaphor and an example of a 'region far from fatherland and home' (*De Rerum Natura* 6, 1105). In a poem that can be confidently dated after Caesar's first invasion and before the death of Caesar's daughter Julia, the neoteric poet Catullus (c. 84 BC–c. 54 BC) refers to the place three times in *Poem 29* where he rails against Mamurra in an invective against triumvirs Caesar and Pompey:

> Quis hoc potest videre, quis potest pati,
> nisi impudicus et vorax et aleo,
> Mamurram habere quod comata Gallia
> habebat ante et ultima Britannia?

> Who can see this, who can stand it, save the shameless, the glutton, and gambler, that Mamurra Mentula should possess what long-haired Gaul had and remotest Britain had before?

> *Poem 29*, 1-4

> Eone nomine, imperator unice,
> Fuisti in ultima occidentis insula
> Is it for this reason, unique commander, you were on that farthest island of the west?

> *Poem 29*, 11-12

. . . where the unique commander is Julius Caesar and the farthest island of the west is Britannia.

And:

> paterna prima lancinata sunt bona;
> secunda praeda Pontica; inde tertia
> Hibera, quam scit amnis aurifer Tagus.
> nunc Galliae timetur et Britanniae.

quid hunc malum fovetis? aut quid hic potest
nisi uncta devorare patrimonia?

First he wasted his patrimony; second the loot from Pontus;
then third the booty from Spain, which even the gold bearing
Tagus knows. Now he is feared by Gauls and Britain. Why
do you indulge this scoundrel? What can he do but devour
well-fattened inheritances?

Poem 29, 18-23

The remoteness and 'edge of empireness' of Britannia (*ultima*) is
emphasised twice, while in all three instances the island is cited as
an example of how the depredations of Mamurra, and of Caesar and
Pompey by extension, extend so far as to include Britannia despite it
being so far from Rome. In the love *Poem 45* of Septimius and Acme,
Britannia is used, with Syria, as a measure of Septimius' devotion:

unam Septimius misellus Acmen
mavult quam Syrias Britanniasque:

Poor Septimius prefers Acme alone to whole Syrias and Britains.

Poem 45 (22-23)

In near contemporary Cicero's (106 BC–43 BC) *Epistulae ad Q. Fratrem*,
written between 60 or 59 to 54 BC, the orator writes to Quintus Tullius,
his brother, who is *legatus* with Caesar's army on the second of his two
British invasions. His words describe for us the dangers, mystery and
intriguing qualities of the place, based, no doubt, on detailed descriptions
penned in earlier correspondence to Cicero from Quintus.

How glad I was to get your letter from Britain! I was afraid
of the ocean, afraid of the coast of the island. The other parts
of the expedition I do not underrate; but yet they inspire
more hope than fear, and it is the suspense rather than any
positive alarm that makes me uneasy. You, however, I can
see, have a splendid subject to describe: topography, natural
features of things and places, manners, races, battles, your
commander himself – what themes for your pen!

In *De Natura Deorum* (2, 34, 88), Cicero cites Britannia (with Scythia) as another exemplum not just of distance and remoteness, but also of the extent of Roman rule. These countries are barbaric (*barbaria*) but their inhabitants nevertheless recognise the work of a rational human being when they see it. In the same treatise (3, 10, 24), he argues that the tides on the Spanish and British (*Britannicus aestus*) coasts ebb and flow without divine intervention.

Britain by the first half of the first century BC was very much on the lips of the educated and literate in and around Rome; it had a place in the vocabulary of philosophers, poets and their côteries, socialites, lawyers, politicians and rhetoricians. In short, it was part of the public narrative; Romans would have expected Britannia to fall to the relentless Roman war machine given that expansionism formed a prominent part of foreign policy at that time. From this perspective, the pressure was very much on Julius Caesar to invade.

Soon after the AD 43 invasion, Emperor Claudius was honoured with the agnomen 'Britannicus' as conqueror of the island. A frieze discovered at Aphrodisias in 1980 shows how dramatically the Romans viewed this: *Claudius subjugating Britannia* is a relief on the south portico of the Sebasteion, Aphrodisias on which Claudius is about to deliver a death blow to a cowering and beaten Britannia. He wears helmet, cloak, and sword belt with scabbard. Britannia wears a tunic with one breast bare, like the Amazons on which she is modelled.

Britannia later appeared on coins issued under Hadrian, as a somewhat more regal-looking female figure. She was soon personified as a goddess, looking not dissimilar to the goddess Minerva. Early portraits of the divinity depict Britannia as a fetching young woman, sporting a Corinthian helmet, and clothed in a white robe with her right breast exposed. She is usually shown seated on a rock, holding a trident, and with a spiked shield propped beside her. Sometimes she holds a standard and leans on the shield. On other coinage, she is seated on a globe above waves: Britain already depicted at the edge of empire, at the brink of the known world. Similar coin types were also minted under Antoninus Pius.

When Roman Britain was divided into four provinces in AD 197, two of them were called Britannia Superior and Britannia Inferior, the latter based at York. The name Britannia survived the end of Roman rule in Britain in the fifth century and provided the name for the island in most

European and various other languages, including the English Britain and the modern Welsh Prydain.

In the ninth century, Bretwalda and Brytenwalda were adopted by some Anglo-Saxon kings to assert a wider hegemony in Britain while inscriptions on coins and titles in charters often included the equivalent title *rex Britanniae*.

Celtic Britain

What kind of Britain would the Romans find when they made their first tentative steps towards occupation in 55 BC? The whole of the island – up to the Forth-Clyde estuaries – was populated by numerous Britonnic tribes – a multi-tribal society in which independent clans ruled smaller autonomous tribes or communities, but with no centralised national government, and, more importantly, no military, political or social cohesion. Many of the tribes, especially the Belgae, appear to have come over in the first century BC from the continent, possibly because of the need for *lebensraum* or indeed because they had been squeezed out as the Romans occupied more and more of what is now France, Belgium, the Netherlands and Germany. We will meet a number of these tribes when dealing with the Roman occupation. They include:

Cantii (Kent) – *Belgae* who arrived with other *Belgae* in the first century BC and were the Romans' first experience of native Britons on British soil. These Celts obviously wasted no time in establishing themselves agriculturally because we know from Caesar that they presided over many farms and lots of cattle, while their lands provided the Romans with plentiful food when they were marooned by a destructive storm in the 55 BC expedition. To establish themselves the Cantii had to displace previous native incumbents, something which they appear to have managed with their superiority in arms, until finally checked in the Claudian invasion some ninety years later.

Belgae Wiltshire and Hampshire – also originally from the continent.

Atrebates – a Belgic tribe settled around today's Berkshire. Related to or a branch of the Atrebates that lived in Gallia Belgica.

Catuvellauni (Hertfordshire) – Belgic tribe, neighbours of the Iceni, they joined in their rebellion. May have been related to the Catalauni who dwelt in the modern Champagne region of France.

Trinovantes/Trinobantes (Essex) – neighbours of the Iceni.

Regnenses/Regni – Belgic tribe, in today's East Hampshire, Sussex and Surrey.

Parisi East Riding of Yorkshire around modern Hull and Bridlington.

Brigantes – a confederacy of tribes spread over most of northern England.

Corieltauvi/Coritani East Midlands including Leicester.

Cornovii Midlands.

Damnonii (Southwestern Scotland).

Iceni East Anglia – under Boudica they rebelled against Roman rule.

Ordovices Gwynedd, Wales.

Silures South Wales – resisted the Romans in present-day South Wales.

Between 700 and 400 BC the Celts, in what was to become Britannia, enjoyed increasing contact with continental Europe, although this internationalism coincided in part with a greater availability of iron, which facilitated land clearance, agriculture and the growth of populations in more and more settlements. The earliest ironsmiths made daggers of the Hallstatt type, but which were distinctly British. The settlements also displayed unmistakably British characteristics, with the traditional round house, the 'Celtic' system of farming with its small fields, and storage pits for grain.

After 600 BC large hill forts began to spring up, suggesting the emergence of powerful and disputatious chieftains and the spread of conflict as increasing populations exerted pressures on the best land. More belligerence was evidenced by 300 BC when swords were making a re-appearance replacing daggers. Finally, in the third century, a British form of La Tène Celtic art was developed to decorate warlike equipment such as scabbards, shields, and helmets, and eventually also bronze mirrors and domestic pottery. During the second century the export of Cornish tin continued as attested, for example, by the Paul (Penzance) hoard of north Italian silver coins.

Further coin finds suggest that south-east Britain was increasingly socially and economically close to Belgic Gaul, resulting in a distinctive culture in Kent and lands north of the Thames which represented a later phase of the continental Celtic La Tène culture. Caesar got it about right when he wrote in his record of the Gallic Wars:

> The inland part of Britain is inhabited by tribes . . . indigenous to the island, the coastal part by tribes that migrated in earlier times from Belgium to procure booty by invasion. Nearly all of these are called after the names of the states from which they originated when they went to Britain; and after the invasion they settled there and began to till the fields. The population is huge; the farm-buildings are found very close together, being very like those of the Gauls; and there are many cattle. They use either bronze, or gold coins, or instead of coined money tallies of iron, of a certain weight. In the midland districts of Britain tin is produced, in the maritime iron, but not much; the bronze they use is imported. There is timber of every kind, as in Gaul, except beech and pine. To them it is wrong to eat hare, fowl, and goose; but they do keep them as pets or for pleasure. The climate is more temperate than in Gaul, the cold seasons more moderate.
>
> The most civilised of all these nations live in Kent, which is entirely coastal, nor do they differ much from the Gallic customs. Most of the inland inhabitants do not sow corn, but live on milk and meat, and are clad with skins. All the Britons, indeed, dye themselves with woad, which gives off a bluish colour, and makes them look more terrible in combat. They wear their hair long, and shave every part of their body except their head and upper lip. They have ten and even twelve wives common to them, even brothers sharing with brothers, and parents with their children; but if there are any children by these wives, they are said to be the children of those who they married when still a virgin.

(Caesar, *De Bello Gallico* 5, 14, adapted from trans.
H. J. Edwards, Harvard University Press, 1917

It is difficult to know with any certainty the population of Britain in the first century BC; however, best estimates give four to five million spread over a wide area with concentrations in the *oppida* (key towns). There is similar uncertainty over the ratio of the sexes. As in any wars, men tend to suffer most in terms of casualties so the male number may have dipped in the conflicts between the Romans and the Welsh tribes and the Brigantes. The Boudican revolt quite possibly redressed the disparity when many women and girls were slaughtered at Camulodunum, Verulamium and London. Warfare leaves a terrible legacy of widows and unmarried girls – Britannia would have been no different in the first century AD; moreover, the occupation itself would have skewed the ratio as largely unmarried, or at least unaccompanied, male legionaries and support personnel flooded onto the island. The Romano-British Cemetery at Trentholme Drive in York supports this with four male skeletons to every one female – similar to Cirencester (5:2) but very different from Lamyatt Beacon near Glastonbury (1:11).

Britannia, then, was clearly very much in the national discourse of the Romans and a prominent feature of the political and military landscape. For Julius Caesar in nearby Gaul it was but a short step away geographically, politically and militarily.

Julius Caesar and His 'Invasions'

Despite the commercial attractions of British tin and other mineral deposits, we know little about anything that happened between Rome and Britannia until the mid-first century BC when an inquisitive Rome arrived in 55 BC with Julius Caesar. Continued expansion meant that the empire had extended its reach from the Alps and Cevennes to the Channel in the five years before the invasion, so Caesar's actions in trying to extend these boundaries would have been by no means unusual. Caesar, of course, was a shrewd reporter and a skilful politician, so it comes as no surprise that he states in his inevitably biased and one-sided Gallic War commentaries that his purported aim in invading Britain, his *casus belli*, was to stifle the military and economic support the Britons had been giving to the Gauls on the mainland. The corollary to this strategy was equally influential; luxury Roman goods available in the import-export markets were valuable bargaining chips for seducing tribes into the Roman political sphere: British chiefs might avail themselves of levels of opulence for home and table unknown or only dreamt about a few years earlier. Archaeological evidence comes in the form of wine jars deposited in the tombs of chiefs and noblemen, silver tableware and bronze-plated furniture. Strabo describes ivory, high-end jewellery and glass. Other exports he mentions include corn, cattle gold, silver, iron, hides, slaves and 'clever hunting dogs'. Numismatic evidence for this commerce comes from the widespread use of silver and gold coinage on the Gallic model throughout south-east England at the time. Less tangible, less traceable entities such as Roman medicine, law and education would also have been attractive to the more enlightened or ambitious Britons as witnessed on their increasingly frequent trips to the Romanised near continent, and even to the city of Rome itself.

Another Side of Caesar

When we think of Julius Caesar we think of an alpha male, a gifted general and a driven and ruthless politician. And that is true, for the most part. There is, however, another side to Britain's first invader.

During the stormy days of the First Triumvirate, Marcus Calpurnius Bibulus proved a thorn in the triumvirate's collective side and exercised his right to veto. On one occasion Bibulus bitchily and publicly referred to Caesar as 'Queen of Bithynia', an allusion to Caesar's alleged dalliance with the king of Bithynia when he apparently lived the life of a girl in the court of King Nicomedes (c. 94 BC–74 BC), and was later referred to behind his back as 'Queen of Bithynia' and 'every woman's man and every man's woman'. The episode continued to haunt Caesar with repeated innuendo and political slur: Licinius Calvus refers to Bithynia as 'Caesar's buggerer'; Curio describes Caesar as the 'queen's concubine' and refers to the 'whorehouse of Nicomedes' and the 'Bithynian brothel'; to Marcus Brutus, Caesar was queen to Pompey's king. Gaius Memmius describes him as cupbearer to Nicomedes along with other catamites. Cicero reminded Caesar in court while he was defending Nysa, Nicomedes' daughter, that 'it is well known what he gave you and what you gave him.' Even his soldiers joined in the fun, singing a typically ribald marching song during the Gallic campaign: 'Caesar had his way with Gaul; Nicomedes had his way with Caesar; behold now Caesar, conqueror of Gaul, in triumph, Not so Nicomedes, conqueror of Caesar.' Even when he was granted the provinces of Gaul and Illyria by the senate, his exultant boast that he would be 'mounting on their heads', that is committing oral rape on the enemy, was met with the quip that that would be rather difficult for a woman to do. Caesar shrugged it off by referring to Semiramis and the Amazons as women successful in war.

There was another, far more lucrative, pretext for the incursion over the Channel; this owes much more to the hoary civic institutions enshrined in the Roman forum than to the misty battlefields and dense forests of Gaul. Caesar's invasions, or more accurately, reconnaissance and intelligence-gathering expeditions, would make a vital addendum to his already impressive *cursus honorum*. The celebrity to be gained by just attempting this foray into the unknown and dangerous world – never mind any success which accrued – would add priceless grist to his political machinations at this time. Caesar would also have been keen to postpone a recall to Rome, where his many enemies could get at him. The invasions of Britannia on the tenuous pretext that it strengthened the security of Gaul would insure against him being recalled on the reasonable basis that his work in Gaul was done. The only risk for Caesar was that, in deploying legions over the unpredictable English Channel, he may leave the mainland territories prone to attack and undo all the good work completed over the last few years. As it turned out this was a risk Caesar, the supreme opportunist, was willing to take, although the prosecution of the two forays turned out to be very unpredictable and uncertain at times.

According to Balsdon, the decision to send an expedition to Britain may have been taken a year before Caesar's armies set sail: 'The notion was in his mind, perhaps, in early 56, indeed when he was at Luca, and it may well have been for this project that those ships had been built on the Loire.' (Balsdon, *Julius Caesar* p. 82) But there were clearly other motives beyond the militaristic.

In Michael Grant's *Julius Caesar* (p. 65) we hear of a probable financial motive: 'Caesar himself like many others hoped for lavish loot of gold and silver and above all pearls.' And then there was the prestige and celebrity brought by conquering this exotic, mysterious land beyond the borders of the world. The British campaign became a kind of publicity stunt, a PR exercise to further his political aspirations. Campaigning against the barbaric Britons in an unknown, wild frontier was sure to impress and spotlight Caesar as the archetypal heroic Roman conqueror.

The Veneti tribe of Brittany may also have been a factor: they enjoyed a monopoly on British trade at the time but Caesar's earlier attempts to disrupt this commerce and glean information through commercial espionage had failed, so stoking his curiosity and desire to investigate further: 'I could not find out anything about the size of the island, the names and populations of the tribes . . . their methods of fighting or the customs they had, or which harbours there could accommodate a large number of big ships.' (*De Bello Gallico* 4, 20)

Cursus honorum

The *cursus honorum or* 'road of honour', was the sequential order of public offices held by aspiring politicians of senatorial rank in the Roman Republic and the early Roman Empire. It was designed for men of senatorial rank and comprised a sequence of age-related military and political administration posts. Each office had a minimum age for election and there were minimum intervals between holding successive offices and laws which forbade repeating an office. These rules were altered at whim and flouted in the last century of the republic. Military operations in Britain would, as noted, have looked very good on the record of Caesar's *cursus honorum*, his CV in effect. See Appendix 9 for more details.

To finance any largesse and to pay his troops, Caesar, like any other ambitious Roman consul-commander, needed money, and lots of it. His desire for plunder he could liquidate and land for resettlement was sharpened by an urgent requirement to pay off the huge debts incurred during the civil wars to pay for troops and bribes, and to settle his veterans. Generally speaking, booty from foreign conquests was recognised as obvious, easy pickings, fuelling a scramble to overrun and despoil rich new territories. Money from booty was also needed by the state to support and finance the expanding urban economies that were generated by the influx of agricultural workers from the surrounding lands. As increasing numbers of foreign territories fell under Rome's sway, the wealth, extravagance, opulence, tax revenues, and ostentatious military triumphs increased. It would all culminate in the bloody civil wars, in which the various triumvirs and their armies relentlessly battled and battered each other, until one general, Octavian, emerged as the victor at the Battle of Actium. By then the republic was ancient history – the empire was its future.

Caesar and Gaul

By 60 BC Caesar was one third of the First Triumvirate, an uneasy and edgy political alliance between himself, Pompey, and Marcus Licinius Crassus. The three effectively held most of the power in Rome. His consulship in 59 BC over, Caesar, to ensure a governorship and continued immunity against prosecution, with the help of the tribune Publius Vatinius, passed the 'Lex Vatinia de provincia Caesaris' which gave Caesar the proconsulship of Cisalpine Gaul and Illyricum – a five-year posting unprecedented in length for a province that was relatively secure. Coincidentally, the current governor of neighbouring Gallia Narbonensis, Quintus Caecilius Metellus Celer, died, and his province was also assigned to Caesar. So Caesar left Rome for Gaul where he spent the next ten years honing his military expertise and seeking glory and the spoils of war. But it was only a matter of time before he would be legally obliged to return to Rome where he would be politically vulnerable, unencumbered by any magisterial and military authority, at which point he would lose that vital immunity against prosecution. It was this predicament which ultimately triggered the crossing of the Rubicon River in 49 BC and the effective end of the Roman Republic.

Caesar was preoccupied with his wars in Gaul from 58 to 51 BC. In this wider context the incursions over the Channel, whatever their official intention, were not that much more than sideshows. His co-duumvir, Pompey, was left to deal with a Rome that was engulfed in bribery scandals, gang warfare, cancelled elections and street fighting. Caesar, that less than impartial source for the Gallic campaign, would have us believe that his campaigns were a pre-emptive, defensive war. In reality, Gaul was, as noted, used by him as an extension to his political ambitions and a means of paying off his substantial debts through booty. In 56 BC things had gone well for Caesar in Gaul, ensuring its near total pacification, and he now badly needed to extend his range of operations if he was to enhance his military reputation, keep himself free from prosecution and, ever the media star, keep his name and image before the Roman public.

Caesar's *Gallic War* comprises seven books, each devoted to one year of campaigning. Roman and Italian merchants and Roman commanders would have communicated what they knew about Gaul and Britain before Caesar's wars. But there still remained much mystery and suspicion, in common with other lands which were largely *terra incognita*. The descriptions of the Greek navigator Pytheas, by Caesar's time some three centuries old, was, as we have seen, the best that might be expected, with the exception of the fantastic description given by Xenophon of Lampsacus. He told the world, as quoted by Pliny the Elder (*Natural History* 4, 95), that in the Gallic north there were people with horses' hooves and huge ears; on the Birds Islands, Xenophon said, people lived on oats and eggs.

Gaul was of considerable strategic importance to Rome and Caesar was doing the state a rare favour when he finally quelled the troublesome natives and secured the Rhine as a natural frontier of the empire. Caesar's war against the Gauls culminated in the decisive Battle of Alesia in 52 BC, in which the total Roman victory resulted in the expansion of the Roman Republic over the whole of Gaul.

Roman Commanders and Their Armies

The first century BC saw significant changes in the organisation of the Roman army and the relationship between rank and file soldiers and their commanders. In the old days, armies were raised in the late spring, fought their battles on the Italian peninsula and laid down their weapons in the autumn to go back to work the farmlands from whence they had come. Looking back on 800 years of Roman history, Josephus remarked that the Romans left the womb ready-equipped for battle. Cicero had already said so much when he asserted that 'glory in war exceeds all other forms of success' – this is what makes a Roman and ensures Rome's eternal fame (*Pro Murena* 9, 22). Rome and the Romans were wired for war; it was in their DNA. Extending the boundaries of empire, not rhetoric or governing lands already subjugated, (*in regendis*), was the essential thing in life: *in propagandis finibus*. Virgil echoes this in the *Aeneid*, Rome's national poem written between 29 and 19 BC, one of the two themes of which is *arma*, arms, first at the beginning with Jupiter's mission statement for Rome (1, 278-230): 'I lay upon Rome boundaries neither of space nor time; I have given them empire without limit', *imperium sine fine dedi*; and then in book 6 when Aeneas in the underworld receives the template and programme for the future of Rome from the shade of his father Anchises. The key message is *parcere subiectis et debellare superbos:* 'spare the defeated and crush the proud'. Cicero's words would have resonated with Julius Caesar and Augustus, and Virgil's with Augustus as they each in their own times deliberated whether to invade or not to invade. The contemporary historian Livy (64 BC – AD 12) lends his support with the unequivocal statement in his *Ab Urbe Condita* (written between 27 and 9 BC) that Rome, through war, will rule the world: Proculus Julius to Romulus, founder of Rome (1, 278f):

> 'Go', he said, 'and declare to the Romans the will of Heaven that my Rome shall be the capital of the world; so let them cherish the art of war, and let them know and teach their children that no human power can resist Roman arms.'

So Rome's very raison d'être, as officially sanctioned, was to conquer and rule, to impose the Roman version of peace on the wider world, to spare those they deemed worthy of sparing and to bring to book anyone they thought arrogant. So absolute and unequivocal was this that it presumably did not occur to many Romans that the mantra itself was the epitome of arrogance, allowing them, theoretically at least, to strut around the world doing as they pleased and exterminating any nation or tribe who was unimpressed with the prospects of Roman *imperium* or who had the audacity to resist or protest. Such an attitude, of course, occasionally had its consequences, as we see in the AD 9 Teutoburger Wald German massacre and the bloody British revolt of Boudica in 60 BC.

Given this national mindset, this obligation to expand, it is hardly surprising that first Julius Caesar and then Augustus, Caligula and Claudius were sorely tempted to extend the empire and to subjugate Britannia.

Warfare, of course, was a fact of life for many Roman men during the monarchy and the early republic; most would have seen service at one time or another unless they were of the lowest orders – freedmen or slaves. Their women would have taken on the responsibility of running the farmstead and the household in their husbands' and older sons' increasingly frequent and lengthier absences. Roman warfare was inextricably linked with politics and economics, with land and the Conflict of the Orders being constant concerns during wars. Economic return on his land gave the soldier the wherewithal to qualify for military service, and to pay for his armour and weapons.

Eligibility for call-up extended from age 17 to 46 *(iuniores)* and 47 to 60 *(seniores)* – the latter usually forming a kind of home guard. By the second half of the second century BC, there were between 380,000 and 480,000 men under arms – three quarters of whom were *iuniores*. The Second Punic War (218–201 BC) saw the army at its greatest strength, with twenty-two legions on hand comprising of (on average) 4,200 infantry and 200 cavalry.

Sixty centuries made up a legion *(legio)* – originally a militia of heavily armed landowner infantry wielding *pilum*, a shield, and a sword *(gladius)*. The legions would be supported by the cavalry, with the wealthy *equites* initially in eighteen centuries – thirty-two centuries of slingers and other auxiliaries provided further back-up. The original *legio* was divided into two in the early republic, each the responsibility of one of the two consuls. By 311 BC there were four legions, reinforced by troops provided by Rome's Italian allies and by mercenary archers. By the middle of the republic, the legions were generally divided into cavalry, light infantry, and heavy infantry.

The Roman war machine needed to be constantly fuelled by new recruits, a fact which created something of a vicious circle. By the end of the third century BC approximately one third of Italians south of Rome had been subdued, and were Roman citizens; they were, therefore, eligible for military service. These citizens were supported by troops supplied by allies, often as auxiliary forces. However, the casualties sustained in continuous bloody wars – not to mention the total disasters at Lake Trasimene and Cannae for example – often meant that Rome had to keep on conquering if it was to maintain her steady supply of recruits, and thereby keep her forces up to strength. Once the Romans were on this treadmill they could not get off as war inexorably had to follow war.

The Punic Wars (264–146 BC) changed everything. There were now serious manpower shortages, caused by heavy casualties and the poverty created by widespread depredation of Roman land and farms. It is estimated that over 120,000 Roman citizens perished during the three wars – a casualty rate that would have crippled most nations. Slaves were enlisted, as an emergency measure, to make up the losses. The lands acquired by the elite and the rich were increasingly worked by slaves – captured, in their droves, by conquest – meaning less land was left for the indigenous farmer and no work was left for the peasant workforce. Therefore, peasants seeking work poured into the towns and cities. Land-owning soldiers found their lands devastated or confiscated on their return from the battlefield, or else they faced high taxation, rents and growing debt; this meant that they too headed for the towns. State land distribution ceased in 170 BC, but demand for land did not. The inevitable result was that commanders saw an opportunity to offer the chance to salvage countless livelihoods as they were now able to raise armies independently, tempting recruits with their private beneficence and the distribution of private land.

Military campaigns were increasingly extensive and costly, taking men away from their land and families for long periods as Rome's expansionism continued apace; new, far-away territories required permanent garrisons. Now that much of the Italian peninsula was under Roman control, booty and land from close-to-home conquests were considerably less plentiful. The low-hanging fruit was all gone: the pressure to recruit further afield was relentless.

In 107 BC, Gaius Marius saw the need to accept volunteers (*proletarii*) without the traditional land or wealth qualification, and the need to have the state pay for the equipment and weaponry for the war against Jugurtha in Africa. These were groundbreaking and highly untraditional changes: soldiers now lived and died for the army – crucially, they now had no land to return to. The legion was their lives, and they developed an intense loyalty to their commanders. Hitherto these *proletarii* were only conscripted as a last resort, in times of crisis (*tumultus*). The new revolutionary changes all coincided with the senate's failure to align the new, permanent professional armies to the state and its unwillingness or inability to pay pensions to veterans on retirement.

It is unlikely that Marius anticipated one of the major consequences of his military reforms. As we have seen, the new non-land-owning class of soldiers now had no lands to go back to, so they inevitably grew dependent on their generals for lifelong support. At the same time, the state had no means of paying adequate discharge payments to its burgeoning armies. Commanders saw an opportunity here: they could recruit and retain armies with the promises of generous pay and pensions which, through long-term mutual loyalty, might well lead to prodigious military and political power for themselves. From now on the soldiery was in the pay of the consuls and generals – and not the state. Individual military leaders could exercise significant political power and influence through their armies, perhaps even to effect revolutionary change in Rome.

Julius Caesar was one of the early beneficiaries of this new order with its close bonds between commanders and men, and the expeditions to Britannia were attempts to exploit the hoped-for financial and military benefits on offer.

The Invasion of Julius Caesar 55 BC

After Gaul, Britain, that enticing island over the intimidating English Channel, was next to come into Caesar's sights in 55 BC. Caesar obviously believed that this diversion from the main event had a good chance of bringing in the booty and enhancing his popularity back home and his reputation as a prominent military commander; he was seduced by the kudos perceived success would bring him. What is more, invasion (of sorts) might also allow him to deal with the troublesome Gallic connection: the Belgae of northeastern Gaul had raided Britain, establishing settlements, and Diviciacus, king of the Suessiones, had had the temerity to wield power in Britain as well as in Gaul. This unacceptable activity had been going on for some time: Gallo-Belgic coins found in Britain predate 100 BC, and perhaps are as early as 150 BC; they were minted in Gaul and found mainly in Kent. More significantly, Caesar had reason to believe that the Britons had embarrassed and compromised his campaigns in Gaul. They had lent support to the efforts of the mainland Gauls against him and provided safe harbour for fugitives from the Gallic Belgae fleeing to Belgic settlements in Britain. Moreover, he believed that the Veneti of Armorica, who controlled seaborne trade to the island, depended on military aid from their British allies in their conflict against him in 56 BC (*De Bello Gallico* 3, 8-9). Strabo adds that the Venetic rebellion was fomented to prevent Caesar from travelling to Britain and disrupting their trade (*Geographica* 4, 4). Caesar believed that the much-dreaded druids had their origins in Britain before spreading to Gaul (*De Bello Civili* 6, 13), where they enjoyed significant political power.

Caesar's planned invasion, however, had to be postponed until the August due to an uprising in eastern Gaul which needed quelling. Since winter was rapidly approaching, Caesar had to scale back his operation to a 'reconnaissance expedition', which was all that could be realistically accomplished in the time available if he was to avoid wintering in Britain, marooned by the weather.

Caesar dispatched a tribune, Gaius Volusenus, as a scout in a single warship to reconnoitre the Kent coast between Hythe and Sandwich, but Volusenus was unable to land, since he 'did not dare leave his ship and entrust himself to the barbarians', and after five days returned to give Caesar what little intelligence he had gleaned. Crucially, he had failed to identify a suitable harbour; had he done so he would have prevented the damage Caesar's exposed ships would later suffer at high tide and obviated the need for the deep-water disembarkation forced on the Romans at Walmer, the selected landing point. Envoys from some British tribes, tipped off by merchants, came to offer alliances but Caesar sent them back, along with his ally Commius, king of the Gallic Atrebates, to win over as many other states as possible.

The Evidence for Pegwell Bay

In 2017, research led by Dr Andrew Fitzpatrick, of the University of Leicester's School of Archaeology and Ancient History, seems to prove that the landing took place at Pegwell Bay on the Isle of Thanet. It had never previously been considered because the location was separated from the mainland until the Middle Ages; but the location matches Caesar's own personal account: its visibility from the sea, the existence of a large open bay and the presence of higher ground. His army immediately constructed a fort there. Iron weaponry, including a javelin, and other artefacts dug up at neighbouring Ebbsfleet overlooking the bay suggest that it was a Roman base dating to the first century BC. The site is now more than 900 metres inland, but at the time of Caesar's invasions it was closer to the coast.

Fitzpatrick adds that

> the Wantsum Channel [which separates it from the mainland] was clearly not a significant barrier to people of Thanet during the Iron Age and it certainly would not have been a major challenge to the engineering capabilities of the Roman army . . . Caesar describes how the ships were left at anchor at an even and open shore and how they were damaged by a great storm. This description is consistent with Pegwell Bay, which today is the largest bay on the east Kent coast and is open and flat. The bay is big enough for the whole Roman army to have landed in the single day that Caesar describes.

At Portius Itius (Boulogne), Caesar assembled a fleet of eighty transport ships, big enough to carry Legio VII and Legio X, along with warships. Another eighteen transports of cavalry were due to sail from Ambleteuse. That the legions travelled without baggage or heavy siege machinery confirms that the invasion was for surveillance only. Dubris (Dover), with its natural harbour, was rejected at the last minute as a beachhead because the Britons on the cliffs above were able to rain down their javelins on the Romans from up there.

The exploratory fact-finding operation was beset by bad luck from the outset when atrocious weather wrecked most of the Roman fleet.

The massed chariots of the Britons on the Kent clifftops put the fear of the gods into the two legions below as they tentatively approached in their vessels. The ships off Walmer were sitting too low in the water due to their loads, preventing them from getting close enough inshore so the troops had to disembark in deep water, all the while under attack from the enemy. They had to be urged on by the *aquilifer* (standard bearer) of the Xth legion who jumped into the shallows shouting: 'Jump down mates, unless you wish to betray your eagle to the enemy. As for me, I'm going to do my duty to the state and to my general.'

The Romans finally repulsed the British with *catapultae* and slings fired from the warships into their exposed flank; but strong winds had delayed the cavalry so they could not finish them off. We have archaeological evidence for a camp set up by the Romans; they received ambassadors and had Commius, who had been arrested by the Britons as soon as he had arrived in Britain, returned to them. Within four days the natives were giving hostages, but things only got worse for Caesar when the ships carrying the cavalry were scattered and forced to turn back to Gaul by the storms. Food was running short, his beached warships were taking on water, and his transports, riding at anchor, were smashing into each other. Some ships were wrecked, and many others were rendered unseaworthy by damaged rigging or other vital equipment. Caesar's journey back to Gaul was threatened.

The British strategy was to detain Caesar in Britain over the winter and starve him into defeat. The Britons then ambushed one of his legions as it foraged near the Roman camp; the foraging party was relieved and the Britons were again beaten off, only to regroup after several days beset by storms with a larger force to attack the Roman camp. This attack was also driven off in a costly rout, deploying cavalry that Commius had gathered from pro-Roman Britons and a Roman scorched-earth policy. The British sent envoys but Caesar, to avoid a winter crossing, set off back to Gaul. Here is Caesar's version of the invasion:

> When the ships had been beached and the camp thoroughly well entrenched, he [Caesar] left the same forces as before to guard the ships: he himself then set out for the point where he had reached before. When he got there he found that even more Britons had assembled there from every direction, and that they had entrusted the supreme

26

command and conduct of the campaign to Cassivellaunus, whose territories are divided from the coastal states by the river Thames, about eighty miles from the sea. Before this there had been continuous wars between Cassivellaunus and the other states; but our arrival had moved the Britons to appoint him commander-in-chief for the conduct of the whole campaign.

The enemy's cavalry and charioteers engaged in fierce conflict with our cavalry on the march, with the result, however, that our troops proved their superiority in all respects, and drove them into the woods and uplands; but, pursuing too eagerly after slaying several of the enemy, they lost some of their own men. After an interval, however, when our troops were off their guard and busy entrenching the camp, the enemy suddenly dashed out from the woods, and charging the detachments on outpost duty in advance of the camp, they did battle fiercely. Though Caesar sent up two cohorts in support—and those the first cohorts of two legions—and two detachments had taken up post soon after, the enemy most courageously broke through in the middle (as our troops were wrong-footed by the new way of fighting), and retired safely from the field. On that day a tribune, Quintus Laberius Durus, was killed. The enemy were driven back when more cohorts had been sent up.

(De Bello Gallico 5, 11-15)

Caesar's efforts then did little to dispel the island's reputation for mystery and danger and, for most Romans it remained a misty island located beyond the ocean at the edge of the known world – *ultima Thule* – so great was the trepidation it evoked. If Caesar had intended the invasion as a full-scale campaign, invasion or occupation, then clearly it had failed. It also had not fully succeeded as a reconnaissance operation or a show of strength to deter further British aid to the Gauls.

Nonetheless, going to Britain and taking Rome beyond the 'known world' carried such prestige for a Roman that the senate decreed a *supplicatio* of twenty days on the basis of Caesar's report. It may also be that this invasion established alliances with British kings in the area which smoothed and facilitated the later invasion of AD 43.

Supplicatio

If Caesar needed reassurance that his incursions had curried the popular favour he craved in Rome then the voting by the senate of an impressively lengthy *supplicatio* provided that reassurance in spades.

A *supplicatio* is a day of public prayer when the men, women, and children of Rome processed to religious sites around the city praying for divine aid in times of crisis. It also served as a thanksgiving, when a great Roman victory had been won, usually decreed as soon as official intelligence of the victory had been received by a report from the general in command. The number of days of the *supplicatio* was proportionate to the importance of the victory. Sometimes it was decreed for only one day, but more commonly for three or five days. A *supplicatio* of ten days was first decreed in honour of Pompey at the end of the war with Mithridates and this one of fifteen days, after the victory over the Belgae by Caesar, was an honour which Caesar says had never been granted to any one before. Subsequently, a *supplicatio* of twenty days was decreed after his defeat of Vercingetorix.

As noted, Caesar's stated official motive for the invasion was to quell Gallic support from Britain: 'in almost all the wars with the Gauls military support had been offered to our enemy from that country.' However, the possibility of exploiting tin reserves and other mineral resources remains another motive. Cicero refers to the disappointing discovery (from his brother Quintus) that there was no gold or silver to be found in the island, although how this could have been established for certain in such a short and geographically limited visit – particularly as the Romans were hundreds of miles from the recognised source in Cornwall – remains problematic. As it happens, silver was mined from soon after the Claudian invasion although not in the areas penetrated by Caesar. Quintus is on safer ground with the chariots as British weapons of war: 'In Britain I am told there is no gold or silver. If that turns out to be the case, I advise you to capture a war-chariot and hasten back to us at the earliest opportunity.' (Cicero, *Ad Familiares* 7, 7) – to C. Trebatius Testa (who was serving in Caesar's army) on his way to Gaul, from Cumae, April 54 BC.

The chariots were obviously a cause for concern back in Rome as this reference to Trebatius makes clear: 'look out, while in Britain, that you are not yourself taken in by the charioteers' (Ad *Familiares* 7, 6); but not just the chariots . . .

28

The result of the British war is a cause of anxiety for it seems that the approaches to the island are protected by astonishing masses of cliff. Moreover, it is now known that there isn't a pennyweight of silver in that island, nor any hope of booty except from slaves, among whom I don't suppose you can expect any instructed in literature or music.

(Cicero, *Ad Atticus* 4, 17)

Suetonius reports that Caesar was said to have gone to Britain in search of pearls (*Caesar* 47). Caesar did later dedicate a thorax decorated with British pearls to Venus Genetrix in the temple dedicated to her that he later built (Pliny, *Natural History* 9, 116) and oysters were later exported from Britain to Rome (Pliny 9, 169 and Juvenal, *Satire* 4, 141).

When Caesar landed in 55 BC, Britain had an estimated population of between one and four million. The lowland south east with its expansive tracts of fertile soil encouraged extensive arable farming, while communications developed along trackways, such as the Icknield Way, the Pilgrims' Way and the Jurassic Way, and along navigable rivers such as the Thames. North of a line from Gloucester to Lincoln, workable arable land was less in evidence. Settlements were usually built on elevated ground and fortified, but in the south east *oppida* were established on lower ground, often at river crossings, suggesting that trade was increasing in importance. As already noted, trade between Britain and the continent had been growing since the Roman conquest of Transalpine Gaul in 124 BC; Italian wine was being imported via the Armorican peninsula, mostly at Hengistbury Head in Dorset.

The Invasion of Julius Caesar in 54 BC

The following year in 54 BC Caesar went back. This time he was better prepared, he had learnt from his mistakes to some extent, and was working to a more adventurous strategy. For a start he took with him a larger force: no fewer than 600 new, specially built transports and twenty-eight ships of war constructed with the latest Venetic shipbuilding technology. His plan was to win over, or compel, native Celtic tribes to pay tribute and give hostages in return for non-aggression. Sadly, there is no truth in the story told by Polyaenus that Caesar defeated Cassivellaunus' men while defending a river crossing by striking fear in their hearts when he deployed an armoured elephant complete with a turret from which archers and slingers let loose:

> When Caesar's fording of a wide river in Britain [the Thames] was opposed by the British king Cassivellaunus, at the head of a strong cavalry force and many chariots, he ordered an elephant, an animal till then unknown to the Britons, to enter the river first, mailed in scales of iron, with a tower on its back, on which archers and slingers were positioned. If the Britons were terrified at so extraordinary a spectacle, what shall I say of their horses? Amongst the Greeks, the horses bolt at the sight of an unarmed elephant; but armoured, and with a tower on its back, from which missiles and stones are continually hurled, is a sight too formidable to bear. So the Britons with their cavalry and chariots took flight, leaving the Romans to pass the river unmolested, their enemy routed by the appearance of a single beast.
>
> (Polyaenus, *Strategemata* 8, 23, 5 – adapted from the translation by R. Shepherd, 1793.)

The five legions and 2,000 cavalry were conveyed in ships better suited to amphibious beach landings, being broader and lower. Portus Itius (somewhere in the Nord-Pas-de-Calais) was the port of departure.

Caesar left Titus Labienus at Portus Itius to ensure the lines of supply. Interestingly and astutely, the naval ships were joined by a trade delegation in the shape of a flotilla of commercial vessels looking to secure business with the Britons. The fleet totalled 800 ships. If nothing else, this civilian contingent proved that, for them at least, Caesar's earlier invasion had dispelled all the anxiety and superstition relating to this strange place at the end of the world; money spoke and for the hopeful merchants Britannia was now a former *terra incognita*, stripped of its ancient terror.

The Britons offered no opposition to the landing. Caesar delegated protection of the beachhead to Quintus Atrius and made an immediate night march some twelve miles inland where he clashed with the British forces somewhere on the River Stour. The Britons were driven back and regrouped at the hillfort at Bigbury Wood, Kent, only to be defeated again.

Bad news came when Caesar heard from Atrius that his anchored ships had (again) been smashed against each other in a storm with the loss of forty vessels. He returned to the coast to repair his fleet, working day and night for ten days, and building a fortified camp around them. Labienus was ordered to send more ships.

When Caesar returned to the Stour river crossing he found the British forces waiting for him. Cassivellaunus (again) was the leader of the British combined forces; he had a chequered past having previously been at war with most of the other British tribes, and had recently deposed the king of the mighty Trinovantes, exiling his son. But the Britons were repelled and routed by the Roman cavalry when they attacked a three-legion foraging party under Gaius Trebonius.

Cassivellaunus knew his limitations. Realising he was unlikely to defeat Caesar in open battle, he resorted to guerrilla warfare, relying on the mobility and speed of his 4,000 chariots and his superior knowledge of the local terrain. Caesar reached the Thames at the one fordable place available to him – only to find that it had been fortified with sharpened stakes, both on the shore and under the water; the far bank was defended.

British opposition then collapsed. The Trinovantes sent envoys promising Caesar aid and materiel, grain and hostages. Mandubracius was restored as their king. Five more tribes, the Cenimagni, Segontiaci, Ancalites, Bibroci and Cassi, surrendered to Caesar, and, crucially, revealed to him the location of Cassivellaunus' stronghold – the hill fort at Wheathampstead, which was duly besieged.

Cassivellaunus responded by sending word to his allies in Kent, Cingetorix, Carvilius, Taximagulus and Segovax, the 'four kings of Cantium', to stage a diversionary attack on the Roman beachhead to draw Caesar away. But this failed, and Cassivellaunus sent ambassadors to negotiate a surrender. Caesar was anxious to get back to Gaul so an agreement was mediated by Commius, the terms of which were that Cassivellaunus give hostages, agree an annual tribute, and undertake not to make war against Mandubracius or the Trinovantes. Later Commius switched sides, fighting in Vercingetorix's rebellion over in Gaul.

After a number of unsuccessful engagements with Caesar's forces, Commius cut his losses and fled back to Britain. Sextus Julius Frontinus, in his *Strategemata*, describes how Commius and his followers, with Caesar in pursuit, boarded their ships. Although the tide was out and the ships still beached, Commius ordered the sails be raised. Caesar, still some distance away, assumed the ships were afloat and called off the pursuit. Some reject this, positing instead that Commius was sent to Britain as a friendly king as part of his truce with Mark Antony. Commius established a dynasty in the Hampshire area, evidenced from coins of Gallo-Belgic type. Verica, the client king whose exile was to prompt Claudius' conquest in AD 43, styled himself a son of Commius.

What the two British expeditions lacked in military success or benefit they more than made up for in propaganda value, although many back in Rome criticised them as expensive and over-ambitious exercises in expansionism. The senate decreed another *supplicatio,* this time for twenty days. Furthermore, Caesar learnt something important from his invasions: the tactical value of the war chariot, something new to the Romans. Caesar describes them as follows:

> This is how they fight with their chariots: firstly, they drive about in all directions and throw their weapons and generally break the ranks of the enemy with the very fear inspired by their horses and the noise of their wheels; and when they have insinuated themselves in between the troops and cavalry, they leap from their chariots and fight on foot. The charioteers in the meantime withdraw a little way from the battle, and place themselves in the chariots so that, if their comrades are overpowered by the enemy, they can offer a ready retreat to their own troops. Thus they display in battle the speed of horse, [together with] the solidity of infantry; and by daily practice and exercise attain expertise that they, even on a slope and steep place, can check their horses at full speed, and manage to turn them in an instant and run along the pole, and stand on the yoke, and then get back with the greatest speed to their chariots again.

During the civil wars, Caesar made use of a kind of boat he had seen used in Britain, similar to the Irish currach or Welsh coracle. He describes them as thus: 'The keels and ribs were made of light timber, then, the rest of the hull of the ships was wrought with wicker work, and covered over with hides.'

Caesar then returned to Gaul having made no actual conquest. The timing was fortuitous because he reached Gaul just in time to see the beginnings of a significant Gallic revolt which threatened not just his earlier conquests but the military reputation on which he relied so heavily. But, just as importantly, his restoration of Mandubracius crucially marked the beginnings of a system of client kingdoms in Britain, so drawing the island firmly into Rome's sphere of political and military influence. Diplomatic and trading links developed further over the next century, always threatening the eventuality of permanent conquest. While the mysterious and misty island at the edge of the world remained unconquered, Caesar certainly benefitted from the excitement and sensational publicity his two missions would have generated around the Roman Empire, evidence for which can be detected in Cicero's letters. In crossing the Channel, Caesar had ventured beyond the world known to Romans – the *orbis terrarum* – and he had brought Britain under the sway of Rome, albeit tentatively for the time being.

As we know, Caesar's invasion of Britain was part of a much bigger campaign: the nine-year battle for Gaul waged between 58 and 51 BC. As stated above, our main source is Caesar's own despatches. Roman generals were obliged to send despatches, *litterae*, reporting their activities to the Roman senate; they might also write extensive reports, or *commentarii*; Caesar's *De Bello Gallico* is a literary example of this – it is obviously propaganda, 'bigging-up' the author. These documents would also serve as a vehicle to remind the Roman public of his accomplishments in the name of their city. The work may also have been intended as a retort to political opponents of Caesar who questioned the necessity of such a costly war which, at the time, was apparently one of the most expensive in Roman history. In summary, Caesar describes how he campaigned across modern France, Belgium, and west Switzerland, and how he twice crossed what the Romans regarded as major boundaries: the River Rhine, which he presented as the border between the Gauls and the Germans, and the perilous sea that was believed to encircle the Roman world.

The Significance of Caesar to Roman Britain and to York

To quote Tacitus (*Agricola*, 13): 'It was, in fact, the deified Julius [Caesar] who first of all Romans invaded Britain with an army: he overawed the natives by a successful battle and took control of the coast; but it may be said that he revealed, rather than left, Britain to Rome.'

Tacitus (c. AD 56–c. AD 120), with the benefit of 150 or so years of hindsight, was right. Caesar adumbrated and exposed the potential benefits a viable invasion might bring to Rome. So much so that by the time of the Claudian invasion, the military was in possession of far more and far better intelligence which extended into territory way beyond Caesar's south-east corner. Much of this would have come from the extensive network established by Roman merchants who no doubt pushed relentlessly further and further north, softening up the increasingly comfortable better-off locals with their luxury items and sumptuous fare. Caesar can take credit for much of this, providing a much-publicised spearhead for increased commercial and economic development extending over a much wider area than his actual sphere of operations.

The campaign was not without its examples of bravery. The first century AD historian Valerius Maximus, in his *Memorable Words and Deeds* (3, 2, 23), tells of the bravery of Marcus Caesius Scaeva, a centurion under Caesar, who, deserted by his comrades, held his position alone against a horde of Britons on a small island, before finally swimming to safety.

Bigger issues claimed attention. The turmoil and anarchy preceding the Battle of Actium in 31 BC and the subsequent establishment of the principate under Octavian, now Augustus, obviously caused matters relating to imperial expansion and international diplomacy and trade to be, at best, paused. It was not until things started to settle down politically that Britain re-emerged as an issue to be dealt with and reappeared on the imperial agenda.

Britain in the Early Empire

So the Roman Republic dissolved, amid much bloodshed and corruption, and re-emerged as the Roman Empire after Octavian's decisive victory at Actium. The story of Britain's relationship with Rome during that period up to the Claudian invasion is one of procrastination, hesitation and false starts descending, under Caligula, into nothing short of farce. Nevertheless, much good diplomatic work was achieved, not least, as noted, the establishment of a number of client kingdoms and the beginnings of the process we call Romanisation in the south-east corner of Britain. When Claudius did invade his progress was rapid, because a number of the noblemen and decision makers already enjoyed a cordial relationship with Rome and were only too happy to facilitate Claudius' progress. Indeed, Claudius was fortunate enough to be able to benefit from and exploit Caesar's diplomatic and commercial legacy.

Imperial Aspirations

The emperor Augustus, as Octavian, (r. 27 BC–AD 14) toyed with the idea of invading in 34 BC: 'he had set out to lead an expedition into Britain also, and had already advanced into Gaul . . . when some of the newly-conquered people and Dalmatians along with them rose in revolt' (Dio 49, 38). In 27 BC we hear that:

> These were the actions of Augustus at that time. He also set out to make an expedition into Britain, but on reaching the provinces of Gaul hesitated there. For the Britons seemed likely to make terms with him, and the affairs of the Gauls were still unsettled, as the civil wars had begun immediately after their subjugation. He took a census of the inhabitants and regulated their life and government. From Gaul he proceeded into Spain, and established order there too.
>
> (Dio 53, 22)

And in 25 BC:

> Augustus was planning an expedition into Britain, since the
> people there would not come to terms, but he was detained
> by the revolt of the Salassi and by the hostility of the
> Cantabri and Astures. The former dwell at the foot of the
> Alps . . . whereas both the other tribes occupy the strongest
> part of the Pyrenees on the Spanish side, together with the
> plain below.
>
> (Dio 53, 25)

Cassius Dio (c. AD 155–c. 235) interestingly gives us another explanation
for Octavian's first projected invasion, claiming that he was anxious to
emulate his adoptive father, Julius Caesar, particularly after the success
in Illyricum seemed to give him an opportunity to add to his military
triumphs. However, trouble in Pannonia, Dalmatia and northern Italy
put a stop to that.

To this we can add Strabo's comments made about the same time.
First, he says that the Romans were loath to invade because they believed
the Britons to be too weak a force to cross over and threaten Roman
rule on the European mainland; and second, that the potential return on
exacting tribute was already outweighed by the tax revenues payable
from the island (*Geographica* 2, 5, 8). Strabo repeats this assertion at 4,
5, 3, adding that British leaders had been in Rome making offerings to
Augustus at the capitol – in effect giving over the whole island to Rome.
The significance of this being that these influential Britons represented
a powerful pro-Roman faction in the island. It would be interesting to
know what the Brigantes and other, less compliant, tribes made of all
of this.

But there was another source of information, at least for the literate
and chattering classes. We have seen how Lucretius and Catullus
reference Britannia, and, in the case of Catullus, Julius Caesar himself,
in the late republic. In the early empire two pro-Augustan poets,
Virgil and Horace, mention the island in the context of imminent or
accomplished invasion; it was everybody's expectation that Britannia
was going to fall to the Romans. We have *ultima Thule* from Virgil in
the *Georgics* (1, 30) as an example of Augustus' global suzerainty: 'the
boundless ocean's God thou come, Sole dread of seamen, till far Thule

36

bow Before thee' and 'Even now I long to escort the stately procession to the shrine and witness the slaughter of steers; and see how Britons raise the crimson curtain they are woven into' in the same poem (3, 25). Horace gives us much the same: 'O shield our Caesar as he goes To furthest Britain, and his band, Rome's harvest! Send on Eastern foes Their fear, and on the Red Sea strand!' (*Odes* 1, 35, 29-31) – *in ultimos orbis Britannos*. Far off Britain was within the reach of Augustus and spoken of in the same lines as other outposts of empire. Augustus, however, may not have thanked Horace for verifying that he would not become a god unless or until he conquered the Parthians, the Persians and the Britons.

Moreover, the debacles visited on the Romans by the Clades Lolliana (17 BC) and at Teutoburger Wald (AD 9) were eloquent reminders of the huge risks involved in oversees aggression and most likely deterred Augustus from further risky expansionism in the north west.

So, all the plans of Augustus came to nothing and relations with Britannia and its tribes proceeded on the basis of diplomacy and trade agreements. Sporadic references to Britannia include British kings who sent embassies to Augustus in Rome, and kings received by Augustus as exiles – Dubnovellaunus and Tincomarus. Tacitus (*Agricola* 13) gives an example of cordial relations and at the same time rekindles the mystique of Britannia in his reports that some of Tiberius' (r. AD 14–37) ships were blown off course to Britain during his German campaigns in AD 16; they were promptly sent back whence they came by local rulers, the startled Romans telling tales of hurricanes, strange birds, monsters and figures half man half animal, imagined or otherwise.

The diplomacy and commerce continued until AD 40 when an exile from the Catuvellauni, Adminius, son of Cunobelinus, fled to the court of Caligula and led the ever-unpredictable Emperor Caligula (r. AD 37–41) to plan an invasion of Britain. The gossipy imperial biographer Suetonius (c. AD 69–after 122) tells that, characteristically for Caligula, it was a complete shambles and that the 'invaders' never actually left Gaul. Caligula ranged his siege engines on the Gallic coast facing Britannia, then, to everyone's astonishment (or maybe not), ordered his troops to gather seashells from the beach – such was the booty due to Rome (Suetonius, *Caligula* 44-46; Dio Cassius, *Roman History* 59, 25). This they did, a lighthouse was erected, a bounty of four gold pieces was announced and he bid the troops 'go rich and go happy!'

Verica and Client Kingdoms

Verica was a British client king in the years before the Claudian invasion of AD 43. Numismatic evidence suggests he was king of the Atrebates tribe and a son of Commius. He succeeded his elder brother Eppillus as king in about AD 15, reigning from Calleva Atrebatum, Silchester. He was recognised as *rex,* king, by Rome and appears to have had long-standing and amicable trade and diplomatic links with the empire.

His territory was threatened from the east by the Catuvellauni, led by Epaticcus, brother of Cunobelinus, who conquered Calleva in about AD 25. After Epaticcus' death c. AD 35, Verica regained some territory, but Cunobelinus' son Caratacus assumed power and conquered the entire kingdom some time after AD 40.

Cassius Dio (60, 19) says that Bericus (Verica) was exiled from Britain around this time and fled to Claudius. Suetonius (*Claudius* 17) refers to demands by the Britons that Rome return 'certain deserters'. As *rex,* Verica was nominally an ally of Rome, so his exile gave Claudius a pretext, if he needed one, to invade Britannia and restore Verica to power.

The Roman client kingdoms in Britain were indigenous tribes who had elected to ally themselves with the Romans, seeing, no doubt, that discretion was the better part of any valour. It protected them from Roman aggression by assuming Roman protection, protection which at the same time deterred land-grabbing expansionist interference from other hostile tribes. The Romans sometimes created or enlisted client kingdoms when they felt arm's length influence without direct rule was appropriate or desirable.

The system, as we have seen, began when Julius Caesar restored Mandubracius as king of the Trinovantes, after he had been deposed by Cassivellaunus and then supported Caesar's second invasion of Britain in 54 BC. The arrangement ran from 54 BC–c. AD 39. Caesar also established the Catuvellauni as a tributary state of Rome. Since AD 10, both areas were ruled by Cunobelinus, who lost control to an anti-Roman faction led by his son Caratacus around AD 39; this was to prompt that farcical 'invasion' of Caligula's.

We have established that it seems likely Augustus adopted a policy of client kingdoms with regard to Britain as being sufficient to keep the island under control, in preference to a full-scale invasion with its financial and manpower costs; at the same time it chimed well with his general foreign policy of containment rather than expansion of the Roman Empire. Financially, the treasuries of Augustus and Tiberius after him would continue to benefit from the customs duty brought in by the flood of imports from the continent as evidenced by excavations of pottery and grave goods around Colchester and other places including Silchester with the Atrebates; Bagendon (Cirencester), Dobunni; Leicester, Coritani; and North Ferriby, Parisi.

Client kingdoms were particularly successful in the south east and included those ruled by Cogidubnus of the Regnenses (55 BC–AD 70s), Prasutagus of the Iceni (roughly Norfolk; c. AD 47–60); Cartimandua of the Brigantes and Boduocus of the Dobunni. The antecedents of the Regnenses, the Atrebates, had been client kingdoms of Rome since Caesar's first invasion in 55 BC. Following the Roman conquest, Cogidubnus, who at some point received the Roman names Tiberius Claudius, ruled what had been the lands of the Atrebates. His people were now referred to as Regni or Regnenses. Cogidubnus was especially loyal to the Romans and after his death, probably in AD 73, the kingdom was absorbed into the Roman province of Britannia.

AD 47 saw the measured governor and commander in chief Aulus Plautius giving way to Ostorius Scapula, a belligerent hawk if ever there was one; Ostorius Scapula exemplifies what happens when client kingdoms go wrong. Tacitus describes his uncompromising policy to 'tame everything this side of Trent and the Severn' (*Annals* 12, 31-40) as ill-advisedly 'reducing the nearest part of Britain into a province', which involved disarming those tribes which Plautius had trusted to retain their weapons. Result: the first Iceni rebellion which Ostorius put down only after a close-fought battle. Prasutagus was installed as king after the revolt of the Iceni. The Iceni were allowed quasi-independence, with the expectation that the kingdom would revert to Roman control on Prasutagus' death. However, the king, invoking an agreement made with the Romans earlier, insisted on leaving control of his kingdom to his daughters. When he died in AD 60, the Romans denied all knowledge, choosing to skate over any small print or codicil, and seized control, thus inciting a second, more challenging, Iceni rebellion under Prasutagus' wife Boudica. After ruthlessly quashing Boudica's revolt, the Romans simply administered the territory as part of Britannia.

Much later when the Romans withdrew behind Hadrian's Wall in AD 164, they left the Votadini as a client kingdom, a buffer zone against the Picts to the north. The Votadini were a Brythonic people who lived under the direct Roman rule between Hadrian's Wall and the Antonine Wall from AD 138 – 162. They maintained their client status until the Romans withdrew from Britain in AD 410.

Client states were a critical element in what we now call Romanisation.

Romanisation, 'Romanitas' and Civilisation

The concepts of 'Roman-ness', *Romanitas*, dictated much of what Romans did in their daily lives and how they did it. They formed the backbone of Roman identity. By the time Eboracum, York, was founded in AD 71 the empire was a very big and varied place; it had evolved over 800 years – the same time span between the English Middle Ages and 2021 – and it was made up of people from all over the known world. Because of this diversity, there was now no such thing as a Roman, as an identifiable entity or concept. The Roman man and woman was forever changing and evolving, socially, culturally, religiously and politically – a moving object, in place and in time. The Roman back in fourth century BC Italy was very different, and quite unrecognisable from, for example, the Roman in first century AD Eboracum.

Indeed, Romanisation as a process was a truly versatile, diverse and variegated concept and phenomenon. Romanisation intentionally blurred the distinction and the realities between the Roman and the native. Just how far and in what way the Romans imposed their culture and national superiority on a given territory depended on what they found there – the opposition, the local politics and demographics. The process, and results, of how Romanisation was adapted in Egypt, for example, were very different from how its counterpart was adapted in Britannia. Nowhere was the local tradition and way of life mutually exclusive with Roman ways, nowhere were local ways of doing things erased completely in favour of the Roman. Romanitas was imposed throughout the empire but in varying ways and degrees. The Romans had a knack of taking the best from a given conquest, place or procedure and repurposing it to their own benefit as subjugators, but at the same time allowing the locals to continue to function as far as was possible in their traditional ways. Brendel (1979) sums it up when he says that 'Roman' culture was by definition a cosmopolitan fusion of influences from diverse origins rather

41

than purely the native culture of Rome itself. Haverfield (1912, p. 18) had said 'First, Romanization in general extinguished the distinction between Roman and provincial ... . Secondly, it did not everywhere and at one destroy all traces of tribal or national sentiments or fashions.' It was 'a two-way process of acculturation: it was the interaction between two cultures' (Millett 1990). Acculturation worked from the top down, with the predominantly urban upper classes adopting Roman culture first and the old tribal ways persisting for the longest among the peasantry in rural areas. In short, Romanisation was osmotic, nuanced, eclectic and syncretic.

Religions too received varying levels of tolerance and makeover. What is termed *interpretatio Romana*, 'Latin translation' (Tacitus, *Germania* 43, 3), was an important factor in Romanisation; it describes the Roman tendency to replace the name of a foreign god or goddess with that of a Roman deity which was considered comparable. It started off with the substitution of Greek gods and goddesses with Roman equivalents bearing Roman names, but it soon extended into other cultures as the Romans came into contact with them, so the German 'Wodan', for example, was called 'Mercurius' by Roman writers.

In the *Germania* reference above, Tacitus describes two German gods worshipped as twin brothers and youths as being just like [our] Castor and Pollux, 'according to the Roman interpretation'. He also mentions the worship of Hercules and Mars. For the Romans, the translation from Greek to Roman allowed the Roman deity the inherent prestige and intellectual kudos implicit in the Greek version. Looking, Janus-like, the other way, *interpretatio Germanica*, for example, permitted the Germanic tribes to assume a Roman appearance, which was valuable in obtaining the status and benefits of a Roman citizen should they be desired. *Interpretatio Romana* was, therefore, part of the process of Romanisation, a step on the way to Romanitas. Rome was generally quite relaxed when it came to tolerance of religious practices of defeated populations: one way of allowing foreigners access to the Roman gods was through *interpretatio Romana*, which associated Roman deities with local gods and goddesses, and permitted the grafting on of local divinities.

But certain qualities and emblems of Roman identity can be recognised which are commonly and consistently attributable to Romans, wherever and whenever they were. Some of those qualities fall conveniently under the term 'Romanitas', a word that was never actually used by the Romans themselves until the third century AD by Roman writer, Tertullian. Tertullian's use was pejorative: he coined it to describe his fellow Carthaginians who mindlessly aped Roman ways. Juvenal (AD 50–after 127) had said much the same, vilifying his fellow Romans who were slaves to the ways of Greeks and to all things Greek; to Juvenal, Greece was polluting and diluting 'Romanitas':

> What is more sickening than this: no woman thinks herself beautiful unless she's changed from being a Tuscan to a little Greek bit ... . Everything has gone Greek: however, it's even more grotesque when Romans have no Latin. They show their fear, their anger, their joys and their worries in Greek; they pour out every secret of their souls in this tongue ... . You might allow this in a young girl, but will you still be Greeking it when you're pushing eighty-six? Such a way of speaking is surely not right for a little old lady.
>
> (Juvenal, *Satires* 6, 184-191)

Martial (AD 41–102) shared Juvenal's exasperation:

> Laelia, you don't live in Greek Ephesus, or Rhodes, or Mitylene, but in a gaff in a posh part of Rome; and although your mother was a dusky Etruscan who never wore make-up; and although your father was a hard man from Aricia, you, and I'm ashamed to say it are a citizen of Roman Hersilia and Egeria – yet you keep assailing me in Greek!
>
> (Martial, *Epigrams* 10, 68)

The concept of 'Romanitas' brought with it an air of respectability and nobility in tune with the 'grandeur that was Rome'; it came to mean quintessential 'Roman-ness' – what it means to be a Roman and how the Romans regarded themselves; it defined a true Roman; it embodied the Roman ideal.

Despite the blandishments and exoticism promised by foreign influences, there was always an element of conservatism and traditionalism running through the marrow of the Roman people. This evolved over time into a national character which had its roots in the early humble, agricultural days and was characterised as demonstrating hard work, honesty, exuding *gravitas* (dignified, serious or solemn conduct) and being diligent in every way; moreover, the true Roman lived by and respected the *mos maiorum*, the way the ancestors had gone about things. The Roman was expected to be dutiful, to exhibit *pietas,* in every sphere of life: towards family, friends, country, fellow citizens, comrades in arms and gods. It was widely held that 'Romanitas', *gravitas* and *pietas* did indeed define the best of Romans.

With the invasion of Britannia came multitudes of Roman businessmen and government officials often with their families in tow. Roman troops from across the empire, as far as Spain, Syria, Egypt, and the Germanic provinces of Batavia and Frisia (modern Netherlands, Belgium, and the Rhineland area of Germany), were garrisoned in Roman towns such as York, and many formed relationships or, when it was officially permitted, married local Britons. The Roman army alone and their families and dependents amounted to an estimated 125,000 people, out of Britannia's total population of 3.6 million at the end of the fourth century. There were also many migrants in other professions, such as sculptors from Roman Syria and doctors from the eastern Mediterranean. This diversification defined Britannia's cultures and religions, while the populace remained mainly Celtic, but with a Roman way of life.

There is often an uneasy relationship between diversity and xenophobia. History lessons told every Roman schoolboy and girl about the arch-conservative Cato the Elder (234–149 BC). As champion of the *mos maiorum* and despiser of things Greek, Cato spoke out sternly against what he saw as a period of moral decline and the erosion of the sturdy principles on which Rome had lain her foundations. Among other things, he identified the growing independence of the women of Rome as an ominous ingredient in this. The defeat of Hannibal at Zama in 202 BC, the victory over the Macedonians at Pydna in 168 BC and the final extinguishing of the Carthaginian threat in 146 BC all allowed Rome to relax more and encouraged an unprecedented influx of Greek and eastern influences and luxuries into a receptive Rome. In 191 BC, Cato defiantly addressed a Greek audience in Athens in Latin.

Cicero too (106 BC–43 BC) was another stickler for good old-fashioned 'Romanitas'. The Latin language, or rather the ability to speak it, and the practice of Roman law were equally potent badges of Roman-ness:

Ordinary men, born in obscurity, take to the sea and they go to places which they have never seen before; places where they can neither be known to the men among whom they have arrived, nor where they can always find a lawyer. However, due to their singular faith in their Roman citizenship, they think that they will be safe, not only among our own magistrates, who are constrained by fear of the law and of public opinion, but also with our fellow citizens who are joined with them, among many other things, by a common language and laws; but wherever they come from they think that this will protect them.

(Cicero *in Verrem* 2, 5, 167)

In *Brutus*, 37, 140, he is even more explicit, declaring that it is shameful for a man or woman not to know Latin; a facility for Latin was a mark of the good Roman citizen. Suetonius tells us that the emperor Tiberius believed it important that soldiers in the Roman army be able to speak Latin following an incident when he refused a Greek soldier permission to reply in Greek when summonsed to give evidence. The conquering or occupying Roman army was the prime vehicle for, and deliverer of, 'Romanisation' when it consolidated the lands into the Roman Empire: speaking Latin was a key element in that 'Romanisation'. There is good evidence that some foreign troops and mercenaries in the Roman army learned Latin.

Wills had to be written in Latin; tombstones for Roman soldiers, be they Roman or foreign, throughout the empire were always in Latin, except for Roman Egypt where Greek was allowed. To the Romans, Latin was the only language of any significance; it would not have occurred to them to learn a 'barbarian' tongue – Latin symbolised civilisation. In about AD 30, the historian Valerius Maximus reported how Roman magistrates throughout the Roman world used Latin as a weapon in upholding Roman *maiestas*, greatness, when they insisted that court proceedings be in Latin and that the Greeks use interpreters to translate into Latin. Speaking Latin inculcated respect for Roman power and symbolised Roman-ness. Latin was an enduring emblem of 'Romanitas'.

In the Roman Empire, about 400 towns enjoyed the rank of *colonia* – showcases of Roman culture and models of the Roman *modus vivendi*.

The native population of any province could see from these how they were expected to live. The status of *Colonia civium Romanorum* brought with it full citizen rights while the fledgling citizens were required to dedicate a temple to the Capitoline Triad: Jupiter, Juno, and Minerva, the deities venerated in the temple of Jupiter Best and Biggest on the capitol in Rome. York was one such *colonia*.

Tacitus leaves us in no doubt regarding the zeal with which his father-in-law, Agricola, championed and promoted in deeds as well as words Romanisation and Romanitas:

> He [Agricola] wanted to accustom them [the Britons] to peace and leisure by providing delightful distractions. He gave personal encouragement and assistance to the building of temples, piazzas and town-houses, he gave the sons of the aristocracy a liberal education, they became eager to speak Latin effectively and the toga was everywhere to be seen. And so they were gradually led into the demoralising vices of porticoes, baths and grand dinner parties.

A cynical Tacitus, though, can see it all from a different perspective as is clear from this razor-sharp observation: 'The naïve Britons described these things as "civilisation", when in fact they were simply part of their enslavement.'

Invasion by the Romans, then, would, as a matter of course, involve the gradual but indelible Romanisation of, and the inculcation of Romanitas within, the conquered territory: Britannia was no exception and we shall see how Eboracum played its part in that process.

Claudius the Invader

Of the multitude of books and papers which deal with the invasion of 43 BC, very few actually explain the reasons why Claudius took that history-changing decision to invade and occupy this *terra incognita* of ours – an operation which everyone close to the seat of power in Rome knew would be costly in terms of time, money and casualties. Many commentators mention the invasion as a simple, isolated act, an event in a historical bubble, without recourse to much background detail which gives it its context within the politics, foreign policy and military objectives in the wider Roman Empire.

Why Did the Romans Invade Britannia Anyway?

Why did the Romans feel the need to conquer Britannia? After all, the empire already stretched from the Sahara to the north German plains, from the Caucasus to the English Channel, and the Channel formed a good, natural, defendable, dependable frontier. A cautious Augustus had reined in the unquenchable hunger for booty; lucrative conquest – so rampant in the later republic – was increasingly hard to come by anyway and he had learnt sobering lessons from the humiliating and costly massacre of Varus' legions in the Teutoburger Wald in AD 9, and before that from the lesser-known Clades Lolliana in which, in 17 BC, tribes led by the Sugambri from near what is now the Dutch-German border on the right bank of the Rhine, ignominiously defeated a Roman legion under the command of Marcus Lollius.

Augustus wielded complete control; he also retained control of the Roman army – enabling him to prevent a return to the bloody turmoil of the civil wars by covetous, power-hungry, often out-of-control generals. He maintained a policy of limited expansion, largely preserving the new empire within its existing borders. This was in the face of hawkish conservative calls to invade Britannia to the west and Parthia in the east and an absolute need to ensure that the legions were usefully employed to the benefit of the political establishment and Rome's stability rather than to its detriment. As far as many Romans could see, there was little out there now which would earn a return on expensive military campaigns; lucrative booty and fertile lands not under Roman control were clearly in short supply beyond what was already embraced by the empire.

So, why bother? Augustus had the financial resources to satisfy and resettle veterans out of his substantial windfalls from the Ptolemaic Empire; he was, as noted, naturally unwilling to allow ambitious commanders any opportunity to fuel insurrection on the back of victorious and lucrative military campaigns.

Britain was not without resources such as copper, gold, iron, lead, salt, silver, and tin, all in high demand in the Roman Empire. The Romans could depend on advanced technology to find, develop and extract valuable minerals on a scale unparalleled again until the later Middle Ages. But economics was not really a viable motive or an incentive – the Roman Empire already enjoyed riches-a-plenty and the natural resources in Britannia were only going to increase those reserves incrementally.

The answer to why the Romans invaded was as much to do with politics and celebrity than anything else. Claudius became emperor by default: the ugly assassination of his predecessor, mad, bad Caligula, had left no obvious successor. Despite his undoubted intelligence and impressive literary skills, Claudius has always been seen, quite unjustly, as a bit of a buffoon (no thanks to Robert Graves), an imperial embarrassment. He would never have been anyone's first choice to lead mighty Rome out of a perilous power vacuum. On accession, to correct this perception Claudius was in desperate need of a high-profile action, an event on an imperial, global scale, which would raise his political and military stock. Britannia was an obvious target, and so the invasion was on.

Claudius the Man

On 24 January AD 41, Caligula and his family were unceremoniously murdered; the Praetorian Guard, ever faithful to the Julio-Claudians, needed someone new to guard: Claudius was available and so they proclaimed Claudius emperor. Claudius, whom everyone found easy to ridicule, was, in his early days, looked after by his grandmother Livia, wife of Augustus: Suetonius shows, through various letters, how Livia agonised over how to accommodate him in the imperial firm while the Piso decree recognises the *discipulina* (education) he received through Livia; she was clearly at pains to give him at least a chance to get on in life.

But for whatever reason – frustration, disappointment, embarrassment – his mother, Antonia Minor Augusta, was, to modern sensitivities, cruel to Claudius, who suffered from what was probably cerebral palsy, calling him a 'monster', a 'half-complete creation', and describing others she considered stupid to be dafter even than Claudius. Despite Livia's efforts to help, Augustus and Livia were embarrassed by Claudius, as shown by a letter from Augustus to Livia in which the emperor deliberates over the extent to which he should allow Claudius to officiate at public events and be seen, indeed gawped at, in the imperial box with him, Emperor of Rome. He urges Livia to show Antonia the letter, confirming for us that she too was exercised by this issue. To a Roman, particularly an elite and successful Roman, *virtus* was a hallmark of *Romanitas;* a deficiency of *virtus* was seen as weakness, a lack of manliness: disability of any kind, mental or physical, precluded *virtus* – they were mutually exclusive. Claudius' *virtus* was seriously compromised and, on the face of it, Claudius never stood a chance in the alpha male world at the pinnacle of Roman power politics.

However, Claudius was nothing if not a determined man and, having made the decision to invade, scored a resounding political and military victory in AD 43 when he conquered Britannia, extending the northern boundary of the empire and eclipsing alpha male Julius Caesar's forays some ninety years earlier. The subsequent lavish victory parade in AD 44 gave Valeria Messalina, his third, mercurial, wife, her first opportunity to shine, and to display her new privileges as first lady of Rome. Their son, Tiberius Claudius Caesar, was given the additional name Britannicus in honour of his father's achievement, Claudius having modestly rejected it when offered it by the senate.

Claudius was a notable historian and an avid student of Greek culture; his teachers included Livy and Sulpicius Flavus. He even had an impact, albeit short-lived, on Roman epigraphy; according to Suetonius (*Claudius* 41-42): 'He invented three new letters and added them to the alphabet, maintaining that they were greatly needed ... . These characters may still be seen in numerous books, in the daily gazette, and in inscriptions on public buildings.'

The new letters were Ɔ or ƆC/X (antisigma) to replace BS and PS, just as 'X' stood in for CS and GS; Ⅎ (an inverted 'F' or digamma) to represent consonantal 'U'; and Ⱶ (a half 'H') as a short vowel sound used before labial consonants in Latin words such as 'optimus'.

Claudius would have been persuaded by the high regard in which the potential subjugation and annexing of Britannia were held. We have seen how Julius Caesar won prestigious *supplicationes* for his two forays into the unknown; the indecisiveness of Augustus and the aborted invasion by Caligula would surely have been a source of great disappointment, embarrassment even, to the public in Rome. Nevertheless, the triumphs bestowed on Claudius when he came home victorious; and the highly visible, tangible victory arches dedicated to him were just the start in a series of events reflecting and highlighting the prestige in which Britannia was held as an asset and as a conquest. Some years later, under Trajan, the appointment of two eminent senators as governors of Britannia – T. Avidius Quietus and L. Neratius Marcellus (from AD 103) – lend further evidence, were it needed, of how highly Britannia was regarded back in Rome. The subsequent attention bestowed on Britannia by the highest profile generals in emperors Hadrian and Antoninus, who honoured the island with two of the most significant and expensive frontier defences (provisioned by and reinforced at York) in the empire, were good news stories which contributed to a much-needed feel-good factor back in Rome and in Britannia itself. Indeed, this was maintained and followed by Emperor Septimius Severus who launched punitive attacks into Caledonia from his fortress in York in attempts to quell the northern unrest once and for all. The elevation of York to headquarters of the northern command, its promotion to the status of *colonia* and the upgrading of the fortress to capital of Britannia Inferior making it, with London, one of the two superior cities of the province and one of the empire's significant places – all these things built up the high reputation of Britannia in general and to York in particular. Add to these the important fact that Britannia was, when circumstances in the wider empire permitted, garrisoned generously and expensively with troops and materiel. The legions here gained fame when they declared that Constantine the Great be appointed Emperor of Rome at his headquarters in York on the death of his father, Constantius in AD 306

So, the Claudian invasion of Britain did not just happen. It was never a mere inevitability waiting to take place. The invasion of Britain was conceived as a necessity for Claudius on a personal and political level which later assumed an important place in the strengthening and security of the Roman empire at its northern extremes, often spearheaded by the fortress at York.

The Roman Media

Britannia was a very long way from the seat of power and government. Given communications at the time there must have been a real sense of isolation felt in, for example, London and York – a sense of isolation which has rarely been acknowledged or analysed in histories of Roman Britain. So, how did the Romans get their news about what was going on around them not just in Rome, but in the far-flung four corners of the empire and in all points in between? How did they get the breaking news that their emperor, Claudius, had won a victory in Britannia? Obviously, word of mouth, chatter and speculation played a big part as did official pronouncements from the senate. However, the most systematic medium was the *Acta Diurna*, first published in 59 BC. This was a kind of daily gazette, a daily record, which recorded official events, ceremonies, speeches in the senate, military activity and lawsuits. Indeed, it was the Roman equivalent to today's online news reports. Public notices and significant births, marriages and deaths were included later.

Its readership extended well beyond Rome into the provinces. The news the *Acta* carried was carved on stone or metal and displayed on message boards in public and busy places such as the Forum Romanum: Rome's equivalent of billboards or outdoor digital screens. Just like yesterday's papers and web posts today, the *Acta* had a short, dispensable life: the notices were taken down after a few days and, with a commendable anticipation of future scholarly needs and curiosity, archived. Scribes sometimes made copies to be dispatched to provincial governors to keep them up to speed with events at the heart of government and Roman power. In the later empire, they were used to announce royal or senatorial decrees and goings-on at court. *Publicare et propagare* appeared at the end of the texts tagging them as a form of press release.

Julius Caesar's expeditions, the disappointing news about the Augustan and Caligulan invasions, the triumph of Claudius in newly subjugated Britannia, the ultimate victory over Boudica, and Agricola's victory at Mons Graupius would certainly have made 'the front pages', as it were, to satisfy the good-news needs of the Roman public from

51

Gaul to Egypt, from Persia to Spain. What today we call 'spin', and 'fake news', would, of course, have been integral factors in much of the content.

Claudius the Invader

Any doubts Claudius may have had about a Britannia expedition evaporated when, as we have described, the usurped and exiled Verica, client king of the Atrebates who had been exiled after a revolt by the Catuvellauni came to him for help as a *rex*, a king and an ally of Rome. Furthermore, Cunobelinus and his sons Togodumnus and Caratacus were busy upsetting the Roman established status quo in the south and Cunobelinus had already expelled another son, Adminius, whom Rome had installed and who was making entreaties to Caligula for reinstatement. The refusal of the Romans to extradite British refugees and the shambolic non-invasion by Caligula did nothing, of course, to help Roman prestige around the world. This was Claudius' chance for fame in the name of Rome and for approval in the eyes of Romans throughout the empire – and he took it with alacrity.

The invasion marked the start of the Roman occupation of Britain. It was only after 365 years of controlling (largely) civilising (mainly) and developing (constantly) that the Romans eventually deserted Britain to defend mother Rome from the circling barbarians. The AD 43 invasion and subsequent occupation was, broadly speaking, an unmitigated success by any military, colonising or imperial standards.

Our first-hand sources for the actual invasion are, to say the least, scant. Tacitus does allude to it briefly in the *Agricola* but the relevant part of his *Annals* is lost. That leaves an epitomised description by Cassius Dio (60, 20) with all the drawbacks that an epitome gives.

Aulus Plautius was appointed commander-in-chief and first governor of Britannia. The invasion force comprised four legions: the IX *Hispana* posted in from Pannonia on the Danube frontier, the II *Augusta* from Strasbourg, the XIV *Gemina* from Mainz, and the XX *Valeria Victrix* from Neuss supported by 20,000 auxiliary troops from Thrace, and Batavia in Germany. The II *Augusta* was commanded by Vespasian who was to emerge as emperor in AD 69 during the turbulent Year of the Four Emperors. The Claudian invasion was not without its problems, however: the old superstitions and horror stories about this strange *terra incognita* spread like wildfire amongst the troops who mustered on the beaches of Gaul terrified of what they were about to do: to them it was just like sailing off the edge of the world. They mutinied, causing the invasion to be delayed by a month or so. Nevertheless, once reassured that the world did not actually end where they stood, reassured significantly by Claudius' influential freedman and high-flying secretary Narcissus – and eventually encouraged at seeing this former slave acting the role of general – they shouted out a war cry '*Io Saturnalia!*' and off they went. Saturnalia was the Roman festival in which social roles were reversed for the day – slave became master and master acted the slave.

Superstition

The Roman legions on the beach, then, were initially paralysed by fear and superstition. The Romans were by nature a superstitious people; in everyday life superstition was rife and omnipresent. We saw it intruding during Caesar's invasions and we see it repeated here with Claudius; we will see it again during the Boudican revolt. In a world where it was widely considered unpropitious for a black cat to enter your house or a snake to fall from the roof into your yard, where it was unlucky if a statue of a god was seen to sweat blood, where a horse was born with five legs, a lamb with a pig's head and a pig with a human head, where a rampant bull ran up three flights of stairs, and a cow talked, and where a statue laughed uncontrollably, a horse cried hot tears, in a world where it was inauspicious to sneeze in the presence of a waiter holding a tray or to sweep the floor when a guest was standing up, where it was *de rigueur* to whistle when lightning flashed, in such a world it should come as no surprise to hear that you should only clip your nails on market days – and even then starting with the forefinger and doing it in silence and never at sea. This was a world which surprised itself that it ever stepped outside, never mind conquered the world. Pliny records that in certain Italian towns it was forbidden by law for women to walk through the streets carrying a spindle. Certain days of the year were avoided by betrothed couples when choosing their wedding day, and the groom had to carry his bride over the threshold to avoid any chance of an unlucky stumble.

Nevertheless, it is important to remember that the Romans were probably no more superstitious than other contemporary cultures and societies. Indeed, if we look at the old wives' tales recounted by George

Orwell from an English rural childhood around 1900 in *Coming Up for Air*, can we say they are any less absurd or irrational than the Romans'? Take for example:

> swimming was dangerous, climbing trees was dangerous ...
> all animals were dangerous ... horses bit, bats got in your
> hair, earwigs got into your ears, swans broke your leg ...
> bulls tossed you ... raw potatoes were deadly poison, and so
> were mushrooms unless you bought them at the grocer's ...
> if you had a bath after a meal you died of cramp ... and if
> you washed your hands in the water eggs were boiled in you
> got warts ... raw onions were a cure for almost anything.

Back on the beach with the invading armies, panic and potential mutiny evaporated in flash when that rallying cry rent the Channel air: the invasion force set sail in three waves, landing at Rutupiae (Richborough), Dubrae (Dover) and Lemanae (Lympne), and possibly also at Bosham Harbour near Fishbourne – a legionary helmet of Claudian date has been found in the harbour there and now resides in Lewes Museum. The delay had the unexpected, but welcome, effect of persuading the Britons that the invasion was off, so they relaxed and got on with the all-important business of bringing in the harvest. Meanwhile, materiel was being shipped over and quietly warehoused at Rutupiae with its extensive camp – the lines of supply were being methodically established.

The Britannia legions

These are the legions which at one time or another served in Britannia:

Legio II *Augusta* – The Second Augustan Legion
Legio VI *Victrix* – The Sixth Victorious Legion
Legio VIII *Augusta* – The Eighth Augustan Legion
Legio IX *Hispana* – The Ninth Spanish Legion
Legio XIV *Gemina* – The Fourteenth Twin Legion
Legio XX *Valeria* – The Twentieth Legion, Valiant and Victorious
Legio XXII *Deiotariana* – The Twenty-Second Deiotarian Legion
Legio XXII *Primigenia* – The Twenty-Second Firstborn Legion

The II, IX, XIV and XX probably all came over in the invasion force. Legio VI *Victrix* and the Legio IX *Hispana* served in York with the former replacing the latter around AD 120 with the arrival of Severus. The mysterious fate of the IXth is dealt with below.

The IXth Legion Before Britannia

Before coming to Britannia the legion may have fought in the siege of Asculum (modern Ascoli Piceno, Italy) during the Social War in 90 BC. Julius Caesar, as governor of Cisalpine Gaul in 58 BC, inherited the four legions, the VII VIII IX and X, that were already based there. It seems that the IXth may have been stationed in Aquileia 'to guard against attacks from the Illyrians' and saw action in the assault on the Helvetii and in the Gallic wars.

Amid the wreckage of the republic, the IXth fought in the battles of Dyrrhachium and Pharsalus (48 BC) and in the African campaign of 46 BC. Caesar then cashiered the legion and settled the veterans around Picenum on the Adriatic coast. After Caesar's assassination, Octavian recalled the veterans of the IXth to quell the rebellion of Sextus Pompeius in Sicily. After defeating Sextus, they were posted to Macedonia. The IXth remained with Octavian in his war of 31 BC against Mark Antony and fought with him in the battle of Actium. With Octavian, now Augustus, the legion was sent to Hispania to take part in the offensive against the Cantabrians (25–13 BC). Their name *Hispana* comes from this time.

After this, the legion probably formed part of the Imperial Army in the Rhinelands that was campaigning against the Germanic tribes. Following the abandonment of the eastern Rhine area after the disastrous Battle of the Teutoburg Forest in AD 9, the IXth was relocated to Pannonia.

The Legio IX inscription from York is a superb fortress inscription from one of the main gates of the Roman fortress and one of the best examples of epigraphy to emerge from Roman Britain (*Roman Inscriptions of Britain* (*RIB*) 665). It was found 7 metres down in King's Square, at the corner of the square and Goodramgate – within a few metres of the site of the Roman south-east gateway. The inscription reads:

The Emperor Caesar Nerva Trajan Augustus, son of the deified Nerva, Conqueror of Germany, Conqueror of Dacia,

pontifex maximus, in his twelfth year of tribunician power,
six times acclaimed emperor, five times consul, father of his
country, built this gate by the IXth Legion Hispana.

At the start of the Claudian invasion the Britons were somewhat
elusive, playing a game of cat and mouse – dodging the invaders by
retreating into bogs and impenetrable forests, declining all offers
of battle. Eventually, Aulus Plautius found his prey, disorganised as
they were, subduing first the Catuvellauni led by Togodumnus and
then Caratacus. Fort constructed, Plautius moved forward first to do
battle on the River Medway, and then on the Thames. The Medway
battle was won by a flanking movement by the auxiliary Batavians –
special forces who were expert in swimming in full armour. Vespasian
commanded Legio II and, along with Hosidius Geta, defeated the
Britons in an unusually protracted two-day battle. Togodumnus was
killed, but Caratacus lived to fight another day out west, taking his
forces with him and leaving the rest of the army rudderless after the
death of his brother. On the Thames, the Britons failed to organise an
effective rearguard action and were cut off by the Romans who had
crossed unchallenged.

   Aulus Plautius paused, waiting for his emperor to arrive and take over
the command at this high-profile critical juncture: Claudius eventually
joined Plautius with reinforcements, artillery and terrifying elephants
for the attack on Camulodunum, the Iron Age *oppidum* which was the
Romans' key objective. At the time it would have consisted of motley
groups of insalubrious timber, wattle and daub huts. Trade, however,
was flourishing: excavations have revealed fine imported ware from
Gaul and red Arretine from Italy as well as the glass Strabo mentions.
Slaves too, captured from other tribes, were on the manifests: a six-man
slave chain has been found at Lord's Bridge in Cambridgeshire. How
great a change awaited Camulodunum, though, when the Romans later
colonised the place with temples, a forum and other powerful symbols
of their civilisation and projections of Roman power.

   This was Claudius' big moment; this is what he had planned the
invasion for: personally taking the war to the enemy and capturing their
royal capital, thus placing him amongst the great Roman commanders
of the past, not least Julius Caesar whose efforts he now truly eclipsed.
Claudius would now be a credible and memorable member of the Julio-

Claudian *gens*: the people of Rome and of the Roman Empire would see how he extended that empire by adding a new province, compensating for the theatrical shambles that Caligula had orchestrated and, in doing so, restoring the glory of Rome in this very visible theatre of war.

Claudius led from the front and, according to Cassius Dio, the stronghold fell after sixteen days allowing Claudius to enter the *oppidum* in triumph. Suetonius is less enthusiastic (*Claudius* 17), an impartial Josephus even less so, giving all the glory to Vespasian (*Bellum Judaicum* 3, 1, 2). Roman armies at this time were in the habit of hailing their emperor as *imperator* when he had won a significant conflict; Dio tells us that, in the case of Claudius, this happened more than once so we might assume that Colchester was not the only successful outcome in his three weeks in Britain. Cogidubnus was installed as a client king for the kingdom of Verica (Sussex); he received two tribes to control and was honoured with the title *rex et legatus Augustii in Britannia*, elevating him to native prince and Roman official. Eleven other tribes of south-east Britain surrendered to Claudius with no loss and the Romans proceeded to infiltrate further west and north into the territory of the Durotriges and Belgae of Dorset and Wiltshire retaining Camulodunum as a springboard for the incursions. The Romans duly established their new capital at Camulodunum and Claudius returned to Rome, his job done, the victory celebrated with coins and triumphal arches in Rome, Boulogne-sur-Mer, Claudius' departure point for Britain, and Cyzicus in Anatolia.

The Arch of Claudius in Rome was a triumphal arch built to honour Claudius' successful invasion of Britannia. Sadly, it has not survived, but happily, the inscription can still be seen at the Capitoline Museum. The arch was dedicated in AD 51, although a preview of sorts could be seen on the reverse of coins issued in AD 46–47 and AD 49 depicting it surmounted by an equestrian statue between two trophies. The reconstructed inscription, which can also be found on the arches celebrating the same events at Boulogne-sur-Mer and at Cyzicus reads:

> The Roman Senate and People to Tiberius Claudius Caesar Augustus Germanicus, son of Drusus, Pontifex Maximus, Tribunician power eleven times, Consul five times, Imperator 22 times, Censor, Father of the Fatherland, because he received the surrender of eleven kings of

the Britons defeated without any loss, and first brought barbarian peoples across the Ocean into the dominion of the Roman people.

ILS 216 *(Corpus Inscriptionum Latinarum, CIL* 6, 920)

The Triumph

Military service demonstrated patriotism, *pietas* and responsibility; it was also prestigious, offering the *gens* and the family palpable opportunities for glory that were visible in decorations, citations, prizes and, the pinnacle of them all, a triumph processing through the streets of Rome. Moreover, military service allowed the proud and patriotic Roman to demonstrate his *virtus,* his bravery and virtue. Glory and kudos were boosted by the complex system of decorations, *dona militaria,* and rewards that was established to reflect military success. Discipline and loyalty too were also strengthened by a tangible and noticeable array of benefits which included elevation to the rank of centurion where, after Marius, the pay was double that of the common soldier and the booty share was sizeably bigger. Gratuities, pay rises, better rations and promotion all contributed, as did social mobility for the common soldier and political success for the elite. Make no mistake though, the average pay for the average soldier or sailor was niggardly: he could earn three times more doing manual labour at twelve asses per day; it took until the time of Julius Caesar for a soldier's remuneration to be raised to ten asses per day in 49 BC. Pay was probably introduced around 406 BC after the wars with the Veii, but it was never meant to provide a living wage – rather it was more of a contribution to the cost of food, equipment and clothing. Increasingly, booty was the financial answer. In the empire, symbolic spears, the *hasta pura,* crowns, collars, *phalerae* and *phiale,* and standards, *vexilla,* were also there for all to see. The *spolia opima* was, of course, a highly prestigious and rare award.

The origin of the triumph remains something of a mystery, with its roots probably in an old Latin rite which, over time, absorbed various Etruscan and monarchical influences. The ceremony was in three parts: the first was focused on the army and the commander, assembled on the Campus Martius with praise heaped on the commander and individual soldiers who had shown conspicuous gallantry. Next came the procession along the traditional route which took in the Porta Triumphalis, the Circus

Maximus, the Palatine, Forum and the Capitoline ending at the temple of Jupiter Optimus Maximus. The procession had three parts: the booty and prisoners of war, the general accompanied by magistrates, and the army. The general rode in a four-horse chariot; he was decked out in a purple and gold tunic and a purple toga; he carried a laurel branch and an ivory sceptre; on his head was a laurel crown; his face was painted red.

You also earned the right to wear triumphal dress in public: the *corona triumphalis* (a gold coronet in the shape of a laurel wreath with gold ribbons); an ivory baton; the *tunica palmata* (a tunic embroidered with palm leaves); and the *toga picta* (painted toga), a toga dyed purple with an embroidered gold border, a robe believed originally to have been the official dress of the early Roman kings. The only other Romans entitled to wear these were the emperor, the two consuls in office and other magistrates when presiding over games.

A bronze statue of the triumphator was erected in the Forum of Augustus. The beneficiary also had the right to erect a further statue of himself in triumphal attire in the vestibule of his own house, which might also be kept on display by his descendants. The honours were degraded towards the end of Tiberius' rule and under Nero (r. AD 54–68), who also awarded them to *delatores* (deployed by these emperors to frame out-of-favour senators for treason and the like), but they were redeemed by Vespasian (r. AD 69–79) who had himself been awarded *ornamenta triumphalia* by Claudius during the invasion of Britain. Under the Antonine emperors (AD 98–180), the winners of triumphal honours lost the right to wear triumphal dress, which was now reserved for the consuls and for the emperors themselves, but they retained the distinction of a public statue.

The British Forces Opposing Rome

What sort of armies were the Romans up against? The Romans were usually a highly trained and disciplined fighting force with effective tactics and strategies; they routinely built camps as they proceeded (as we will see) and they possessed good equipment and a range of battle-proven weaponry; their lines of supply and stores were, by and large, well organised – as evidenced, for example, by the excavation of three quarters of a million nails unearthed at the site of the Inchtuthil legionary base.

Not so the Britons. No standing army – just levies of independent tribes, mainly farmers, with wavering loyalty, disunity and differing objectives. The Britons had absolute dependence on their lands and so many combatants had to keep one eye on the seasons and weather so that sowing and harvesting times were not missed.

The Romans' short-term strategy of subjugation must have been to establish legionary fortresses, auxiliary forts and roads to connect them all. A location somewhere in the vicinity of York, with Brigantes on one side and Parisi on the other, will have been earmarked for a northernmost fortress based on earlier reconnaissance of the island. So, Aulus Plautius got on with his task of subduing Britannia, advancing inland. The IXth penetrated the northeastern territories of the Catuvellauni into the Coritani lands in modern Leicestershire and Lincolnshire, establishing a fortress at Lincoln (Lindum Colonia). Within four years of the invasion, an area south of a line from the Humber to the Severn estuary was under Roman control, a line traced by the Roman Fosse Way. The XIVth marched north west, quelling the remaining pockets of Catuvellaunian resistance before conquering the Dobunni in what is Gloucestershire today. The II *Augusta,* under Vespasian, went south west as far as Exeter and South Wales (*Agricola* 13, *Histories* 3, 44; Suetonius, *Vespasian* 4), where, en route, they conquered first the Belgae of Wiltshire and Hampshire and then the Durotriges in Somerset and Dorset, assisted by the *Classis Britanniae* 'the British Fleet', whose role it was to build a naval supply depot at Chichester in the lands of the Regnenses and to provide naval support where required. Of the twenty or so British *oppida* taken in this campaign, the undoubted jewels in the crown were the formidable Maiden Castle (Dunum) near Dorchester, Hod Hill, north east of Blandford, Waddon Hill and Spetisbury Rings in north Dorset. In AD 49, the XXth moved west from Colchester and built a fortress at Gloucester (Gleva) in order to keep an eye on the troublesome tribes in the Welsh foothills. The XIVth were installed further north at Wroxeter (Viroconium) with the IXth over at Lincoln. The principal sea ports were at Richborough (Rutupiae), Bosham near Fishbourne and Fingringhoe in Essex, Hamworthy at Poole and Topsham near Exeter. The tribes of the Brigantes were taken on board under Cartimandua. By AD 49 the Romans had reached what was presumably their primary objectives: the Trent; the Severn and the Dee. Then they paused.

One thing all three legions now had in common was that they each faced hill country and all the military challenges that uplands and their inhabitants presented; the hills of Wales, Derbyshire and the Pennines were to prove no exception. Indeed, so formidable an obstacle did they present that real progress was hindered for the best part of a generation. A three-year foray into Wales from AD 57 was aborted. By the end of AD 69, through the reign of Nero and the Year of the Four Emperors, not much had changed: the west was confined behind a line from Newport through Shrewsbury to Chester; the north through Lincoln, Derby and Chester.

On the plus side, Tacitus describes the infighting and divisiveness that was characteristic of the British tribes and particularly of the confederation that was the Brigantes. Their inability to unify was ultimately largely responsible for their conquest: 'and so they fight individually, and all are conquered'; nevertheless, 'the natives are generally compliant and toe the line, so long as their trust is not abused.' Divided and ruled the Britons clearly were.

Plautius remained governor of the new province until AD 47 when he was replaced by Publius Ostorius Scapula. Dio records that, on his return to Rome, 'Plautius for his skillful and successful conduct of the war in Britain not only was praised by Claudius but also obtained an *ovatio* – ovation'. Unusually, and contrary to protocol, the emperor walked with his governor friend to the capitol on the big day.

Ovationes

An *ovatio* was a diluted form of a triumph, triumph-lite. Augustus had changed the rules regarding triumphs when he reserved the honour exclusively for members of the imperial family, so Claudius was honouring Plautius with the next best thing. In an *ovatio*, the conquering commander entered Rome on a caparisoned horse instead of the triumphal chariot; he did not redden his face with red lead as was the practice in a triumph in imitation of a terracotta image of triumphant Mars, but he did follow the same route through the city. Plautius' *ovatio* was to be the last time the distinction was granted to anyone outside of the imperial family. Claudius was, though, distantly related to Plautius through his first marriage to Plautia Urgulanilla.

Nepotism apart, this *ovatio* shows just how important the conquest of Britannia was to Roman foreign policy and prestige at home.

The Brigantes

Of all the British tribes, the one that interests us most is the Brigantes because York was established in Brigantian territory. Little is known of the Brigantes before the Roman invasion. Ptolemy helps us locate them in his *Geographia* (2, 3, 4) when he cites Eboracum as one of the nine places in Brigantian territory. This allows us to locate them in the old counties of Lancashire, the North and West Ridings of Yorkshire, Cumberland, Westmoreland and Durham. Ptolemy mentions two places, Camulodunum and Rigodunum, which were originally pre-Roman hill forts at Almondbury and Ingleborough; there was another at Barwick-in-Elmet and an *oppidum* at Stanwick near Richmond – a fortified royal centre. Because the Brigantes were a confederacy of clans rather than one united tribe it led to tribal and family rivalries and many a power struggle. This, of course, was a significant weakness militarily and diplomatically and something of a gift to the invading Romans.

Archaeological evidence suggests some wealth and culture among the tribal hierarchies, no doubt bankrolled by Roman subsidies paid to keep them down and quiet. A prestigious horned-head-shaped terret or harness ring found at Aldborough and an enamelled belt plate unearthed in York are in the Yorkshire Museum. Apart from the aristocracy, most of the Brigantes lived in rudimentary circular houses about 15 metres in diameter on farmsteads; good examples have been found at Naburn, close to York.

Stanwick (between Richmond and Gainford) probably represents the pinnacle of Brigantian wealth and power. Today an excavated section, some of it cut into rock, of the ramparts of the huge Iron Age trading and power centre can still be seen. Some four miles long, the defences covered 766 acres. After the Roman conquest, the Brigantian capital relocated to Aldborough. Archaeology tells us that the Brigantes were trading in Roman goods with French ceramics and Italian glass; Roman roof tiles have also been unearthed. Evidence of military activity comes by way of a hoard of decorated metalwork, which included chariot fittings, harness mounts and a sword scabbard. The ditch next to a gateway has yielded a sword still in its scabbard and a skull nearby, traumatised with life-changing wounds.

The absence of written records relating to the Brigantes before the Roman conquest makes it difficult to give a cogent history of their political, religious and social activities, but it seems probable that their rise to power came gradually rather than suddenly by conquest. Territorially speaking, the Brigantes were the largest tribe in Britain, encompassing sub-tribes such as the Gabrantovices on the Yorkshire coast, and the Textoverdi in the upper valley of the River South Tyne near Hadrian's Wall. The names Portus Setantiorum and Coria Lopocarum suggest other groups, the Setantii and the Lopocares, located on the Lancashire coast and the River Tyne respectively. The Carvetii, who occupied what is now Cumbria, may have been another sub-tribe.

Ptolemy names nine principal *poleis* or towns belonging to the Brigantes, these were:

Epiacum	Whitley Castle, Northumberland
Vinovium	Binchester, County Durham
Cataractonium	Catterick, North Yorkshire
Calatum	Burrow, Lonsdale, Lancashire
Isurium Brigantum	Aldborough, North Yorkshire
Rigodunum	Castleshaw, Greater Manchester
Olicana	Ilkley, West Yorkshire
Eboracum	York
Cambodunum	Slack, West Yorkshire

There was also:

Wincobank, near Sheffield

Bremetenacum Veteranorum, Ribchester, Lancashire

Calcaria, Tadcaster, North Yorkshire

Luguvalium, Carlisle, Cumbria – probably a settlement of the Carvetii

Coria Corbridge, Northumberland – possibly a settlement of the Lopocares

The first we hear of the Brigantes after the Roman invasion is when, according to Tacitus (*Annals* 12, 32), in AD 47, Publius Ostorius Scapula had to abandon his campaign against the Deceangli of North Wales because of annoying and worrying 'disaffection' among the Brigantes, whose leaders had been allies of Rome. Some of those who had taken up arms were executed while the rest were pardoned.

Aldborough is built on the site of a major Romano-British town, Isurium Brigantum. Isurium was probably the headquarters of the Legio IX *Hispana* although no structural evidence for any fort has been found. Isurium Brigantum was at the crossing of Dere Street over the River Ure, the Roman road from York to the Antonine Wall via Corbridge and Hadrian's Wall. The modern village does retain part of the Roman street plan and St Andrew's Church stands on the site of the forum. Isurium Brigantum was the capital of the Brigantes after AD 160, one of the most northern Roman urban centres – a *civitas* – probably founded in the late first century or early second century. In terms of civic status, it was on a par with Exeter, Leicester, Chichester and Canterbury.

In Britannia generally all was not well. The area corresponding roughly to modern-day Wales continued to prove particularly intractable with fierce resistance coming from the Silures, Ordovices and Deceangli. In addition, Caratacus and his guerrilla attacks were a real problem as he proceeded to shift his allegiance to the Silures and then to the Ordovices (in modern Powys). In the north and east of England the Brigantes and the Iceni continued to be troublesome. AD 50 saw things came to a head when Publius Ostorius Scapula defeated Caratacus in the Battle of Caer Caradoc, Caratacus' last stand. Caratacus' wife, son, and daughter were captured and his brother surrendered; Caratacus fled to the Brigantes, but a fickle Queen Cartimandua handed him over to the Romans in chains and he was dispatched to Rome to become a reluctant star in Claudius' triumph. This was another significant feather in Claudius' military cap; Ostorius, however, had to make do with triumphal insignia.

Intractable Wales and Duplicitous Cartimandua

It is unlikely that Ostorius had much time to bask in his new glory: the Silures would not lie down, continually harassing the Romans, fired by the Roman's tactless assertion that 'the Silures must be exterminated', which may have resonated with some of the more educated tribesman as an echo from the rumours they may have heard of Cato's similarly doom-laden 'Carthage must be destroyed'. Their guerrilla campaign culminated in an attack on a large detachment of legionaries under a *praefectus castrorum*, which had been detailed to construct forts in Silurian territory. The unit was cut off and only narrowly survived, but with the loss of the prefect and eight centurions – a significant defeat by any measure (Tacitus, *Annals* 12, 38). Other embarrassments included the ambushing of a foraging party and then of the auxiliaries dispatched to rescue them: Ostorius had no option but to deploy his legions. Then there was the luring into a trap of two auxiliary cohorts which were taken prisoner; the shrewd Silures cleverly shared out the hostages and their booty amongst neighbouring tribes, thus currying favour locally and building up an alliance against the Romans.

Ostorius died soon after – exhausted by his reversals: *taedio curarum fessus* (*Annals* 12, 39); the Silures were saved the promised extermination and lived to fight another day – much to the dismay of the Romans. Ostorius was hastily replaced by the experienced and successful Aulus Didius Gallus (14, 1); he advanced into Wales, but the Silures continued to triumph, not least with a significant victory against the XXth legion. Didius managed to subdue the Welsh border country but then halted. Significant a victory as this was, Didius could not afford to relax, and now faced a renewed threat from the Brigantes. Cartimandua's former husband Venutius, a passionate hater of the name of Rome, *Romani nominis odium,* assumed the mantle of leader of British resistance against Rome.

In Rome at this time there was considerable tumult. Claudius died in suspicious circumstances and was succeeded by the mercurial and unpredictable Nero. Suetonius (*Nero* 18) records that the emperor was presumably running out of patience with the persistent unrest in Britannia and considered pulling out altogether. If this rumour had reached Didius it would be no surprise if he reverted to a strategy of containment. Alternatively, it is quite possible that Nero's negative attitude was shaped by the pandemonium caused by the Boudican revolt. Whatever the reason, Nero, in the end, was astute enough to see that a withdrawal would reflect well on Claudius but would rebound on himself – he would be seen as the emperor who presided over a failure.

In Britannia, the next seasoned general as governor – one Quintus Veranius – planned another punitive assault on Wales. Veranius, however, died in office, paving the way for Gaius Suetonius Paulinus.

Tacitus had asserted that the guerrilla warfare waged by the Silures and other disaffected tribes was only dealt with by a policy of building fortresses (*Annals* 12, 32); these would be supported by the establishment in AD 49 of a *colonia* at Camulodunum where *agri captivi* – the lands of the defeated – were requisitioned on which, six years after the invasion, Roman veterans who were coming up for retirement could be settled. This was not only a consolidating defensive tactic, it was also intended as a big step towards the Romanisation of southern Britain. Cunobelinus would have been a major loser here with his lands suddenly being subsumed into the emperor's private estates. As an exercise in Romanisation it clearly failed; on the contrary, it caused seething and rebellious discontentment amongst the Catuvellauni and the Trinovantes.

Cartimandua had probably been leader of the Brigantes well before Claudius invaded and may be one of the eleven monarchs who surrendered to Rome without a fight, as proclaimed on Claudius' triumphal arch. She was now considerably wealthy, due to her shrewd support of Rome and her betrayal of Caratacus; however, Venutius attacked the Brigantes, only failing to defeat them when the Romans sent Caesius Nasica and the Legio IX *Hispana*, to reinforce the queen.

Cartimandua had married Vellocatus, former armour-bearer to Venutius, and made him her king. Although Tacitus records that Cartimandua was a trusted ally of Rome's and acknowledges her *nobilitas* – nobility – he savages her character in much the same way as back in Rome the establishment Augustan poets, Horace, Virgil and Propertius, had trashed the memory of Cleopatra VII in the early days of the empire. Tacitus describes Cartimandua's treatment of Caratacus as evilly intentioned, and highlights her obscene wealth and luxurious lifestyle; he slurs her liaison with Vellocatus as adulterous, driven by rage and lust: it is a disgraceful act, *flagitium,* which shook the very foundations of her dynasty. Cartimandua is *regina,* queen, (a dirty word in Rome, thanks to Rome's vexed relationship with Cleopatra) and is duplicitous in her behaviour towards Venutius and his family. Tacitus disparages the power that she wields as being ignominious to men. The historian's vitriol here is indicative of his, and of many Romans like him, unfettered disgust at duplicity, particularly duplicity in a woman.

The next powerful woman, the next British queen the Romans encountered, Boudica, was to prove even more belligerent and somewhat less compliant.

Druids

A druid was a member of the higher class in ancient Celtic cultures. We associate them with religious leadership, but they were also legal experts, judges, bards, medical professionals, and political advisors. Druids were literate but they have left us no written records because, inconveniently for us, they were not permitted to produce written accounts of themselves.

As we have said, in AD 58 Gaius Suetonius Paulinus was appointed governor of Britain, replacing Quintus Veranius, who had died in office. Suetonius was another eminent commander, having been, amongst other achievements, the first Roman to cross the Atlas Mountains. His objective in AD 60 Britannia was to indulge in a spot of ethnic cleansing and religious intolerance: the subjugation of Mona, Anglesey, and extermination of the druid community there. In doing so, Suetonius would bring an end to the island's status as a haven for disaffected refugees. Druidism was feared by the Romans, not least because of its reputation for focusing opposition to Roman rule and for its veneration of the human head, which often led to routine decapitation of corpses after battle. This terrifying headhunting can be seen depicted on Trajan's Column. According to Caesar (*De Bello Gallico* 4), druidic convention ruled that anyone found guilty of theft or other petty criminal offences could find themselves sacrificial victims, although if such criminals were in short supply, innocents would do just as well. A form of sacrifice recorded by Caesar from his experiences in Gaul was the burning alive of victims in a large wooden effigy, now often known as a wicker man. According to Tacitus, the druids had a reputation for 'soaking their altars in the blood of prisoners and using human entrails in their divination'; human sacrifice in other words. Reports of druids performing human sacrifice are found in Lucan, *Pharsalia* 1, 450-58; Caesar, *Gallic Wars* 6, 16, 17.3-5; Suetonius, *Claudius* 25; Cicero, *Pro Fonte*io 31; Cicero, *De Republica* 9, 15. The demonisation of druids by the Romans may be seen as an attempt to justify colonialisation and the suppression of so-called barbarians.

But they were not totally savage: Strabo tells us about those who studied moral philosophy. Nevertheless, Diodorus Siculus records that:

> These men predict the future by observing the flight and calls of birds and by the sacrifice of holy animals: all orders of society are in their power ... and in very important matters they prepare a human victim, plunging a dagger into his

chest; by observing the way his limbs convulse as he falls and the gushing of his blood, they are able to read the future.

Paulinus' soldiers lined up opposite an armed force among which were 'women dressed in black robes with dishevelled hair like Furies, brandishing torches. Next to them were the druids, their hands raised to the skies, screaming fearsome curses.'The Romans were at first paralysed with fear, understandably, but then pulled themselves together, attacked, slaughtered all before them and hacked down the sacred groves.

As noted, by and large, Rome was receptive to many of the religions it encountered in its conquests, allowing a mutual absorption of the imperial with the local. This tolerance and syncretism, however, had its limits – and anything the Romans encountered which excited their innate superstition or was considered a vehicle for sedition was not tolerated. Druidism, obviously, fell into that category. According to Pliny the Elder, Tiberius (r. AD 14–37), enacted laws banning druidic practices, and those from other native soothsayers and healers, a move which Pliny believed would bring an end to human sacrifice in Gaul. Suetonius claimed that Augustus had decreed that no one could be both a druid and a Roman citizen, and that this was followed by a law passed by Claudius which 'thoroughly suppressed' the druids by banning their religious practices.

Suetonius also tells that another, purely personal, reason for Paulinus' assault on the druids was to match rival general Corbulo's achievement in winning Armenia for Rome. Gnaeus Domitius Corbulo (c. AD 7–67) was a populist Roman commander, brother-in-law of Caligula and father-in-law of Domitian. Nero, scared of Corbulo's reputation, ordered him to commit suicide, which the general carried out, exclaiming *Axios,* 'I am worthy', and fell on his own sword.

The Boudican Revolt, AD 60–61

One way in which local tribes could guarantee peaceful co-existence with Rome was to bequeath to the Romans their lands on the death of the monarch. As noted, Prasutagus, prosperous king of the Iceni did just that, citing Nero as heir but with a codicil naming his daughters as co-heirs. The Iceni had been on friendly terms with the Romans since the early days of the invasion, but on the king's death in AD 60 these same Romans chose to ignore the small print in the king's will, divided up the legacy, took over the kingdom and plundered it. Indeed, Suetonius relates (*Augustus* 48) that Augustus had ordained that many years before client kingdoms (*reges socii*) were always 'integral parts of the empire' (*membra partesque imperii*). Perhaps it was naive of the Iceni to expect an extension of the special relationship after Prasutagus' death, but the aftermath of the Roman decision was shocking, brutal and highly provocative: Prasutagus' daughters were raped, Queen Boudica, his wife, was flogged, the family was treated as slaves and his Roman creditors called in their loans, loans which the Iceni had been led to believe were gifts; grants made by Claudius were also revoked. Boudica was comprehensively humiliated and outraged.

Elsewhere in Britannia, the time was ripe for revenge and rebellion: the Iceni were joined by the disaffected Trinovantes, the tribe that had been ignominiously displaced from the native capital Camulodunum and enslaved as labourers to help in the construction of the *colonia* in AD 49–50 with its Temple of Claudius, a citadel unmistakably symbolic of oppressive Roman rule, a beacon of Romanisation, which was the focus of an imperial cult dedicated to Claudius with the burden of cost on the native aristocracy. Furthermore, the Romans settled it with a large contingent of army veterans, which would provide a permanent insurance against rebellion, in effect making it a small piece of Rome in Britannia. What they failed to do, however, was fortify the place.

On the eve of the uprising the omens were not good for the Romans: 'the statue of Victory in Camulodunum crashed to the ground as if in flight; there were lamentations, though no mortal man had uttered the words or the groans'; hysterical women chanted, heralding impending doom, 'at night there was heard to issue from the senate-house foreign jargon mingled with laughter, and from the theatre more cries; a ghost town on the Thames was seen to be in ruins and the Channel turned blood red; shapes like bodies were washed up.' More crucially, Camulodunum was not only not fortified but largely undefended – Suetonius Paulinus had fatefully posted the garrison legion, the XXth, to the Welsh borders. The procurator was found wanting: when the Roman inhabitants clamoured for reinforcements, Catus Decianus sent a mere 200 auxiliary troops.

In AD 61, the Iceni under Boudica advanced on the *colonia*. Camulodunum was sacked and the temple fell after two days; the *saevitia,* savagery, of Boudica's forces was uncompromising. The sounds of human sacrifice rang around the sacred groves. The IXth legion under Petillius Cerealis rushed to relieve the defenders but was annihilated. Catus Decianus fled to Gaul. Only the IXth's cavalry escaped to fight another day. Suetonius reached Londinium – then an important but undefended trading port – calculating that it was impossible to defend with the meagre forces at his disposal. The awful decision to abandon Londinium was made and those left behind were slaughtered in the carnage that ensued. Excavations have revealed a thick red layer of burnt detritus covering coins and pottery dating before AD 60.

Euphoric and drunk – metaphorically and actually – on their easy successes, the Britons then devastated Verulamium (St Albans), a stronghold of the pro-Roman Catuvellauni. According to (an exaggerating) Tacitus, up to 80,000 men, women and children were slain in the orgy of destruction visited on the three towns by Boudica's forces. The Britons were not in the habit of taking prisoners – they had no interest in selling slaves – they showed no quarter; the only options were rape, slaughter, hanging, burning alive and crucifixion. Dio's account is even more graphic: he says that the noblest women had the length of their bodies impaled on sharpened spikes and their breasts were hacked off and sewn onto their mouths, 'to the accompaniment of sacrifices, feasts, and lewd behaviour' sacrilegiously performed in sacred places, such as the groves of Andraste, a British goddess of victory.

Suetonius Paulinus hurriedly assembled a force of around 10,000 men and prepared for battle, the Battle of Watling Street, to salvage what he could of the Roman occupation. His army included his own Legio XIV

Gemina and units from the XX *Valeria Victrix*; Legio II *Augusta* under Poenius Postumus, near Exeter, did not respond to the call for assistance either because Postumus was petrified at the prospect of fighting Boudica or, more likely, because he (sensibly) did not want to leave the south west unprotected. Whatever, his insubordination would have fortuitously detained some tribes in the south west preventing them from joining Boudica.

The 10,000 were massively outnumbered by Boudica's 230,000 – no doubt another huge exaggeration but Boudica certainly enjoyed a substantial superiority; as Dio says, even if the Romans were lined up one deep, they would not have reached the end of Boudica's line. However, British complacency was to be their undoing: so casual, so confident was Boudica's army of victory that women were allowed to attend the battle as grandstand spectators in wagons on the edge of the battlefield. Boudica herself rallied her troops from a chariot, her violated daughters beside her, in a rousing speech, anticipating another easy victory.

Unfortunately for the Britons, there was to be no victory; Boudica was soundly defeated. The Britons were hampered by their poor manoeuvrability and their inexperience of disciplined open-field tactics. Moreover, the narrow battlefield restricted the numbers Boudica could deploy at any one time, thus diminishing her numerical advantage. The Britons were felled in their droves by the Roman javelins which rained down on them.

Women and domestic animals were slaughtered while Boudica's retreating warriors were hampered in their collective flight by the wagons nearby, all full of those hapless spectators. According to Tacitus (exaggerating again), 80,000 Britons died that day to the Romans' loss of 400. No doubt there was more rape and other atrocities; the fate of Boudica's daughters is not recorded. Some say Boudica herself committed suicide by poisoning; Dio disputes this, or at least paraphrases the detail out of the same story, and claims that Boudica fell ill and died, and was buried at great expense and with full honours.

Postumus fell on his sword, his leaderless legion along with the IXth joining Suetonius. The IXth was reinforced with 2,000 infantry from Germany, eight cohorts of auxiliary infantry and 1,000 auxiliary horse. Catus Decianus was replaced by Gaius Julius Alpinus Classicianus. Suetonius instigated vicious slash-and-burn reprisals on every tribe involved in the rebellion, but he was eventually replaced by the more conciliatory Publius Petronius Turpilianus, in the interests of averting another revolt. The pretext for Suetonius' (the commander) removal was that he had apparently 'lost' some of the ships of the Roman fleet. If Suetonius, (the biographer), is to be believed, the crisis, as noted, almost made Nero, now emperor, abandon Britannia for good.

Iceni territory was amongst the lands laid waste by Suetonius Paulinus with many surviving rebels sold into slavery, and 'whatever tribes still wavered or were hostile were ravaged with fire and sword'. The prospect, and reality, of famine became all the more real because the Britons had not bothered to sow seeds for the year's harvest, over-optimistically and naively assuming they could live off plundered Roman supplies. It is likely that Britannia went into recession, even depression: the fields were empty and the agricultural workforce was severely depleted through war casualties, disability and enslavement.

What little evidence we have of Romanisation immediately after the revolt comes from the rebuilding of London, as a civil rather than the military community destroyed by Boudica. In the '70s there was reconstruction work at Verulamium and civic projects at Exeter and Cirencester. But it was the new procurator, Gaius Julius Alpinus Classicianus from 61 to 65 who salvaged the increasingly tenuous Roman hold on Britannia. He was a man with experience of motives for rebellion and the consequences of repression, gained through his father-in-law, Julius Indus, a distinguished provincial from the Trier region. Classicianus saw what the destruction of these huge swathes of Britannia would do to his tax revenues: his intervention was pivotal in the future of Roman Britannia.

In the short term, the Romans had to win back the hearts and minds of those members of the British aristocracy who were pro-Roman or, at least, not anti-Roman. They had obviously lost much goodwill and sympathy during and after the revolt, particularly following Suetonius' savage reprisals. Classicianus' critical report, especially in relation to Suetonius Paulinus, led to an inquiry presided over by the freedman Polyclitus. Tacitus loathed Polyclitus, because, as a snob, the historian loathed all freedmen and their new powers, alien as they were to the *mos maiorum* – the way your forefathers did things – the mantra of the conservative Roman. He despised Publius Petronius Turpilianus, the new governor (62–63) because of what he saw as disgraceful turpitude when he failed to rush headlong into more conflict with the barbaric Britons. But between Classicianus and Turpilianus, it cannot be denied, they restored much-needed order to southern Britain and southern Britain never rose in revolt ever again.

Tacitus hints of some success here when he says, not without a sneer, that the Britons were beginning to enjoy the fruits of peace and the allurements of civilisation under Trebellius Maximus, governor AD 63–69. The Britons were turning into Romans. . .

Mos Maiorum

An unwritten, but nevertheless powerful, code subscribed to by conservative Romans who believed that in all things their ancestors did it best and they did it in the right way. The code prescribed social norms and laid down values for the true Roman to follow. According to some, Rome had been declining in so many ways since the third century BC. We have already encountered Cato the Elder; to Cato and others like him the waging of war was one answer to all manner of political and social issues.

Here are the key pillars of the *mos maiorum*:

Fides
Trust, trustworthiness, good faith, faithfulness, confidence, reliability and credibility.

Pietas
Respect towards the gods, homeland, parents and family, which required the maintenance of relationships in a moral and dutiful manner. Cicero defined *pietas* as 'justice towards the gods' (*De Natura Deorum* 1, 116). It was the principal virtue of Aeneas in Virgil's national poem, the *Aeneid*.

Religio and *cultus*
Religio was the bond between gods and mortals, as carried out in traditional religious practices for preserving the *pax deorum* ('peace of the gods'). *Cultus* was the active observance and the correct performance of rituals.

Disciplina
The military character of Roman society explains the importance of *disciplina*, as related to education, training, discipline and self-control.

Gravitas and *Constantia*

Gravitas was dignified self-control. *Constantia* was steadiness or perseverance. In adversity, a good Roman must maintain an emotionless disposition.

Virtus

Virtus enshrined the ideal of the true Roman male.

Dignitas and *auctoritas*

Dignitas and *auctoritas* were what you got by displaying the values of the ideal Roman in the form of priesthoods, military rank and magistracies. *Dignitas* was reputation for worth, honour and esteem. Thus, a Roman who displayed their *gravitas, constantia, fides, pietas* and other values of a Roman would be exhibiting *dignitas* among his peers.

The Romans showed breathtaking arrogance and naivety in the run-up to the rebellion. History should have told them that much of what they were doing in the years before AD 60 was politically inept, provocative, inflammatory, diplomatically disastrous and certain to end badly. The maulings Rome took in the Clades Lolliana in 17 BC and in the Teutoburger Wald in AD 9 were still relatively recent, but any lessons learned there seem to have been forgotten. The only good that came out of the Boudican revolt was the programme of civic and fortress building which the Romans undertook to defend against the rebellious Brigantes and Welsh tribes. Eboracum was one of those fortresses which benefitted, and as such became a major player in the defence of Roman Britain and the civilising and Romanising which went with it.

The Road to York: Why York?

From the Romans' point of view the abiding impact of Boudica's revolt was, quite simply, to increase their resolve of the Romans to subdue and Romanise Britannia – a feat which was to a large degree accomplished under Gnaeus Julius Agricola (AD 40–93), governor AD 77–84. The establishment of fortress York in AD 71 with the IXth as its garrison is one earlier powerful manifestation of that policy and objective, and an unmissable projection of Roman power. The penetrating advances into the Derbyshire hills and the east Pennines are two more.

There were also economic benefits to taking the northern reaches of Britannia – for example, the exploitation of the raw materials latent in this decidedly inhospitable region. But the prime motive was military. The belligerent Picts and Scots, the Brigantes and the Parisi were kept down by stationing the Roman IX Legion to the south at York; consequently, most of the Roman settlements north of the Humber were military stations. The Romans built military settlements in the Pennines at Ilkley, Castleshaw and Slack to control the Brigantians, and temporary Roman military camps on the North York Moors at Cawthorne and Goathland. There were, however, signs of incipient civilising as seen in Roman villas around Derventio, Petuaria and in the area around present-day Bridlington; these suggest a degree of settled and civilised Romano-British concord.

Marcus Vettius Bolanus (c. AD 33–76) was governor of Britain AD 69–71. The increasingly restless Brigantes presented Bolanus with a second insurrection in the shape of Venutius. We have seen how Cartimandua, Venutius' former wife and queen of the Brigantes, had been a client ruler loyal to the Romans for twenty years; the Romans had defended her against an earlier revolt by her ex-husband. This time, however, Bolanus could only send auxiliaries. Cartimandua had to get out, leaving her kingdom in the hands of the seriously anti-Rome Venutius. Friendly buffer state had instantly turned into a significant military threat. Northern protection for the Romans offered by the Brigantes was a thing of the past: Roman policy in Britannia would have to change dramatically.

Back in Rome, by the end of AD 69 Vespasian had emerged from the civil war turmoil, establishing himself as emperor at the expense of the other three pretenders to the throne, and set about restoring control over troublesome tribes fomenting trouble around the empire; one of the tribes on the hit list was the Brigantes. The XIVth *Gemina* was again withdrawn from Britain in AD 70 to help put down Batavian unrest on the lower Rhine, and the mutinous Marcus Roscius Coelius was replaced as commander of XX *Valeria Victrix* by Gnaeus Julius Agricola. Bolanus remained as governor until AD 71. The poet Statius (c. AD 45–c. 96) tells (*Silvae* 5,2) how Bolanus established forts, watchtowers, walls and ditches and captured a breastplate from 'a British king', which suggests that he reconquered some of the territory lost in the Brigantian revolt. In his *Agricola* (8, 16), Tacitus suggests that Vettius Bolanus was not really up to the job, saying that

> he governed more mildly than suited so turbulent a province . . . nor did Vettius Bolanus, even as the civil wars wore on, trouble Britain with discipline. There was the same lethargy with regard to his operations against the enemy, and similar unruliness in his camp. Bolanus was an honourable man and nothing about him made you dislike him but he had won popularity at the expense of control.

Caution, however, is required with these accounts which cannot be regarded as wholly objective or impartial: Tacitus was Agricola's son-in-law and Statius' poem is a eulogy to Bolanus' son, Crispinus.

Bolanus was succeeded by Quintus Petillius Cerialis (c. AD 30–after 83); he went on to be governor of Asia in AD 75–76. Vespasian, having quelled uprisings in Judaea and the Netherlands, appointed Cerialis governor of Britannia; Cerialis, a relative of Vespasian, was accompanied by the II *Adiutrix*, until then garrisoned in Nijmegen and formed from the I *Classica*, a legion levied by Nero among the marines of the Classis Misenensis, but later completed by Galba. Cerialis stationed the legion at Lincoln, replacing the IXth which was posted to Eboracum. Cerialis was supported by Gnaeus Julius Agricola, commander of XX *Valeria Victrix*, later to be governor. Agricola dealt efficiently with the Ordovices and took Anglesey. In preparation for the continued drive north he established the fortress at Chester – strategically important for incursions into North Wales and access to the Irish Sea and as a springboard for assaults on the Brigantes from the west.

Cerialis, like Vespasian, was a veteran of Britannia: he had his first experience here as legate of Legio IX *Hispana* under governor Gaius Suetonius Paulinus. In the Boudican rebellion, Cerialis suffered a serious reverse when attempting to relieve Camulodunum which was taken by the Britons before he arrived. Tacitus (*Annals* 14, 32) says: 'The victorious enemy met Petillius Cerialis, commander of the ninth legion, as he was coming to the rescue, routed his troops, and destroyed all his infantry. Cerialis escaped with some cavalry into the camp, and was saved by its fortifications.'

The appointment of the dynamic Cerialis was one of the key strands in a more aggressive, proactive policy. To Tacitus this was the start of a succession of great commanders and armies (*Agricola* 17), boosting morale in the province and invigorating the soldiery. Another key factor was the construction of that legionary fortress at Eboracum, a strategic fortification that was both defensive and offensive; it was built on the site of a short-lived Roman base established under Vettius Bolanus. A fort at Danum (Doncaster), at a strategic crossing over the River Don, was also built. The Romans were methodically and patiently inching north, advancing along the road that ran along the Wolds from Lindum Colonia (Lincoln) and then crossing the Humber to land at Petuaria, (Brough) on the north bank, west of modern Hull, the capital of the Parisi tribe. Cerealis capitalised on the goodwill of the pro-Roman Parisi who afforded him access to the adjoining Brigantian territory. He moved up from Brough to Malton (Derventio), east of York, where evidence for a vexillation fortress has been found, and to Isurium Brigantum (Aldborough) – the Brigantian stronghold, later capital, – and finally to Eboracum.

The date for the new fortress is AD 71; it was of wooden construction in the traditional playing-card plan, occupying about 25 hectares. York was identified as a significantly strategic site on the confluence of the rivers Foss and Ouse and on a strategically important glacial moraine above the surrounding marshy Vale of York. Bolanus' construction apart, it seems probable that the Romans found little if any pre-existing native settlements here; this gave them a blank canvas on which to work. Virgin land and meadow scrub enabled them to build their *castra* (forts) exactly how they wanted them. The Romans, of course, were experts in these civil engineering projects. Later, military builders could refer to technical camp building handbooks such as the *De Munationibus Castrorum – On the Fortifications of a Military* Camp by Pseudo-Hyginus from the middle of the second century; this was a practical, detailed manual on how to lay out a military camp, written specially for the high-ranking officer. For example, the author explains how much space is needed for each soldier or horse. In the fifth century, Vegetius added to the expertise with his *De Re Militari* and its *Epitoma rei militaris, About things Military* – a veritable military encyclopedia including how to fortify and organise a camp. Of course, neither would have been available to the surveyors (*agrimensores*) or *architecti*, chief engineers at nascent York, but it is very likely that other, similar works which are not extant, would have been on hand and consulted on site.

The IXth was duly installed here as the vanguard in the new governor's strategy to subdue the island north and west of York. The fortress and its garrison allowed the Romans to monitor potential uprisings by both the Parisi to the east and south and the Brigantes to the west and north. From now on Eboracum would be the jumping-off point and supply centre for military activities in and well beyond the immediate vicinity. It was the largest town in northern Britain and, in time, prospered to become command headquarters for the north, capital city of Britannia Inferior and win the status of *colonia*.

From York, Cerialis attacked the Brigantian canton on both flanks then pushed north to Cataractonium (Catterick), and then on to the huge British fortification at Stanwick near Richmond and Piercebridge in the Tees Valley, which is the site of the fortified river crossing where Dere Street crossed the River Tees. In addition, we have evidence of marching camps way to the west in the Stainmore Pass. From all of this we clearly see the rapidity and efficiency which characterised Roman military progress: roads, forts and bridges were built with seeming effortless ease to facilitate the now relentless Roman advance up through Britannia. A veritable *blitzkrieg*. At least twenty-eight forts were built from North Yorkshire up to the Tyne and from the Mersey to the Eden. Cerialis may also have penetrated some way along the Chester to Carlisle road if the evidence provided by three marching camps is anything to go by.

Cerialis then campaigned through most of Brigantian territory, with mixed success according to Tacitus who records 'many battles, some very bloody' (*Agricola* 17), probably including a major action against Venutius. Tacitus (*Agricola* 17) reports the Roman progress in glowing terms:

> When however Vespasian had restored unity to Britain as well as to the rest of the world [in AD 69], the presence of great generals and crack armies crushed the enemy's aspirations. They were at once panic-stricken by the attack by Petillius Cerialis on the Brigantes, said to be the most prosperous tribe in the entire province. There were many battles, some very bloody, and his conquests, or at least his wars, consumed a large part of the territory of the Brigantes. Indeed he would have totally overshadowed the activity and renown of any other successor; but Julius Frontinus was equal to the task, a great man as far as greatness was then possible, who subdued with his army the powerful and belligerent tribe of the Silures, overcoming the difficulties presented by the terrain and the bravery of the enemy.

Julius Frontinus

Sextus Julius Frontinus (c. AD 40–103), civil engineer, author, soldier and senator, was a major player with Quintus Petillius Cerialis in suppressing the Gallic revolt of Gaius Julius Civilis in AD 70 and later tells us (*Strategemata* 4, 3, 14) that he received the surrender of 70,000 Lingones, a Gallic tribe. He succeeded Cerialis as governor of Britain (AD 74–77) where he subjugated the Silures of South Wales, built a fortress for Legio II *Augusta* at Caerleon and most probably engaged the Brigantes. He was also a capable civil engineer with special expertise in aqueducts and water supply for which he was appointed to the highly prestigious office of *curator aquarum* (supervisor of the aqueducts of Rome) by Emperor Nerva; he was also a noted military strategist. In AD 99 he was made *consul ordinarius* with Trajan – a high honour which illustrates the regard in which he was held. Works include *De Aquaeductu* and *Strategemata*, a manual of examples of military stratagems from Greek and Roman history, for the use in the field by commanders.

How to Win a Siege or Prosecute a War – the Roman Way

There was, of course, plenty of advice to be had on strategy and tactics and the right and proper way to prosecute a war. Apart from Julius Caesar expatiating on the conflict in Gaul and the civil wars, there was the *Strategikos* of Onasander, Polybius' work on camps (*Histories* 6, 19-42), the *Strategemata* by Frontinus, the *De Re Militari* of Vegetius, and the Byzantine historian Zosimus (fl. AD 490s–510s). Taking siege warfare as an example, Onasander recommends restraint when it comes to plunder, and not to threaten massacre as both just lead to a more defiant and intractable enemy; prisoners of war should be spared, at least for the duration of the war, for the same reasons. Indeed, all prisoners should be shepherded into the besieged city to exacerbate food shortages and hasten starvation. Onasander is not averse to brutality when it is necessary (*Strategikos* 38). Zosimus (*Historia Nova* 1, 69) records how Lydius, at the siege of Cremona in AD 278, evicted all the prisoners, young and old; the Romans sent them back, only for Lydius to hurl them to their deaths into a ravine. Frontinus advocated terrorising the besieged (*Strategemata* 2, 9, 2-5).

The pursuit of terror tactics and *blitzkrieg* generally was a strategy not lost on Britannia's next governor, Gnaeus Julius Agricola, in his first year in charge, according to Tacitus (*Agricola* 20).

How did the locals react to the overrunning of their islands, or more likely on a local level, to the occupation of their native lands and what did the Romans do to get them on side? The tribes obviously reacted differently to the Romans depending on their individual circumstances and long-term objectives. As we have seen, some, such as the Brigantes and Iceni, rebelled but over the next ninety years, although force was always a key option and threat, other methods were at the Romans' disposal with which to retain control – mollifying tactics which the Romans knew all about from their centuries of conquest and Romanisation. These included bribery, goodwill, taxation, timely demonstrations of military might and power, and installing Roman and allied settlers. The Romans, it must be said, may not have had to try that hard to bring potentially winnable natives under their influence. All the circumspect but vacillating Briton had to do to see the fruits of collaboration was to pick up those reports from over the Channel and hear about opportunities for social mobility, comparative wealth, luxuries, even power and high status. The benefits of peace and cooperation were obvious, particularly when seen against the current lifestyle the tribes endured, notable for its constant inter-tribal and internecine warfare.

Julius Frontinus, as the next governor (AD 74–77), obviously believed that Cerialis, his predecessor, had succeeded in taming the north; this allowed him to focus on subduing the ever-turbulent Silures by sea and land, eventually bringing South Wales to heel, as shown by the evacuation of Gloucester and the establishment of a fortress at Isca Silurum, Caerleon, for Legio II. He appropriated good farming land from the defeated Silures while he constructed auxiliary forts in the territory of the southwestern Demetae who posed little problem. But the Ordovices in Snowdonia were a different matter, only to be addressed by the construction of the fortress at Deva, Chester, to garrison II *Adiutrix*, bringing the number of legions concentrated here to three.

AD 79 was a year of consolidation with the territory of the Votadini and Selgovae, north of the Tyne-Solway isthmus, firmly in the Romans' sights. The Tavus (Tay) was reached: it seems likely that the plan was to execute a pincer movement from Carlisle and Corbridge concluding at Inveresk on the Forth and then advancing to Stirling via Strathallan and Strathearn and on to the Tay.

It was, however, Julius Agricola, the next governor who would lead this campaign (AD 78– 85). As we know, Agricola had been in Britannia twice before, as military tribune between 58 and 62 under Suetonius Paulinus and as commander of the XXth under Petilius Cerialis, so he was familiar with the territory and with the locals.

Agricola, ignoring cautionary advice and much to the probable consternation of the enemy, started as he meant to go on: he hit the ground running by attacking, and annihilating, the Ordovices (*Agricola* 18, 3). Anglesey, the target aborted all those years before by Suetonius Paulinus, was next with Agricola creating more astonishment and surprise by deploying special forces in the shape of the Batavians – those expert, fully armed, kit-carrying swimmers – when everyone was expecting a conventional invasion by ship. So, in two short operations Agricola had eloquently established his credentials: he had surprised and beaten his enemy with little Roman loss, he had established his reputation with his troops, he had conquered hitherto refractory territory, and he had impressed Vespasian at the expense of Corbulo.

Much of Agricola's overall success as governor can be attributed to a judicious blend of aggression towards recalcitrants and adept selling of the benefits of Roman rule, seductively promoting the Roman brand. Tacitus embodies it in this description of Agricola's management in AD 79: *Agricola* 21 is something of a template for the process of Romanisation as promulgated in Britannia by Agricola, although it must be viewed with the inevitability in mind that Tacitus was keen to 'big up' his father-in-law; just as interestingly Tacitus, as previously noted, cynically saw the process as just another form of servitude in which the locals turned soft:

> The following winter passed without disturbance, and was employed in salutary measures. For, to accustom to rest and repose through the charms of luxury a population scattered and barbarous and therefore inclined to war, Agricola gave private encouragement and public aid to the building of temples, courts of justice and dwelling-houses, praising the energetic, and reproving the indolent. Thus an honourable rivalry took the place of compulsion. He likewise provided a liberal education for the sons of the chiefs, and showed such a preference for the natural powers of the Britons over the industry of the Gauls that they who lately disdained the tongue of Rome now coveted its eloquence. Hence, too, a liking sprang up for our style of dress, and the toga became fashionable. Step by step they were led to things which dispose to vice, the lounging around, the bath, the elegant banquet. All this in their ignorance, they called civilization, when it was but a part of their servitude.

The processes which Tacitus describes were obviously long term, developing and evolving over time. Much of Britannia would have been seduced by the blandishments of Romanisation, and York too would have succumbed, and benefitted. For the rest of his governorship Agricola penetrated further and further north, absorbing parts of southern Caledonia and culminating in the battle of Mons Graupius in AD 84 (in the Grampian Mountains, perhaps at Bennachie by Inveruric) and all the while sowing the seductive seeds of Romanisation. As well as those who fought to the bitter end in the mountains, many of the Caledonians took refuge in the surrounding forests and mountains torching their houses and even going so far as to kill their own wives and children in fear of and to obviate Roman reprisals. On the following day Tacitus records, 'the hills were deserted, houses smoking in the distance, and our scouts did not meet a soul.' This was not be the last time the Scots were to suffer from scorched earth, slash and burn, and *blitzkrieg*.

Agricola had delivered the military part of his mandate with clinical precision and efficiency. Now throughout the province public buildings were constructed, Roman education was introduced, the attractions of civilisation Roman style were permeating the British aristocracies, slowly percolating down through the lower orders. The glue which held it all together, though, was unmistakably first and foremost military, as evidenced by the three fortresses at Eboracum, Caerleon and Chester and the two walled *coloniae* at Lincoln and Gloucester. Britannia was now a *bona fide* part of the Roman Empire, and York was a major place and had a significant role to play in that new outpost of empire.

Agricola was peremptorily recalled to Rome one year after his great achievement at Mons Graupius. Details after Tacitus for the next 300 or so years are comparatively thin but we can piece together a lot of what happened from archaeological evidence. In the years after Agricola's departure the Romans pulled back to the more defensible line along the Forth-Clyde isthmus while there may have been troop reductions and withdrawals to repel crises elsewhere in the empire. A programme of fort rebuilding seems to have been undertaken along the new frontier.

Agricola was clearly a major force in the early occupation of Britannia. It is important to look more closely at the achievements of the governor and of his son-in-law, Tacitus, author of his biography, to give context to the pivotal role York played in his strategy to subdue and contain the north of England and southern Scotland.

Gnaeus Julius Agricola

Gnaeus Julius Agricola (AD 40–93) was born in the *colonia* of Forum Julii (Fréjus), Gallia Narbonensis; as it happened, he began his military career in Britain, serving as military tribune (*tribunus laticlavus*) under the governor Gaius Suetonius Paulinus from 58 to 62. Most likely he was attached to the Legio II *Augusta*, but was selected to serve on Suetonius' staff and would have fought in the suppression of Boudica's revolt in AD 61. Following that he was appointed quaestor in the province of Asia in 64, then plebeian tribune in 66, and praetor in 68. He judiciously backed Vespasian during the Year of the Four Emperors in 69 for which he was rewarded with the command of the Legio XX *Valeria Victrix*, stationed in Britain, to replace the wayward Marcus Roscius Coelius.

Coelius was the legate of the Legio XX *Valeria Victrix* in 68. He was at loggerheads with the provincial governor from AD 63, Marcus Trebellius Maximus. Trebellius continued the policy of consolidation and made no new territorial conquests. He also continued the Romanisation of Britain, restoring Camulodunum after the rebellion of Boudica; Londonium grew in stature as a trading centre. By 67, the province was stable enough to allow Legio XIV *Gemina* to be withdrawn, but inertia, and a noticeable lack of opportunities for booty, led to unrest among the legions that remained. Trebellius had failed to restore discipline, and a feud with Marcus Roscius Coelius further undermined his authority. Coelius had grasped the opportunity during the chaos of the Year of Four Emperors to foment mutiny against him. Trebellius lost all authority with the army, which sided with Coelius, and fled to the protection of Vitellius (another of the Four) in Germania sending units from Legio XX to fight for him. Vitellius also returned Legio XIV, which had sided with his defeated opponent Otho (another of the Four), to Britain. Coelius and his fellow legates ruled the province for a short time until Vitellius, now briefly emperor, posted Marcus Vettius Bolanus as new governor to Britannia in late 69 (Tacitus, *Histories* 2, 65; *Agricola* 7).

Agricola's command ended in 73 when he was elevated to the patrician aristocracy in Rome and appointed governor of Gallia Aquitania. He was made *suffect* consul and betrothed his daughter, Julia, to Tacitus. When a magistrate resigned or died during his term of office, a successor had to be appointed for the rest of that year – this was called a *suffectus*. The following year, Tacitus and Julia married; Agricola was appointed to the College of Pontiffs, and returned to Britain for a third time, as its governor (*Legatus Augusti pro praetore*). As we have already noted, the final showdown at the Battle of Mons Graupius in 84 was where Agricola was victorious.

He was recalled from Britain in 85 after serving an unusually long tenure, rewarded handsomely with triumphal honours (one below a triumph), a public statue and a long citation. He retired from military and public life, tactfully declining the proconsulship of Asia under an unpredictable and insecure Emperor Domitian.

Agricola, then, was clearly the right man for the job which he executed with consummate efficiency, if we are to believe his son-in-law, and we probably can. He pursued a model *cursus honorum* and achieved his aim of a consulship with seemingly little trouble. York would have figured large in his life: his second stint here under Quintus Petillius Cerialis coincided with the establishment of the fortress – a major strategic decision in which he would have been involved, and from which he would have orchestrated his attacks on the Brigantes. Throughout his governorship too he would have used York as his command headquarters whence he would have travelled north with his legions into the unchartered north.

York would have benefitted socially and culturally from Agricola's tenure. Agricola was a provincial Roman and he would have empathised with the provincial nature of York and with its provincial inhabitants. He was an ardent advocate of the civilising benefits of Romanisation so York would have gained much from his efforts in this area: for example an orderly programme of urbanisation in the Roman way as well as the diffusion of Roman ideas, culture and of Latin in the higher echelons of society.

Publius (or Gaius) Cornelius Tacitus (c. AD 56–c. AD 120)

Tacitus was a Roman historian of the first order, up there with Livy and Sallust. He was the author of: (AD 98) *De vita Iulii Agricolae (The Life of Agricola)*; (98) *De origine et situ Germanorum (Germania)*; (102) *Dialogus de oratoribus (Dialogue on Oratory)*; (105) *Historiae (Histories);* and (117) *Ab excessu divi Augusti (Annals).* It is, of course, the *Agricola* which is of greatest interest to us: the biography of his father-in-law with particular focus on his governorship of Britannia from his headquarters in York.

Without Tacitus we would be considerably less well informed about early Roman Britain since the parts of the *Histories* and *Annals* which cover Agricola's governorship of Britannia are lost, which only leaves

Cassius Dio writing in the third century; Dio mentions Agricola twice (39, 50, 4; 66, 20, 1) and there are two inscriptions which bear Agricola's name – one from the forum at St Alban's and the other at the fortress at Chester. That is the extent of the literary evidence for early Roman York. Consequently, we owe much to Tacitus: without his *Agricola* most of the detail we have on the early conquest of the north from the base in York would be lost to us.

The Vindolanda Tablets

Vindolanda is extremely important in its own right but it is probably most famous for the Vindolanda tablets, preserved wooden leaf tablets that were, at the time in 1973 and 1993 when they were discovered, the oldest surviving handwritten documents in Britain. They gave us a hitherto unknown papyrus substitute, thin postcard-sized leaves of wood which were inscribed using pen and carbon-based ink with day-to-day book-keeping records and letters. They were scored down the middle and folded to form diptychs with ink writing on the inner faces; the ink was made up of carbon, gum arabic and water.

The 752 tablets dated between AD 90 and 120 offer a highly informative and vivid insight to life guarding the outpost of empire that was Britannia. They are sometimes mundane in their minutiae, but historically they are of seismic importance. They tell us much about the challenges faced by merchants and logistic operators and hauliers as well as military and administrative staff in the day-to-day running of a fort – lines of supply, procurement, materiel, service and social life are all there with first-hand descriptions from those facing the unpredictable and disaffected natives from further north.

Two Roman auxiliary regiments, the Ninth Cohort of Batavians and, before them, the First Cohort of Tungrians, are the stars of the tablets. Among the 400 officers and other ranks named, the Batavian prefect Flavius Cerialis features prominently, together with his wife Sulpicia Lepidina, who received the celebrated birthday party invitation from her friend Claudia Severa, wife of Cerialis' colleague and fellow hunting aficionado, Aelius Brocchus. The tablets shed priceless light on officers and their families, their friends, and their colleagues; it reveals the daily grind of ordinary soldiers; their names and duties; military routine, duty reports, leave, and deserters; the supply of food, drink and other goods;

merchants and contractors; army wife life; visitors and entertainment; as well as leisure activities such as hunting and religion. The first tablet excavated (No. 346) in 1973 happened to be about socks, sandals and underpants:

> I have sent you ... pairs of socks from Sattua, two pairs of sandals and two pairs of underpants, two pairs of sandals ... . Greet ... ndes, Elpis, Iu ... enus, Tetricus and all your messmates with whom I pray that you live in the greatest good fortune.

Other tablets are more edifying: one of the letters is from one slave to another regarding payment for some items needed for the all-important Saturnalia festival; there is an account of food supplies possibly for the fort commander's residence: it includes fish sauce (the ever-popular *garum*), lard for cooking, beer and barley for the household's livestock. In another letter, a man complains to a friend that he has yet to hear back from his previous letter. Tablet No. 164, a memo, is especially interesting:

> the Britons are unprotected by armour. There are very many cavalry. The cavalry do not use swords nor do the wretched Britons mount in order to throw javelins.

As is No. 343, possibly from a civilian trader complaining, somewhat fawningly, to the governor that he had been flogged by a centurion:

> he beat me all the more ... goods ... or pour them down the drain. As befits an honest man I implore your majesty not to allow me, an innocent man, to have been beaten with rods and, my lord, inasmuch as I was unable to complain to the prefect because he was detained by ill-health I have complained in vain to the *beneficiarius* and the rest of the centurions of his unit. Accordingly I implore your mercifulness not to allow me, a man from overseas and an innocent one, about whose good faith you may inquire, to have been bloodied by rods as if I had committed some crime.

We also hear from such demanding characters as, for example, Octavian (No. 343), a merchant dealing in wheat, hides and sinews, possibly a civilian contractor. At this time soldiers were not officially permitted to marry on service, but many did, building relationships with local women and starting families with them. One of the most fascinating tablets shows that wives of officers clearly did accompany their husbands on service overseas: Claudia Severa sent that famous birthday party invitation to her sister Lepidina asking her to make her day special by coming along on 11 September on tablet No. 291:

> On 11 September, sister, for the day of the celebration of my birthday, I give you a warm invitation to make sure that you come to us, to make the day more enjoyable for me by your arrival, if you are present. Give my greetings to your Cerialis. My Aelius and my little son send him their greetings. [A second hand writes] I shall expect you, sister. Farewell, sister, my dearest soul, as I hope to prosper, and hail. [Written on the other side, in the first hand] To Sulpicia Lepidina, wife of Cerialis, from Severa.

Claudia's handwriting also appears in Nos. 292 and 293; here, she seeks permission to visit Lepidina:

> . . . greetings. Just as I had spoken with you, sister, and promised that I would ask Brocchus and would come to you, I asked him and he gave me the following reply, that it was always readily permitted to me, together with ... to come to you in whatever way I can. For there are certain essential things which ... you will receive my letters by which you will know what I am going to do ... I was ... and will remain at Briga. Greet your Cerialis from me. [Written in the second hand] Farewell my sister, my dearest and most longed-for soul. [Written on the other side, in the first hand] To Sulpicia Lepidina, wife of Cerialis, from Severa, wife of Brocchus.

Apart from providing copious and invaluable information relating to provincial military life and administration, the tablets give us a fascinating insight on literacy among officers and their wives, rank and file soldiers, and civilian contractors. Most of this would have been recognisable to soldiers and their families garrisoned at York.

One of the Vindolanda tablets gives us our earliest written reference to York, datable to about AD 100, occurring as Eburacum, as it does in the *Antonine Itinerary* and *Ravenna Cosmography*, two Roman 'road atlases' that list place names along the highways of the empire.

Most importantly, though, there is nothing to suggest that the daily life on Hadrian's Wall adumbrated by the tablets was so very much different from what was going on in York, mundane as some of it might have been. The tablets give a clear and revealing picture of garrison life throughout the province.

Fortress York

Eboracum – The Name

The root of the early name was Eburos, an ancient British personal name, suggesting that the site was founded by someone called Eburos. An alternative theory is that the name is based on the ancient British word Eburos meaning yew, a sacred Celtic tree from which the personal name Eburos derives. The Britons, therefore, called the place Eburacon. During the Roman occupation there was a Gaulish tribe called the Eburorovices – the 'Warriors of the Yew Tree'. The Romans Latinised this into Eburacon or Eboracum and the boar became emblematic of the town (the Latin ebur – whose genitive eboris contains an O – is 'ivory', referring to boars' tusks). As noted, one of the Vindolanda tablets gives us our earliest written reference to York, datable to about AD 100, occurring as Eburacum, as it does in the *Antonine Itinerary* and seventh-century *Ravenna Cosmography*. The Vindolanda reference is one of thirty or so literary and epigraphic references to York. The form Eboracum is more common, occurring, for example, in the works of the second-century BC Greek geographer Ptolemy (2, 3, 17 Εβορακον) and on several stone inscriptions from York. See Appendix 8.

When the Anglo-Saxons replaced the Romans in the sixth century, they made Eboracum the capital of Deira, a Northumbrian sub-kingdom. Eboracum was corrupted by the Anglo-Saxons into Eoforwic and Evorwic meaning 'wild boar settlement'. In 876, Halfdene the Dane made Eoforwic the capital of the Viking Kingdom of York. The Vikings mispronounced Eoforwic as Jorvik. In the late Viking period the name Jorvik was shortened to York, although 'Yerk' is also known.

Roman Fortifications

The word for a fort is *castrum* (plural *castra*) but this Latin word is something of a catch all for different types of fortification. Confusingly, in English *castrum* can apply to a fort, camp, marching camp or fortress. The diminutive *castellum* was used for fortlets, as occupied by a detachment of a cohort or a century.

The Romans could build a camp even when under enemy attack in as little as a few hours. They had a repertoire of camp plans, selecting the one appropriate to the length of time a legion would spend in it: tertia castra, quarta castra, *etc.* – a camp for three days, four days, *etc.*

Castra were essential to security while an army was on the move, which it often was; their construction at the end of a day's marching followed a text-book plan with every man knowing his particular responsibility and the position of his billet. See Polybius 6, 27-32 for a detailed description. Apart from his weapons, each soldier carried two stakes used to construct a palisade inside a ditch which was dug at each night stop.

Josephus describes the daily routine in *The Jewish War* (3, 5, 1):

> as soon as they have marched into enemy territory, the Romans do not fight until they have fortified their camp; nor is the fence they construct poorly built or uneven ... their individual places [in the camp] are not assigned at random; but if the ground happens to be uneven, it is first leveled: the camp is four-square, and many carpenters are ready with their tools to build the buildings for them.

More permanent camps were *castra stativa* (standing camps). The most temporary of these were *castra aestiva* or *aestivalia*, summer camps, in which the soldiers were housed *sub pellibus* or *sub tentoriis*, 'under tents'. For the winter, the soldiers retired to *castra hiberna* containing barracks and other buildings of more solid materials, with timber construction gradually being replaced by stone over time.

The camp allowed the Romans to keep a rested and supplied army in the field, a massive advantage which neither the Celtic nor Germanic armies enjoyed: they had to disperse after only a few days.

The Romans could call on a number of other fortifications in the field, depending on what was required in a given campaign or in a particular military scenario. They include

Temporary (vexillation) forts
Roman vexillation forts are rectangular enclosures set up and occupied on a purely temporary basis by a campaigning army of between 2,500 to

4,000 legionary and auxiliary troops. They flourished soon after the conquest in AD 43, when the highly mobile Roman army had not yet established the boundaries of its occupation, and then during campaigns to increase and establish its control. All were probably abandoned by about AD 90. Vexillation forts are defined by a single rampart of earth or turf, usually surrounded by one or more outer ditches. Only fourteen examples of vexillation fortresses have been recorded in England.

Forts

There are over 125 known forts in Britannia, most sited for obvious strategic reasons, for example to guard river crossings and ports; establish defensive positions; post troops near or in local communities; assert control over new territories; and form part of a cohesive network providing easy access to reinforcements and military support. The soldiers in the forts would also have assisted in collecting local taxes. The forts provided homes for the garrison, which contributed to the local economy in terms of infrastructure contracts and the soldiers' disposable income, not least in the surrounding *vicus*.

Roman forts varied in size and construction materials depending on strategic requirements and local natural resources. Most conform to the same basic layout, which facilitated a well-practised method of siting and set-up that was pervasive throughout the empire and familiar to all legionaries.

The standard Roman fort was rectangular with rounded corners, 'playing-card' shaped. The perimeters were formed by a system of banks or ramparts and ditches, the banks created by the digging of the ditches on site. Timber came from the surrounding landscape for palisades, and timber walls along the top of the banks.

The interior was laid out with roads at right angles to each other with a central gate in each side allowing access to the fort. The central area would include the headquarters (*principia*), which housed the staff offices, the treasury, and sometimes a shrine. There were also storehouses, granaries, barracks, stables for the cavalry horses and pack animals; wagon sheds, workshops, a hospital, senior officers' quarters and bakehouses with ovens. Bath houses were positioned outside the fort perimeters on account of their fire risk. There were parade grounds inside and outside the forts and areas for physical training and for practising battlefield and combat skills. Many forts were rebuilt in stone after their initial turf and timber construction.

Examples of the many forts in Roman Britain are Caernarfon, Manchester, Lancaster, Catterick, Ravenglass, Cumbria, as well as Housesteads, Vindolanda and Chesters on Hadrian's Wall.

Milecastles
Positioned between forts along frontiers; Hadrian's Wall has an extensive network.

Fortresses
There were three permanent legionary bases in Roman Britain: Caerleon (Isca Silurium), Chester (Deva) and York. The most northerly, albeit short-lived, legionary fortress known in the Roman Empire was at Inchtuthil, west of Dundee.

Marching camps (castra)

Fortress buildings
The original wooden fortress at York was refurbished by Agricola in 81; it was completely rebuilt in stone between 107 and 108 as part of a rebuilding programme which fortified the two other permanent fortresses: Caerleon in 100 and Chester after 102. This suggests that garrisoning rather than campaigning was now very much the order of the day. The early second century saw the start of more long-term rebuilding under Trajan, extending for a century or so into the reign of Septimius Severus. At York, something like over 48,000m^3 of stone was used – mainly magnesian limestone from the quarries at Calcaria, Tadcaster. The Romans used several other types of stone in their buildings including millstone grit and Elland stone (York stone), which was used for floors and roofs as it splits naturally into flat slabs. However, the use of mortar to hold everything together was the real Roman revolution enabling far larger buildings than ever seen before.

The York fortress would have comprised a number of key buildings common to most fortresses around the empire. These included the headquarters *basilica* and barracks, the commander's house (*praetorium*), workshops (*fabricae* – for metal and wood), granaries (*horrea*), meat store (*carnarea*), hospital (*valetudinarium*), veterinary surgeon (*veterinarium*), stables, and the fortress baths. There were also barracks for the special forces: *classici* (marines), *equites* (cavalry), *exploratores* (scouts), and *vexillarii* (carriers of *vexillae*, the official colours of the legion and its units).

The Legionary Baths

There were at least two bath houses in York – the fortress baths and the civic baths. The York fortress baths, nearly 11,000 square yards of them, were, as normal, outside the gates, on the south-east side of the *praetentura* – the 'stretching to the front' – which contained the *scamnum legatorum*, the quarters of officers below general but higher than company commanders, *legati*. The *retentura* – 'stretching to the rear' – contained the *quaestorium*: a strongroom for booty and a prison for hostages and high-ranking enemy captives. Nearby were the quarters of the headquarters guard (*statores*) – made up of two centuries.

Evidence for the legionary baths in York was unearthed in 1991 in excavations in Swinegate and with the discovery of the sewers in Church Street in 1972; copious amounts of waste water from the baths and latrines would have been washed away through these sewers. If the baths at Exeter are comparable then something like 70,000 gallons gushed through every day. The sewer extended for 44 metres and was high enough to allow slaves to crawl along inside to clean it. Silt deposits have revealed seeds and pollen from plants typically at home in limestone landscapes, suggesting that an aqueduct was involved to bring water from limestone country, possibly around Tadcaster (Calcaria) or on the North York Moors.

Other tantalising water-related and bathing finds include a stone fountain unearthed in Bishophill in 1906 – now unfortunately dismantled; a timber lined 6 metre deep well at 58-59 Skeldergate, which was probably used for gardens as well as for drinking if the box clippings (tidy, aromatic and curative) found inside are evidence, and a Roman well languishing under the stage in York Theatre Royal. Excavations of the 115 hectare site of University of York campus expansion at Heslington East show evidence of a bath house.

The Roman Bath Museum is under the Roman Bath public house in St Sampson's Square. The main feature of the museum is remains of part of the legionary bath house in the southern quadrant of the fortress.

This bath house was excavated in 1930–31; it is probably of the early fourth century AD and was originally only viewable through a glass panel in the floor of the public house. Now visible to visitors to the museum are the east corner and south-east side of a *frigidarium* including a cold plunge bath together with part of the *caldarium* (heated room), with an apse and hypocaust system (underfloor heating). The cold plunge bath has a tiled floor with some of the tiles bearing stamps of the two legions that occupied the fortress, the IXth and the VIth. It is probable that the large Roman sewer discovered under Swinegate served this bath house. Set among the museum's excavated remains are descriptive displays, original Roman artefacts and a collection of replica uniforms, clothing, regalia and equipment. The splendidly detailed replica helmets are of particular interest.

Evidence for the public bath house has emerged at the north-east end of Micklegate. The walls were a huge 2.2 metres thick and up to 3.5 metres high. A water pipe found at Wellington Row and a fountain at Bishophill are evidence of the piped water supply to such bath houses.

Bath houses were central to urban living and to military life. They constituted a social and exercise centre where you went to meet and make friends, gossip and generally socialise. But they were not all good news: Seneca the Younger had the misfortune to live in an apartment above a public bath house; in this tetchy letter to Lucilius (*Letters* 56, 1, 2), he gives us a fascinating glimpse into what went on in these places:

> Imagine what a din reverberates in my ears! I have lodgings right over a bathing establishment. So picture the different sounds, which are so loud as to make me hate my very powers of hearing! When your strongman, for example, is exercising himself by wielding lead weights, when he is working hard, or else pretends to be working hard, I can hear him grunt, and whenever he exhales his imprisoned breath, I can hear him panting, wheezy and hissing. Or perhaps I notice some lazy fellow, content with a cheap rubdown, and hear the crack of the pummelling hand on his shoulder, varying in sound according to whether that hand is laid on a flat or hollow part of the body ... . Add to this the arrest of the odd drunk or pickpocket, the noise of the man who always likes to sing out loud in the bath, or the over-keen men who plunge into the swimming pool splashing loudly. Besides all of these . . . picture the hair-plucker with his penetrating, shrill voice which he uses for self-advertising, – continually giving it vent and never shutting up except when he is plucking armpits and making

his victim scream instead. Then the cake seller with his various cries, the sausage man, the sweet seller, and all the vendors of food hawking their wares, each with his own individual yell.

The Multangular Tower

This integral part of the city walls is a multi-period structure at the west corner tower of the fortress. It is in what is now York Museum Gardens and stands with the adjacent stretches of the curtain wall. What greater symbol of Rome's might; what greater projection of Roman power?

The Multangular Tower was probably built no later than 200 to 250. The protruding style of the polygon tower made it easy to fire down on enemy attackers. The commemorative stone (in part inaccurately) at the front reads:

> This tower formed the north west corner of the Roman Legionary Fortress of Eboracum. It was built about 300 A.D. on the site of an older tower. The larger stonework at the top is Medieval.

It is possible to see how the layers differ according to when they were added. Square stone, called *saxa quadrata*, makes up the internal and external skin, a layer of red tiles then acts as a modern-day wall tie does, holding the two layers together and creating a firm structure.

The tower gets its name from its ten sides and was named by a Dr Martin Lister, a member of the Repository of the Royal Society, a group dedicated to documenting the country and human activity. It appeared in a paper published in the *Philosophical Transactions of the Royal Society* in 1807.

Nine building stones of the VIth legion (*RIB* 669) were built into the lower courses of the inner face of the Multangular Tower. They read:

> *a* leg(io) [VI] Vic[t(rix)]*b* leg(io) [VI] Vict(rix) *c* Calp]urni Vict[o]rini *d* Anton(i) Prim(i)
>
> N CXX *e* Anton(i) Prim(i) *f* VNO [...] MNVI [,,,,] VIC *g* [...] *h* LN [ ] XXX *i* [...]

a-e translate as

> *a* [Sixth] Legion Victrix *b*[Sixth] Legion Victrix *c*The century of Calpurnius Victorinus. *d* The century of Antonius Primus (built) 120 (feet). *e*The century of Antonius Primus.

It was originally thought to have been built with three floors and a wooden roof but later, in 1807, a drawing of the tower showed it filled with earth right up to the upper lookout points, maybe to provide more strength and rigidity when under attack. Over time the tower has been referred to as Ellerandyng in 1315 and Elrondyng in 1380.

There was another non-extant similar tower at the south corner as well as six interval towers studding Severus' walls.

The late Roman Anglian Tower is about 60 metres to the north east of the Multangular Tower, built into the fortress wall. It was originally discovered in 1842 and re-excavated in 1970. It is 13 feet high and 14ft 6in square. What was its purpose? It could have been built as a watch tower, or as a replacement for a nearby Roman interval tower. It was formerly known as The Roman Room.

Remains of the Roman *basilica* building, at the north side of the *principia* are visible in the undercroft of York Minster. Heaps of animal bones – pig and sheep – have been unearthed and radiocarbon dated to the late fourth or early fifth century; this and some evidence of metal working in hearths suggest a major change in use of the *basilica* in the final days of the garrison as it prepared to withdraw from York and return to Rome. Excavation at the Minster in the 1960s and 70s suggests that the *basilica* may have endured until demolition well before the late eighth or early ninth century as previously believed.

One of the most significant findings was the toppled 7 metre long Roman column now opposite the south door of the Minster. Substantial remains of painted wall plaster still attached to the adjoining wall were also discovered.

Frontier Walls,
Frontier Wars and the Legions

History is relatively silent around the turn of the millennium, suggesting that, despite Scotland having been ceded by the Romans, Britannia had been effectively subdued and Romanisation was seeping into the fabric of British society. The mighty Roman war machine that had subjugated Britannia was now complemented by an equally formidable administrative engine, the purpose of which was to efficiently subsume and organise new territories fresh from defeat. Julius Caesar had had none of this; Claudius and his successors had it in spades.

However, in around 105 there appears to have been a serious reverse at the hands of the tribes of the Picts of Alba: we have evidence that several Roman forts were torched, with human remains and battle-damaged armour unearthed at Trimontium (Newstead). Auxiliary reinforcements may have been sent from Germany, and an unnamed British war of the time is inscribed on the gravestone of a tribune of Cyrene. Trajan's Dacian Wars may account for troop reductions or even total withdrawal, which led to slighting of the forts by the Picts rather than an unsubstantiated military defeat. Furthermore, the Romans sensibly destroyed their own forts during orderly withdrawals to deny them to the enemy. In either case, the frontier probably moved south to the line of the Stanegate at the Tyne-Solway isthmus around this time.

The Troublesome Brigantes – Again

The tribes making up the Brigantes continued to make trouble for the Romans well into the second century. The Roman satirist Juvenal, writing in the early years of the century (*Satires* 14, 196), describes a Roman father urging his son to win glory by destroying the forts of the Brigantes. Such an action was clearly deemed a pinnacle of military achievement by the Romans. There was a rebellion in the

98

north sometime in the early reign of Hadrian, but details are lost. A revolt by the Brigantes has often been posited as the explanation for the mysterious disappearance of the IXth legion, stationed at York. It is plausible that one of the motives for building Hadrian's Wall from 122 was to confound attempts by the Brigantes to communicate with, and encourage sedition with, the tribes further north. The emperor Antoninus Pius (r. 138–161) is said by Pausanias to have defeated the Brigantes after they fomented a war against Roman allies (*Description of Greece* 8, 43, 4), maybe even provoking the building of the Antonine Wall (142–144).

Trajan died in 117; his reign can be characterised in Britannia as one of withdrawal from Caledonia and consolidation of all territories south of that. Hadrian, his successor, continued in similar vein, reinforcing frontiers and dealing efficiently with troublemakers within those boundaries. He created *municipia* and established *coloniae* throughout his empire. In pursuit of this, Hadrian spent much of his time actually visiting and inspecting his territories rather than getting embroiled in politics in Rome as emperors before and after him often did. For Hadrian it was the establishment of communities, the civil engineering infrastructures and military projects which appealed: inevitably, it was only a matter of time before Britannia figured on his never-ending itinerary, and for Britannia Hadrian had big plans.

Hadrian, like Trajan, was a provincial from the same provincial city as Trajan, Italica in Hispania Baetica. This gave him a less Rome-centric view of his empire – Rome was mightily important but it was not the be all and end all of the Roman Empire, which other emperors believed to be the case. Hadrian's view of his world was more universal; a bigger picture gaze which embraced the whole empire rather than just a few square miles in Italy. Indeed, Hadrian did more than anyone to demonstrate that Rome, even with its prodigious and cumbersome civil service, was a mobile, portable entity: where Hadrian was Rome was. Traditionalists took a dim view of this: to them Hadrian was shirking his responsibilities and they carped, as they had done with an itinerant Nero some sixty years earlier, when he travelled to Greece. In the *Historia Augusta* – a late Roman collection of biographies of the Roman emperors, their junior colleagues, designated heirs and usurpers of the period 117 to 284 – Hadrian is described as 'a little too much Greek', too cosmopolitan for a Roman emperor.

Hadrian and Trajan were two very different men; Trajan's comfort zone was enshrined within the restrictions dictated and imposed by the *mos maiorum*: conservative and averse to too much change too quickly, continuing the age-old tradition of progress through empire-building conquests. Not so Hadrian; Hadrian built in the grand style like Trajan but his buildings were often characterised by aesthetics over utility; Hadrian's love was for Greek culture (and for the Greek youth Antinous). Hadrian was not for expansion; his ambitious focus was on unification and for making the empire a one nation empire in which defence was the order of the day all around the world; seventy-five years of relative peace says that Hadrian's policy was an unmitigated success. There were of course exceptions to this view: for example, the Jews would never have considered Hadrian a champion of their culture but, by and large, Hadrian was what was called 'a good emperor'.

Britannia provides another exception. There is little aesthetic about the great wall that was erected after Hadrian's visit in 122, but it is an unmissable and powerful symbol of defence and defiance, an emblem of Roman power and influence; it has been called the most military barrier in the Roman world by more than one historian. Hadrian may have been attracted by the opportunity to quell disturbances by insurgents from 119 to 121, during the governorship of Q. Pompeius Falco (118–122); these may have been fomented by disaffected collaborators from within. Inscriptions tell of an *expeditio Britannica* involving major troop movements, including the dispatch of a detachment (*vexillatio*), made up of some 3,000 soldiers. Fronto writes about military losses in Britannia at the time. Coins of AD 119–120 attest that Falco was sent to restore order.

A formidable defensive wall was seen as the way to put a stop to this once and for all. *Scriptores Historia Augustae*, Hadrian 9, 2 in the fourth century tells us that Hadrian wanted to build the wall to separate the barbarians from the Romans. The policy to curtail the extension of empire and a need to reduce defence costs, as a wall was a much cheaper way of deterring attacks than financing a border army, were surely other motives; moreover, a wall was just as useful in controlling cross-border trade and for collecting excise and supervising immigration. By the end of 122, Hadrian had done his work and concluded his visit to Britannia. He never saw the famous wall that bears his name.

As befits its high military and political status, Eboracum was visited by the emperors of the day. Hadrian of course came in 122 en route to his great wall project, bringing with him the VIth legion to replace the incumbent IXth. Septimius Severus arrived in 208, using the fortress as his base for his Scottish campaign. The imperial court was based in York until at least 211 when Severus died and was succeeded by his querulous sons, Caracalla and Geta. Severus was cremated in Eboracum.

The later third century saw the Western Empire embroiled in political and economic turmoil with Britannia occasionally ruled by usurpers independent of Rome. Emperor Constantius I subdued these pretenders and came to Eboracum in 306, winning the unfortunate reputation of becoming the second emperor to die here. 'See York and die?' military men and officials must have pondered back in Rome when contemplating postings. His son Constantine was proclaimed as successor by the troops in the fortress. It has long been thought that Constantine rebuilt the south-west front of the fortress with polygonally fronted interval towers and the two great corner towers, one of which – the Multangular Tower – still stands, as we have just seen, in all its glory. However, rebuilding of the defences in the third and fourth centuries is doubted. The Multangular Tower is now thought to date to the early third century, and this dating probably applies to the entire south-west stone defences.

Eboracum was *the* major military base in the north of Britain; politically it was just as important as London: as noted, after the third-century division of Britannia, it became the capital of northern Britain, Britannia Inferior. By 237, Eboracum was elevated to a *colonia*, the highest legal status any Roman city could attain, one of only four confirmed in Britain. At around the same time, Eboracum became self-governing, with a council made up of affluent local merchants and veteran soldiers. In 296, Britannia Inferior was divided further into two provinces of equal status with Eboracum the provincial capital of Britannia Secunda.

The Legion

The word legion derives from the Latin *legio*, meaning a selection, a levy of troops, a legion. We know that four legions were part of the initial invasion force in AD 43 – some 20,000 –25,000 troops. A legion, numbering approximately 5,000 men, consisted of ten cohorts, a cohort was 480 men made up of six centuries, each of eighty men commanded by a centurion. The basic unit was a *contubernium* – eight men who shared a tent when on campaign and a barrack room when in the fortress; ten *contubernia* made a cohort. The legionary troops comprised mostly infantry, but a cavalry unit was also attached.

Legionaries were Roman citizens with all the benefits and privileges that conferred. The soldiers, if they weren't killed or severely disabled, were required to serve for twenty-five years before retirement as a veteran. A long time, but worth waiting for as veteran status brought land in the *colonia* and land unlocked the door to political and social advancement as well as a worthwhile gratuity. Detachments of auxiliary troops were key to the legions – just like reservists in today's British Army; these were recruited from the indigenous populations of the various provinces of the Roman Empire and included special forces such as archers or marine commandos who excelled in swimming with full armour, literally armed to the teeth. Auxiliaries were not Roman citizens; they were enlisted to fight in support in cohorts or *alae* (wings) of 500 men or so. After twenty-five years they retired and were granted Roman citizenship, as were their dependents.

The commanding officer, the *legatus legionis,* was always of senatorial rank, in his thirties serving a three to four year posting as a stage on his *cursus honorum*, the career path taking in pre-ordained military and administrative posts culminating in the consulship. The second-in-command (*tribunus laticlavus*) would also be of senatorial rank and in his early twenties. There were usually five other senior officers: *tribuni augusticlavii* who were equestrians (one down from a senator) and who served for three years. The most important was the camp prefect, *praefectus castrorum*, who looked after the smooth running of the camp, training, discipline and equipment.

The demographics of the Roman army changed significantly between the first and second centuries. In the first half of the first century, sixty-five per cent of the military were from Italy; this had diminished to less than one per cent by the second century, so at any one time the soldiers in York and other major military settlements would have been a very diverse group. This is reflected on a number of headstones and altars. At the same time, we can estimate that the empire-wide Roman army numbered 155,000 legionaries and 218,000 auxiliaries.

The VI *Victrix* Legion

And so Hadrian's wall was built under the auspices of the new governor, Aulus Platorius Nepos, and of the VIth *Victrix* legion, which he brought with him to replace the IXth *Hispana*, the fate and final whereabouts of which remain elusive.

When it arrived with Hadrian in AD 120, the VIth *Victrix* would have been swiftly redeployed to Hadrian's Wall and its hinterland after establishing itself in fortress York and taking the handover from the IXth. It was founded in 41 BC by Octavian and was the twin legion of VI *Ferrata* (Ironclad) which was also known as *Fidelis Constans*, 'loyal and steadfast'.

The legion cut its teeth with Julius Caesar in the Gallic Wars; as noted, it later battled at Perusia in 41 BC with Octavian, fought against Sextus Pompeius in Sicily and at Actium against Mark Antony. In the early days of the empire, the legion participated at the end of the conquest of Hispania in Augustus' war against the Cantabrians, from 29 BC to 19 BC. The legion remained in Spain for the best part of a century and received the surname *Hispaniensis,* founding the city of Legio (León). Soldiers of the VIth and X *Gemina* were colonists of Caesaraugusta – modern-day Zaragoza. After the mid-first century, it was stationed at Neuss under Quintus Petillius Cerealis, soon to become commander of the IXth at York in AD 71. In AD 70, Vespasian dispatched a large expeditionary force to the north: VI *Victrix* was one of the legions involved and at Xanten, where it replaced XXII *Primigenia*, it won a hard-fought battle commemorated in an inscription that mentions the new emperor, Vespasian, and the commander of the VIth, Sextus Caelius Tuscus. Units of VI *Victrix* were deployed to the Danube: one inscription suggests that a subunit of the VIth was part of a task force with the other legions from Germania Inferior, I *Minervia* and X *Gemina* from Bonn and Nijmegen.

Domitian awarded the legion the additional and highly prestigious title *pia fidelis*, dutiful and faithful, after its support for him in the revolt by Lucius Antonius Saturninus – a legionary commander based in Germany. We can see this on many tiles from the York workshops which were stamped with PF as well as VIC. The cognomen *Victrix* (Victorious) dates back to the reign of Nero; when the governor of Hispania Tarraconensis, Servius Sulpicius Galba, declared his intention to overthrow Nero; the legion supported him and he was proclaimed emperor in the VI *Victrix* camp.

From AD 110 to 119, the legion was stationed on the Rhine in Germania Inferior. Around 120, Hadrian relocated the legion to northern Britannia, to reinforce those legions already quelling the resistance there. *Victrix* played a key role and, as we have seen, replaced the IXth *Hispana* at Eboracum. In 122, the legion started work on Hadrian's Wall; twenty years later, it helped construct the Antonine Wall and forts such as Castlecary.

Legio VI was awarded the honorary title *'Britannica'* by Commodus in 184 following his own adoption of the title. From now on, the full name of the legion was VI *Victrix Pia Fidelis Britannica*. The large fort at Carpow on the Tay was occupied from about 184 by Legio VI who completed the fort with the *principia* and *praetorium*. The legate of the legion in the late second century, Claudius Hieronymianus, dedicated a temple to Serapis in Eboracum in advance of the arrival of Septimius Severus in 208.

When Britannia temporarily became part of the Gallic Empire, the legion supported the Gallic emperors (260–274); when Britain became independent again, it supported usurpers such as Carausius and Allectus (286–297). After 297, the province was restored to the Roman Empire, and the soldiers served crown-prince Constantius I Chlorus. As we have seen, when he died in 306 in York, soldiers of the VIth proclaimed his son emperor: Constantine the Great (306–337).

In 402, the legion may have been withdrawn to the continent by Stilicho, the commander of the Roman forces in Western Europe during the reign of Honorius.

The IXth Legion: Where Did it Go?

The legion had a chequered career in its fifty or so years in Britannia. It probably came over with Claudius in AD 43 under Aulus Plautius and was one of two legions that defeated Caratacus at Caer Caradoc. Around the same time, the legion built a fort, Lindum Colonia, at Lincoln. Under Caesius Nasica it subdued the first revolt of Venutius between 52 and 57. The IXth was badly mauled at Camulodunum under Quintus Petillius Cerialis in the rebellion of Boudica (AD 61) when most of the infantry were slaughtered in a disastrous attempt to relieve the besieged city.

Only the cavalry got out; the legion was later reinforced with legionaries from the Germania provinces. When Cerialis returned as governor of Britain ten years later, he took command of the IXth again in a successful campaign against the Brigantes in 71–72. Around the same time, it was the IXth who constructed the new fortress at York as evidenced by finds of tile stamps from the site.

The IXth was part of Agricola's invasion of Caledonia in 82–83 where, according to Tacitus, the legion narrowly escaped total massacre when the Caledonians launched a surprise night raid on its fort. The Caledonians 'burst upon them' and in frantic hand-to-hand fighting the Caledonians entered the camp, but Agricola was able to send cavalry to relieve the legion. Seeing the relief force, 'the men of the IXth Legion recovered their spirit, and sure of their safety, fought for glory', repulsing the Caledonians. The legion also participated in the decisive battle of Mons Graupius. We know that the legion was at York in 107–108, rebuilding in stone the legionary fortress as recorded in an inscribed stone tablet discovered in 1864, but after that the trail goes cold.

Stamped tiles dated 104–120 tell us that it, or at least a detachment thereof, was at Nijmegen (Noviomagus Batavorum) from c. 120. This is supported by a silver-plated bronze pendant, found in the 1990s, that was part of a *phalera* (military medal), with 'LEG HISP IX' inscribed on the reverse. In addition, an altar to Apollo dating from this period was found at neighbouring Aquae Granni (Aachen), erected in fulfillment of a vow, by Lucius Latinius Macer, who described himself as *primus pilus* (chief centurion) and as *praefectus castrorum* (prefect of the camp), third-in-command of IXth *Hispana*. Eric Birley suggests the intention was to move it from York to Carlisle around 126 but that it was then posted to Jerusalem where it disappeared during the Bar Kokhba revolt (132–135), or in the wars of Marcus Aurelius in Parthian Armenia in 161 against King Vologases IV (Dio 71, 2).

Theodor Mommsen believed that the legion was annihilated in northern Britain soon after 108, from the latest datable inscription of the IXth found in Britain; this theory gained some traction from the 1954 novel *The Eagle of the Ninth* in which the legion is said to have marched into Caledonia, after which it was 'never heard of again'.

Mommsen in turn cites the historian Marcus Cornelius Fronto for corroboration, writing in the AD 160s, who told Marcus Aurelius: 'Indeed, when your grandfather Hadrian held imperial power, what great numbers of soldiers were killed by the Jews, what great numbers by the Britons.' (*Parthian War* 2, 220).

Whatever, the IXth *Hispana* is not recorded during the reign of Septimius Severus (r. 193–211): the IXth was seemingly no longer in existence after 197. Two lists of the legions survive from the time, one inscribed on a column found in Rome (*CIL* 6, 3492) and the other a list of legions in existence 'today' provided by the contemporary Dio Cassius, writing c. 210–232 (*Roman History* 55, 23-24). Both these lists date from after 197, as both include the three Parthica legions founded by Septimius Severus in that year. Both provide an identical list of thirty-three legions; neither includes a IXth *Hispana*. It thus appears that IXth *Hispana* disappeared sometime in the period 120–197.

This 1969 limerick gives an indication of the exasperation felt by some scholars over this intractable mystery:

> The fate of the Ninth still engages
> The minds of both nitwits and sages;
> But that problem, one fears,
> Will be with us for years
> And for ages and ages and ages.

What Did Those Legionaries Do All Day and Night?

Obviously, a lot of the time was spent away from the York fortress, any of the fortresses, in combat, subduing fractious tribes, building forts and walls to keep insurgents at bay. When in the fortress we can estimate that the legionary spent a lot of time on guard duty. In a unit of 800 men twenty per cent were on guard once every twenty-four hours, so 160 men every day. In a full legion, then, 1,200 men out of 6,000 would have been on guard every day. Patrols, parades, combat training, cooking, admin, maintenance and cleaning of weapons and armour occupied much of the rest of the time, as in any army: ninety per cent routine boredom, ten per cent action.

Attaining full complement must have been problematic with absenteeism caused by extra-mural exercises, secondments, and illness. One of the Vindolanda tablets (No. 154) records that in one instance of 752 men on the roll, only 265 were actually available for duties.

The northern wall in Britannia was not Hadrian's first defensive barrier; his first and *the* first was built in Germany just before he came to Britain – a timber palisade bolstering the Taunus, Wetterau and Odenwald sections of the German frontier. Other such constructions may have been built by Hadrian in Africa (the Fossatum Africae) and Raetiae (in modern-day Alpine Austria).

Stanwix, near Carlisle, was the largest fort on Hadrian's Wall and that is where the senior officer would have operated from, reporting to the legionary legate at York. The wall helped to provide a period of military stability in Britannia which, in turn, allowed Romansiation to prosper. Wroxeter is a good example where a forum dedicated to Hadrian was built on the site of a complex which was demolished and re-erected over the road. Indeed, we can be sure that Hadrian's visit cultivated a surge in Romanisation province wide just as much as it fostered military calm. London, Leicester and Caistor-by-Norwich also benefitted at the time with new civic buildings while we can be sure that York, Aldborough and Brough-on-Humber too would have seen a vigorous construction programme of public works and amenities. Local administration was increasingly the responsibility of local communities, leaving the army to respond flexibly to any local emergencies. This in turn led to an increasing influx of administrators and service industries to support the infrastructure projects in towns and garrisons, bringing in increasing numbers of Romans from all parts of the empire. The more they came the more Roman ways were inculcated over the length and breadth of the province. Local men and women would also have profited, including many lower down the social scale, to fire the businesses and trades in the towns. The countryside and rural economies would feel the benefits too, working the iron, tileries and ceramics workshops, for example, as well as the land.

Antoninus and His Wall

Publius Aelius Hadrianus Augustus died in 138. He was succeeded by a senator noted for his financial prudence, honesty and devotion to duty: this was Aelius Hadrianus Antoninus Augustus Pius, or Antoninus Pius, who was to rule from 138 to 161. Significantly, an unpredicted resumption of expansionism was to lead to the construction of what we now know as the Antonine Wall, the Vallum Antonini, a 39 mile turf fortification on stone foundations between the firths of Forth and Clyde which was 10 feet high and 16 feet wide. The wall, therefore, pushed forward the frontier of the Roman Empire by some 100 miles and is celebrated as the sole act of expansionism by war in the reign of Antoninus. In fact, his lack of belligerence led scholar J. J Wilkes to write, 'It is almost certain not only that at no time in his life did he ever see, let alone command, a Roman army, but that, throughout the twenty-three years of his reign, he never went within five hundred miles of a legion.' Which just shows that you don't have to be a serial warmonger to be a good Roman.

The wall was, in effect, a potent symbol of the reconquest of southern Scotland from around AD 141. Lines of supply would have been an extension of those used for Hadrian's Wall, leading through the difficult terrain in between the walls all the way back to Eboracum. The wall took about twelve years to complete; within twenty years it was abandoned and the garrison retreated to Hadrian's Wall.

Why did the Romans build this wall when a perfectly serviceable wall already existed only ninety-nine miles to the south? It seems likely that Antoninus, like Claudius before him, was anxious to shine and, despite his innate aversion to conflict, to add a military achievement of some importance to his name. Hadrian's Wall was the subject of ongoing bad press, relating to aspects of its muddled planning and cost. Antoninus' Wall would eclipse this, and Antoninus would overshadow Hadrian: it would be a model of simple but effective frontier building. What is more, Antoninus was, as noted, a traditionalist and we have already seen how traditionalists – those adherents to the *mos maiorum* – were, more often than not, stolid advocates of extending Rome's might through war. A new, more aggressive, policy was clearly needed to put an end to the troubles on the fringe of the empire; a new governor took over in 139, Quintus Lollius Urbicus, a native of Numidia and previously governor of Germania Inferior. Lollius invaded southern Scotland, winning some significant victories, before going on to build the wall. Pausanias may be referring to it when he mentions a war in Britain and an inscription honouring Antoninus, erected by Legio II *Augusta*, the legion which helped build the wall, and a sobering relief showing four naked prisoners, one of them beheaded. The recapture of southern Scotland won for Antoninus the revived ancient salutation of *imperator*; his place in Roman military history assured, he could then get on with the business of keeping the peace around the rest of his empire.

What went wrong to force the abandonment? As well as the uprisings in Mauretania and unrest amongst the Jews and Egyptians, trouble erupted closer to home in the Pennines amongst the Brigantes from 155, now headquartered in Aldborough near York. Fronto was later to say that, although

Antoninus delegated the British campaign to others, he should be regarded as the helmsman who directed the voyage, whose glory, therefore, belonged to him. Moreover, it seems inconceivable that the plague which bears the name of Antoninus, and which wreaked so much devastation within the ranks and conscription potential of the Roman army was not a contributory factor: Roman troops were needed elsewhere and the Antonine Wall was seen as dispensable. For recent evidence of the plague in Britannia see Appendix 12.

Antoninus dealt with the rebellion as coins of 154–155 attest and Pausanias records the punishment meted out on the Brigantes for their attack on 'the Genounian district', the whereabouts of which is unknown.

The first Antonine occupation of Scotland then, ended as a result of further trouble in 155–158, when the Brigantes revolted. With no hope of receiving reinforcements, the Romans moved their troops south; the rising was suppressed by governor Gnaeus Julius Verus. The unrest appears to have continued into 158; there was then extensive military rebuilding under governor Calpurnius Agricola in the north at Corbridge and Chesterholm; in the west at Lancaster, Ribchester and Hardknott; and in the south at Ilkley and Bainbridge, some sixty miles west of York, in what we now call the Yorkshire Dales. What exactly happened is obscure but we know that the Antonine Wall was abandoned in 162 and burnt, and that there was more slaughter at Trimontium (modern Newstead near Melrose). Antoninus reacted by carving up the Brigantian *civitas*, thus emasculating the tribe politically, socially and militarily (Pausanias, *Description of Greece* 8, 43, 4).

All was not lost for the Romans: the large fort at Trimontium was maintained along with seven smaller outposts until at least 180. The second push north and the occupation may have been connected with Antoninus' obligation to protect the Votadini.

Antoninus died of an illness in 161 and was succeeded by his adopted sons Marcus Aurelius and Lucius Verus as co-emperors.

Aldborough (Isurium Brigantum)

Recent archaeological work is telling us that Aldborough was more important than first thought and that its prominence and thriving economy and society had implications for nearby Eboracum.

The Aldborough Roman Museum displays relics of the Roman town, including mosaic pavements. The famous Lupa and Romulus and Remus mosaic is in Leeds City Museum (dated c. AD 300).

The summer of 2011 was a significant time for our knowledge of Roman Aldborough; that was when archaeologists with geomagnetic scanners were able to report the discovery, after two years' work, of what has been dubbed 'the lost amphitheatre of northern England'. They revealed a tiered bank of seats below curving hummocks in a field at the top of Studforth Hill, an oval arena which would have combined spectacles and entertainments with a 360 degree view.

According to Martin Millett, Professor of Classical Archaeology at the University of Cambridge, speaking to *The Guardian* on 17 August of that year:

> Its discovery leaves little doubt that Isurium Brigantium . . . was the civil capital of the Britons known as Brigantes, effectively the population between Derbyshire and Hadrian's Wall . . . York is much better-known for Roman remains . . . but the evidence suggests that it was the military base. Civil power and society, and the most important place for Roman Britons in the northern province, was likely to have been here.

The article, written by Martin Wainwright, continues:

> Aldborough was thought for years to have been a Roman fort because of its impressive town walls, which include a long remaining stretch with curved lookout towers. The strategic position on Dere Street . . . also pointed to a largely military function. But a series of small 19th-and 20th-century excavations, many in gardens and allotments, began to build a more complex picture, and the discovery of the town's Roman name – meaning the 'main city of the Brigantes' – shifted opinion towards a large civilian settlement.

The website www.aldboroughromantown.wordpress.com, concludes:

> Our work seems to show a rather different picture of Isurium Brigantium than hitherto suggested. The town is conventionally seen as geographically marginal in the Roman province, and of secondary importance to York – arguably a second-rate abandoned fort converted to a mundane town.

However, we now begin to see indications of a pattern of planning, with major hillside terracing and grand houses with sophisticated design and decoration; such elements are not yet evident from the archaeology of York itself.

Might it be that we need to rethink Roman Aldborough as a place of more significance and interest with a distinctive character of its own?

In 175, a sizeable force of Sarmatian cavalry, 5,500 strong, disembarked in Britannia, probably to reinforce troops fighting unrecorded uprisings. In 180, Hadrian's Wall was breached by the Caledonians and the governor was killed there in what Cassius Dio described as the most serious war of the reign of Commodus (161–192).

Lucius Aelius Aurelius Commodus was Roman emperor with his father Marcus Aurelius from 177 until his father's death in 180, and then reigned solo until 192. Ulpius Marcellus was posted as replacement governor, and by 184 he had restored the Roman frontier to the Antonine Wall and won a new peace. The turbulent years of the reign of Commodus, who was inaugurated in 183 as consul with Aufidius Victorinus, saw war erupt in Dacia in which two future contenders for the throne, Clodius Albinus and Pescennius Niger, both distinguished themselves in the campaign. In Britannia in 184, despite the new peace, Ulpius Marcellus found that the legionaries were having none of it and revolted against the harsh discipline they were having to endure and acclaimed another legate, Priscus, as emperor (Dio 73, 10, 2). However, Priscus turned them down and Perennis had all the legionary legates in Britain cashiered – a ritual and humiliating dismissal. In 185, a detachment of 1,500 soldiers from Britain who had been posted to Italy to suppress brigands denounced Perennis to the emperor for allegedly plotting to make his own son emperor; Commodus allowed them to execute Perennis as well as his wife and sons. Sextus Tigidius Perennis (AD 125–185) served as Praetorian Prefect under Commodus. He wielded an inflated influence over Commodus and was effectively in charge of the Roman Empire.

The future emperor Pertinax was sent to Britannia to quell the mutiny and had some early success in regaining control, but when a riot broke out among his troops he was left for dead, and asked to be recalled to Rome, where he briefly succeeded Commodus as emperor in 192. The death of Pertinax, in turn, encouraged several rivals to bid for the emperorship, including Septimius Severus and Clodius Albinus. The latter was the new governor of Britannia who started well by winning over the natives as well as four legions which reinforced his claim, making him a significant claimant to the crown. The legions were II *Augusta*, VI *Victrix* and XX *Valeria Victrix* from Britain, and VII *Gemina* from Spain.

The Antonine Plague was the first of three devastating pandemics which ravaged the Roman Empire and the early Byzantine Empire, the others being the Plague of Cyprian (AD 249–AD 262) and the Justinian Plague (AD 541–542).

It was never only the booty which victorious troops returning from war brought back to the homeland and their families and friends. Sexually transmitted infections and other diseases were sometimes incubating in the soldiers and infecting their baggage trains, only too ready to spread into new populations. The Antonine Plague, or the Plague of Galen, which was probably smallpox, took hold during the golden reign of Marcus Aurelius (r. AD 161–180), and devastated the Roman army with direct or indirect effects on every garrison the empire over including York; it may have killed over five million people in the Roman Empire after the army came home from the war in Parthia (161–166). It has even been suggested that a quarter to a third of the entire population of the empire perished, estimated at 60–70 million. For recent evidence of its presence on Hadrian's Wall see Appendix 12.

See York . . . and Die

As Hadrian showed us, the Roman Empire and its many associated bureaucracies and administrations could be a moveable feast, not stuck fast in the city of Rome; Rome could be and was governed by proxy from wherever the emperor happened to be at any one time. And the emperor of the day happened to be in York three times in the early empire, making York the *de facto* beating heart of the Roman Empire three times. Astonishingly, on two of those occasions, the emperor died in the city and both times the death sparked a battle for succession. This first death came when Septimius Severus resided in York between 208 and 211.

Septimius Severus chose York as his base for his north country campaigns against the Caledonii and the Maeatae. This was no ordinary unaccompanied posting – he brought with him his empress, Julia Domna, his sons (the disputatious Caracalla and Geta) and an impressive entourage, including the crack Praetorian Guard, the likes of which would never have been seen in York before. York, then, was temporarily the true epicentre of the Roman Empire because where the emperor was so was government of the empire. Indeed, an imperial edict dated 5 May 210 headed 'Eboraci' confirms this.

In 1818, William Hargrove, local newspaper proprietor, published his *History of York* in which he gushed, 'it was during this residence of Severus that our city shone in its full splendour.' Some 130 years later in 1956, Peter Wenham in his *Short Guide to Roman York* asserted in relation to the funeral of Severus: 'In some sense that vivid spectacle marked a turning point in the history of the civilised world and York was its setting.'

Septimius Severus and Clodius Albinus

Pescennius Niger was proclaimed emperor by the legions in Syria; Septimius Severus by the troops in Illyricum and Pannonia; and Albinus by the armies in Britain and Gaul.

113

In pursuit of this, Albinus virtually stripped Britannia of its garrison to fight his corner on the continent leaving the troublesome tribes in the north to wreak havoc and vengeance as far south as York.

In the autumn of 196, Albinus heard that Severus had appointed his elder son Caracalla as his successor and had convinced the senate to declare him, Albinus, an enemy of Rome. Now with nothing to lose, Albinus mobilised his legions in Britannia, proclaimed himself emperor (Imperator Caesar Decimus Clodius Septimius Albinus Augustus) and crossed from Britain to Gaul, bringing the best part of the British garrison with him. He defeated Severus' legate Virius Lupus, and laid claim to the military resources of Gaul making Lugdunum his headquarters; he was, however, unable to win over the Rhine legions.

On 19 February 197, Albinus confronted Severus' army at the hard-fought Battle of Lugdunum with 150,000 troops on each side, according to Dio Cassius. Albinus was defeated and fell on his sword, or was captured and executed on the orders of Severus. Severus had his naked body splayed out on the ground before him, so that he could ride his trampling horse over it in a final act of humiliation. Albinus' wife and sons were initially pardoned by Severus, but he appeared to change his mind almost immediately afterwards: they were beheaded just as Albinus' corpse had been. Albinus' headless body was thrown into the Rhône, together with the corpses of his murdered family. Severus sent his enemy's head to Rome as a bloody warning to his supporters, mocking the senate for their loyalty to Albinus.

Albinus had clearly demonstrated the major problem that Britannia posed. In order to be secure the island needed a garrison of at least three legions, but these legions constituted a very tempting power base for ambitious rivals. Deploying those legions elsewhere would obviously leave the province defenceless against revolts by the native Celtic tribes and against incursions by the Picts and Scots.

It seems probable that northern Britain, led by York, slumped into anarchy while Albinus battled in Gaul: Dio records that the new governor, Virius Lupus, had to buy peace from the fractious Maeatae. The succession of militarily distinguished governors who were subsequently appointed suggests that the natives generally were posing an intractable challenge. Lucius Alfenus Senecio restored many of the installations at Hadrian's Wall, which had been decommissioned following the uprisings of earlier years. Dio also writes of victories in Britain in 206 and it is therefore likely that he finished the re-occupation of the province and its frontiers. Troubles from the Maeatae and the Caledonian Confederacy necessitated expeditions north of the wall. Senecio seems to have been initially successful as attested by a victory monument he erected at Benwell (*CIL* 7, 513). His report to Rome in 207 describes barbarians 'rebelling, over-running the land, taking loot and creating destruction.' Senecio requested either reinforcements or an imperial expedition, the latter perhaps on an 'if you don't ask you don't get' basis; the emperor, perhaps surprisingly to Senecio, chose the latter, despite being 62 years old and in failing health. As noted, Severus then moved lock, stock and barrel to York with family and hangers-on, making the fortress the centre of operations for a retaliatory campaign further north and, effectively, the seat of Roman power for a time.

Severus' arrival in Britain in 208 awed the enemy tribes; the Caledonians soon sued for peace when they surrendered to the emperor after he personally led a military expedition north of Hadrian's Wall. But the emperor had not come all that way to leave without a victory, and he probably also wished to inculcate in his quarrelsome teenage sons Caracalla and Geta, not just first-hand experience of conflict in a hostile barbarian land, but also the vagaries of provincial administration.

Severus established York as his Imperial capital and centre of operations. He was joined here by Legio VI *Victrix* already incumbent, Legio II *Augusta* from Caerleon and Legio XX *Valeria Victrix* from Chester – together with the auxiliary units based in Britain. He had also brought with him (not unwisely) a reformed Praetorian Guard having replaced the regular guard with 15,000 of his own troops. One of their number was Septimius Lupianus whose sarcophagus reveals that he was recently promoted to legionary centurion. As well as the Praetorians, he was also accompanied by the Imperial Guard Cavalry and his new Roman legion, the Legio II *Parthica*. This gave him a force totalling 50,000 men, together with the 7,000 sailors and marines of the regional fleet. These units arrived in Britain at the great estuary (Orwell) in East Anglia, Brough-on-Humber, South Shields and Wallsend.

To support it all, the fort, harbour and supply base at South Shields (Arbeia) became the main supply depot. The existing site was extended, with huge new granaries being built that could hold 2,500 tonnes of grain. This was enough to feed the whole army for two months.

South Shields (Arbeia)

Overlooking the River Tyne, the fort was founded in 120 to guard the main sea route to Hadrian's Wall; later, it was to become a huge maritime supply base providing logistical support for the wall and, to that end, contains the only permanent stone-built granaries found in Britain. Over 600 troops were stationed there.

The first garrison was the First Wing of Sabinus' Pannonians (Ala Primae Pannoniorum Sabiniana), a 500-strong cavalry regiment traditionally recruited from what is now Hungary. The fort here was expanded with the addition of a further seven new granaries between 222 and 235 and remained occupied during the rest of the third and fourth centuries, with the garrison changing to the Company of Bargemen from the Tigris (Numerus Barcariorum Tigrisiensium) towards the end of the latter. This unit was traditionally recruited from around the Tigris and it is possible that this is how South Shields got its Latin name, the Aramaic Arbeia, which translates as 'place of the Arabs'.

Arbeia is as good a place as any to illustrate the thoroughly cosmopolitan and fluid nature of the Roman world. One epigraph commemorates Regina, a British woman of the Catuvellauni tribe, who was first the slave, then the freedwoman and wife of Barates, a merchant from Palmyra (now part of Syria) who set up a gravestone after she died at the age of 30. Barates himself is buried at the nearby fort of Coria (Corbridge).

Another commemorates Victor, also a former slave, freed by Numerianus of the Ala I Asturum, who also arranged his funeral ('piantissime', with all devotion) when Victor died at the age of 20. The stone records that Victor was 'of the Moorish nation'.

Two more altar stones are of interest:

DEAE BRIGANTIAE SACRVM CONGENNCCVS VSLM

To the sacred goddess Brigantia. Congenniccus willingly and deservedly fulfilled his vow. (*RIB* 1053)

Brigantia was the patron deity of the local British tribe in the area of the wall, who was worshipped throughout the iron-age world as Brigit.

She was the tripartite goddess of wisdom, also known as the Mother of Memory, a daughter of Dana the iron-age Mother Goddess.

Altar to the 'Spirits of Conservation':

DIS CONSERVATORIB PRO SALV IMP C M AVREL ANTONINI AVG BRIT MAX [ET IMP C P SEP GETAE AVG] ...RENS OB REDITV V S

To the gods the Preservers for the welfare of the Emperor Caesar Marcus Aurelius Antoninus Augustus, Most Great Conqueror of Britain, [and of the Emperor Caesar Publius Septimius Geta Augustus, conqueror of Britain], the military unit at Lugudunum paid its vow for their safe return. (*RIB* 1054, AD 211)

From South Shields the ships of the Classis Britannica used the Tyne and eastern coastal routes to get, and keep, the army on the move once the campaign began. Meanwhile, the fort at Corbridge on Dere Street, just south of Hadrian's Wall, was also upgraded, again for use as a major supply base. When all was ready in the spring of 209, Severus launched the first of his two assaults against the Maeatae and Caledonians in the far north of the province.

He was joined by Caracalla, leaving Geta behind in York to look after the imperial administration with the support of Julia Domna, the empress. The immense force marched north along Dere Street, crossing Hadrian's Wall and then smashing through the Scottish Borders, destroying all before it. Any opposition was eradicated.

Severus moved north with 20,000 men in 208–209; Dio records, and exaggerates, that the Caledonians inflicted 50,000 Roman casualties through their guerrilla warfare tactics which prevented the Roman legions from fighting on an open battlefield. Severus was rapidly running out of patience and, his health worsening, ordered his troops to kill everyone (Dio 76, 13-15). The emperor's forces pushed north as far as the River Tay, but for little gain, as peace treaties were signed with the Caledonians. By 210, Severus had returned to York, and the frontier once again reverted to Hadrian's Wall. Colin Martin has suggested that Severus did not seek a battle but instead sought to destroy the fertile agricultural land of eastern

117

Scotland and thereby bring about genocide of the Caledonians through starvation.

The Hand of God

In 2018, archaeologists discovered a hand-shaped Roman artefact described as the 'hand of God' near Hadrian's Wall. It is made of 2.3 kilos of solid bronze and is believed to be associated with Severus' campaign as a tribute to a god of war. The bronze hand may well have been buried in a boggy area close to Vindolanda shortly after the end of the conflict. Archaeologists said the child-sized hand was probably buried as part of a religious ritual to mark the completion of a temple dedicated to the god close by. The hand is associated with a Roman god of Middle Eastern origin called Jupiter Dolichenus – popular with the Roman military. Such hands were often mounted on the top of a pole – and used to bless worshippers during religious rituals. The 4 inch hand originally had an attachment, now missing, that was inserted into the palm. Jupiter Dolichenus was typically depicted holding a thunderbolt in his hand with upraised arm signifying his destructive power. The open hand also symbolises protection and well-being.

'The discovery of Jupiter Dolichenus' bronze hand, deposited as a thanksgiving offering, demonstrates just how serious the conflict was and how relieved the Roman soldiers were that it had ended,' says Andrew Birley, director of the Vindolanda excavations. 'It is further evidence illustrating how deeply religious they were and how seriously they took their relationship with their god.'

Of the nineteen Dolichenus temples discovered so far around the empire, only the two in Rome are not sited at frontier settlements such as Vindolanda.

Severus immediately proclaimed a famous victory, with himself, Caracalla and Geta awarded the (rather premature as it turned out) title 'Britannicus', and with celebratory coins being struck rather hastily to commemorate the event. The emperor, his sons and the armies wintered in York. Next year, in 210, the Maeatae revolted again, joined by the Caledonians. Severus was having none of it and decided to return north again to settle matters once and for all; his orders were unequivocal, as Dio records, with its echoes of the *Iliad*: 'Let no-one escape annihilation at our hands, not even the baby in its mother's womb, let it not escape destruction. The whole people must be wiped out of existence, with none to shed a tear for them, leaving no trace.' (*Epitome of Book* 76, 15)

Ethnic cleansing was on the cards.

This second campaign was an exact re-enactment of that in 209 although it was conducted by Caracalla as Severus was now too ill. What it lacked in good old Roman mercy (remember the paradigm in the *Aeneid*? 'Spare spare the defeated'), it more than made up for with savage atrocities resulting in a peace along the northern border lasting for an unprecedented four generations. The 'Severan surge' then headed south again to winter once more at York, leaving large garrisons in place. Policy had to be reassessed, though, when Severus died in York in February 211.

Severus' immense force of 50,000 men returned to their own bases around the province. The northern border was once more re-established on Hadrian's Wall.

Caledonians, Picts and the Maeatae

Throughout the second century, two major tribal confederations had emerged in the region of modern Scotland by 180. These were the Maeatae based in the central Midland Valley either side of the Clyde-Firth of Forth line and the Caledonians to their north. The Caledonians, or the Caledonian Confederacy, were a Celtic tribal confederacy; the Greek form of the name, Καληδῶνες, gave them their name. Dio gossips that they lived naked in tents and had their women in common. We first met them in 83 or 84 at the battle of Mons Graupius under Calgacus, as described by Tacitus. Presumably Calgacus was leader of a confederacy of tribes rather than just the Caledonians.

In 180 they took part in that invasion of Britannia, breached Hadrian's Wall and were on the rampage for several years, eventually signing peace treaties with the governor Ulpius Marcellus. Confusingly, Roman historians use 'Caledonius' not only to refer to the Caledones themselves, but also to any of the other tribes both Pictish or Brythonic living north of Hadrian's Wall.

In 197, Dio records that the Caledonians supported a further attack on the Roman frontier led by the Maeatae and the Brigantes, probably spurred on by the withdrawal of garrisons on Hadrian's Wall by Clodius Albinus. Dio adds that the Caledonians broke the treaties they had made with

Marcellus a few years earlier (Dio 72, 12). Virius Lupus, the next governor, was obliged to buy peace from the Maeatae rather than fight them.

As shown above the Caledonians re-emerged in 209, when they surrendered to Septimius Severus during his personally led military expedition north of Hadrian's Wall, in search of that glorious military victory.

By 210 however, the Caledonians had resumed their alliance with the Maeatae and joined a fresh offensive. Caracalla was dispatched, slaughtering all and sundry from any of the northern tribes. When Severus died at Eboracum in 211, Caracalla made an unsuccessful bid to take over command, but when his troops refused to recognise him as emperor he made peace with the Caledonians and retreated south of Hadrian's Wall; Caracalla had much bigger fish to fry with his claim for the imperial title. The Caledonians did regain their territory and pushed the Romans back to Hadrian's Wall.

It is not until 305 that we hear anything significant again: Constantius Chlorus re-invaded the northern lands of Britain and a great victory over the 'Caledones and others' is mentioned (*Panegyrici Latini Vetares*, 6 (7) 7, 2), incidentally giving us the first recorded use, in 297, of the Latin word *Picti* (painted people) to describe the tribes of the area.

As far as we know, the Maeatae were settled in lands north of the Antonine Wall; currently, the thinking is that they were centred between Dumyat Hill above Stirling and Myot Hill near Fankerton, Falkirk.

In 360, together with the Gaels from Ireland, the Picts launched a concerted incursion over Hadrian's Wall. The emperor Julian dispatched legions to deal with them but to no avail. The Pictish raids were cutting deeper and ever deeper into the south.

Before the 65-year-old Severus died, he did three things: the first was to order himself a cremation urn. When he got it, he hubristically told it: 'You will hold a man that the world could not hold.' In the second he made sure of his reputation for posterity when, as Dio says, he declared on his deathbed: 'When I took over the state chaos reigned everywhere; I am leaving it at peace, even Britain . . . the empire which I am leaving my sons is a strong one.' The third parting shot had considerably wider repercussions: he was astute enough to set in train a momentous foreign policy decision which was to change the course of history, not just of York but of Roman Britain generally. To neutralise the endless and damaging stream of powerful and rebellious governors in Britain, he proposed dividing the province into Britannia Superior and Britannia Inferior. Eboracum was to be the capital of Inferior. This inspired plan was brought to fruition by Caracalla; it checked rebellion in the province for almost a century, ushering in the Long Peace. Nevertheless, the number of buried hoards found from this period rose significantly, suggesting some ongoing panic and unrest.

Dio describes a scene in which the emperor utters the following wise words to his two sons on his deathbed: 'Agree with each other, make the soldiers rich, and ignore everyone else.' (Dio, *Historia Romana* 76, 15, 2). Before his death, Severus was afflicted by nightmares while the all-important omens were less than promising. William Combe in *The History and Antiquities of the City of York* (1785), and referenced by Drake in *Eboracum* (1788), suggests that Aelius Spartianus reported that a temple to Bellona, a goddess of war, existed just outside Micklegate Bar in the context of Severus' return from Scotland in 221. Aelius Spartianus was a historian who wrote the biographies of Hadrian, Didius Julianus, Severus, Niger, Caracalla and Geta for the notoriously unreliable *Historia Augusta*.

Severus visited the shrine to perform a sacrifice in thanks for his victories, but the soothsayer on duty (an 'ignorant Augur') supplied black instead of white animals. This terrible gaffe could only mean bad luck. Severus was horrified and distraught and returned to his palace while, piling one calamity on another, the black beasts were carelessly allowed to follow close behind to the very doors of the palace. A very bad and unpropitious day for the emperor – he died soon after. Bellona was often recognisable by her helmet along with other accoutrements of conflict: sword, spear, or shield, frequently brandishing a bloody torch or whip as she hurtled into battle in a four-horse war chariot. Bellona's priests were known as Bellonarii; they ritually self-harmed, wounding their own arms or legs and either offered up the blood or drank it themselves in order to become inspired with belligerent zeal.

Severus was cremated in Eboracum; Dio described what would have been a spectacular ceremony attended by the entire imperial family and anyone who was anyone in Roman York: 'His body dressed in military uniform was placed on a pyre, and as a mark of honour the soldiers and his sons ceremoniously ran around it; the soldiers who had gifts put them on the fire while his sons set fire to it.'

The location of the cremation was not recorded, but a hill to the west of modern York, known now as Severus Hill, is associated by some historians as the site where it took place; there is no archaeological evidence to support this. His ashes were returned to Rome in a gilded porphyry. His widow and heirs reportedly hurried back to Rome with unseemly haste to pursue their claims to the imperial throne. Severus was very soon history.

Julia Domna and the Roman Head Pot

These odd pots, head pots, were all the rage in the reign of Septimius Severus. Bits of up to fifty different head pots have been found in York, first made by potters attached to the army from North Africa around 211–212; their popularity was boosted no doubt by Julia Domna's sojourn in the city.

The example in the Yorkshire Museum is beautifully fashioned and, unusually, it is complete and intact. The hairstyle and physiognomy suggest that it is modelled on Severus' Syrian wife Julia Domna (c. 160 –217); she was from Emesa (now Homs), and, as we know, she accompanied him to York along with most of the imperial household.

Dio tells how Domna was proficient at rhetoric and in political and philosophical discussions with the powerful and eminent men of the day. She played an important role in a salon of Roman and Greek philosophers and sophists, including Philostratus, whom she encouraged to write the *Life of Apollonius of Tyana*. She regularly advised her elder son Caracalla in an official capacity; he delegated to her matters of state which he could not be bothered with and her name appeared with his on correspondence with the senate (*CIL* 10, 6009). Among her many offices she was, in 195, made *Mater invictorum castrorum* – Mother of the Invincible Camps – and in 215 was put in charge of the *cura epistularum Graecarum*, *epistularum Latinarum,* and held the office of *a libellis,* the official in charge of receiving petitions. Gibbon says that Domna built 'the most splendid reputation' by applying herself to letters and philosophy.

When Severus died in 211, Julia found herself the mediator between her two fractious sons, Caracalla and Geta, who were supposed to rule as joint emperors, according to their father's wishes as expressed in his will. However, the two young men had a disputatious relationship and Geta was murdered by Caracalla's soldiers. Geta's name was then removed from inscriptions and public records, and his image erased in a *damnatio memoriae.*

Julia Domna committed suicide in 217 in Antioch on the assassination of Caracalla during his campaign against the Parthians. Her decision will have been influenced by the knowledge that she was suffering from breast cancer. She became the first empress dowager to receive the title combination 'Pia Felix Augusta', which probably means she enjoyed greater powers than usual for a Roman empress mother.

The Economic and Cultural Impact of Septimius Severus

Libyan Septimius Severus from Leptis Magna, the first black citizen to hold Rome's highest office, brought to the city a surge of cosmopolitan culture, fashion and prestige on a scale never seen before and probably never since. Before Severus' court arrived, few residents of York would have seen a foreigner, apart from those in the army, never mind Syrians or Mesopotamians; yet almost overnight their city was buzzing with every nationality known to Rome. Severus was also keen to show off and promote his wife, Julia, who sported modish fashions and an up-to-the-minute hairstyle and cosmetics. Indeed, they were York's, maybe Roman Britain's, first celebrities. Different exotic foods, foreign languages also made their debuts here into a very cosmopolitan and trendy Eboracum.

The so-called Ivory Bangle Lady discovered in 2010 was confirmed as a high-status young black woman buried in York during the period Severus was in town – more evidence to contradict popular assumptions that African and other immigrants in Roman Britain were of low status, male and more than likely to have been slaves.

Dio tells us that, as you might expect, Septimius Severus' staff brought with them truly prodigious quantities of supplies to feed and water the armies and the cavalry's horses, the mules for transport and the beasts and birds for sacrifice and augury. Moreover, all the soldiers had to be paid, so enormous amounts of coinage would be handed out over time; this would soon find itself boosting the local economy as the 30-40,000-strong soldiery spent their salaries in the local markets, shops, taverns and brothels. Severus obviously anticipated this as he had also brought the Imperial Fiscus Treasury (the personal chest of the emperors of Rome) and key senators, turning the *principia* – the headquarters of the legionary fortress in York – into the Imperial Roman capital.

A large number of hoards dating to the Severan period have been found in Britain, including several from around York. The Overton Hoard (in the Yorkshire Museum) is one of the more celebrated and sheds light on how life in Roman York and its environs were impacted by the events associated with the Severan presence in the city. The latest and least worn of the coins are dated to 193–211. The earliest coins in the hoard are much older, dating to the reign of Vespasian in 69–79.

Unsurprisingly, given the sheer size of the settlement, food and drink and their provision were always hugely important in York. Archaeological evidence tells us much about food consumption and diet in the garrison, with significant signs of cereal crops and animal husbandry. A first-century warehouse fire in 39–41 on Coney Street in the *vicus* revealed that spelt wheat (*triticum spelta*) (sixty per cent of the charred grains), barley (twenty-five per cent) and rye (twenty-five per cent) were the most common cereal grains at that time. Meanwhile, the ditch at 5 Rougier Street yielded eighty-nine per cent spelt wheat and eleven per cent barley. The brewing of beer would probably have consumed the barley.

We should not forget weeds, many of which were found in grain deposits or brought in on, or in, the dung from beasts driven to York for market, or in their hay. Seeds for edible plants such as opium poppies, coriander, dill and savory, which were in use as seasoning agents, have been found on the General Accident site.

In research carried out by Terry O'Connor from the University of York, a sampling of 7,306 excavated animal bones revealed that in the late second and early third centuries, cows at sixty-nine per cent were by far the main source of meat with sheep (seventeen per cent) and pigs (fourteen per cent) providing much less. Minor sources of meat came from chicken and geese, with an insignificant quantity of wild fowl, deer and hare. O'Connor's research also revealed evidence of marrow extraction from cattle bones and of smoking the beef. A delicacy at the more ostentatious dinner parties was the well-known *glis glis*; no evidence of this dormouse has been found but digging on the General Accident site has yielded what may have been a tolerable alternative – the garden dormouse *eliomys quercinus*, which was native to Gaul.

As for seafood and fish, we can thank the General Accident site again for evidence of crab and herring, no doubt originating from the east coast or Humber estuary. Apart from the imports of olive oil, fish sauce (*garum*) and wine there is evidence of olives, grapes and figs coming in.

Romano-British 'hunt cups' depict hunting scenes, and *mortaria* (mixing bowls) have been excavated from the city and large millstones have been found in rural sites outside the *colonia* at Heslington and Stamford Bridge.

Dining scenes can be seen on the tombstones of Julia Velva, Mantinia Maercia and Aelia Aeliana to cater for their needs in the afterlife; they are shown reclining on a couch and being served food and wine. Furthermore, several inhumation burials from Trentholme Drive contained hens' eggs placed in ceramic urns as essential grave goods for the deceased.

The Romans, military and civilian, would not have gone for long without their staples and favourites: olive oil, wine and *garum* would have been in high and immediate demand. This, of course, spawned the importation and local (Roman) manufacture of cooking and storage vessels, flagons and platters for such commodities and for dining. The Romans – and the Britons – enjoyed their wine as much as anyone. In York, four examples of beakers inscribed with appropriately convivial exhortations have been discovered: they urge '*da mihi*', 'give to me!'; '*misce mihi*', 'mix for me!'; '*nolite sitire*', 'don't be thirsty!', and '*vivatis*'; 'a long life to you!' (*Eboracum* Nos. 151 a–f). Olive oil and wine were imported in large *amphorae* – wine from south-west Gaul, oil from southern Spain; numerous sherds from *amphorae* found in and around York attest to this. There was locally produced pottery but it seems to have been of low quality: the Romans with their finer tastes and higher standards required something better and so the legionary potters, *figuli,* made their own – usually of red earthenware of a standard design. Detritus from the Aldwark, Heworth and Peaseholme Green areas attest to the existence of kilns. We call much of it Ebor Ware, the production of which flourished periodically from the late first century to the early third. Another popular brand was Samian Ware which would have come from other kilns in Britannia and from around Toulouse, Clermont-Ferrand and Trier in Gaul.

Samian Ware, or *terra sigillata,* is a general term for the ubiquitous fine-red Roman pottery roughly translated as 'sealed earth', i.e. 'clay bearing little images' (*sigilla*), much of it made in Italy and in Gaul, and used and deposited throughout the empire. A mould has been found in York.

Glass came in from Italy, Gaul and the Rhine lands, and later from London. Unusual green-glazed vessels were imported from Gaul too, while decorated colour-coated purple sheen jars and beakers flooded in from around Cologne. Wellington Row gets the prize for the largest deposit of pottery with 20,000 or so sherds excavated there; twenty-five per cent of these originated from the mid-second to early third centuries and were imported. By the time we get down to third-century layers the figure rises to thirty-six per cent.

One importer was the *signifer*, standard bearer, Lucius Duccius Rufinus whose tombstone was found in 1688 at Holy Trinity Church in Micklegate. He was bringing in wine from the Rhône Valley. His epitaph reads: 'Lucius Duccius Rufinus, son of Lucius, of the Voltinian tribe, from Vienne, a standard bearer of the Ninth Legion, 28 years old. He is laid here.'

And then there was Lucius Viducius Placidus, a merchant, *negotiator*, from Velioccasses (Rouen) whose name we find etched onto a tablet found at Clementhorpe. This is important because it is a rare example in Britannia of a commemoration of a building erected by a private individual – ARCUM ET IANUM – an archway and doorway, probably part of a temple. We can only guess but he probably traded in olive oil, wine and pottery one way, and, as exports, jet, grain and beef the other way. His building tells us that trade was good and lucrative.

What could the Britons offer the Romans? Grain – ever an anxiety for the empire – was a critical export, which the Romans seem to have exploited to feed other parts of the empire near to Britannia. More exotic, exclusive and somewhat rarer, however, was jet.

Jet (*gagates*)

Jet is a black mineraloid, the compressed remains (fossilised wood) of ancestors of the monkey puzzle tree (*Araucariaceae*), found in abundance in the cliffs and on the moors around Whitby and used since the Bronze Age to make beads and other jewellery. Jet enjoys the greatest celebrity and has done since Roman times with copious pendants, earrings, rings hairpins and brooches unearthed, reaching its zenith 1,400 years later during the reign of Victoria after the death of Prince Albert. The jet found around Whitby is of early Jurassic (Toarcian) age, approximately 182 million years old. The hardest, purest, saltwater jet comes from a seven-and-a-half-mile stretch of coast around Whitby which yields some of the best deposits the Earth has to offer. Whitby jet is light in weight making it perfect for fashioning into jewellery; it has a hardness of 3.5-4 on the Mohs hardness scale.

Eboracum was the place to go for Whitby jet, or *gagates* in Latin. In Whitby it would have been harvested from the beach or cut from underwater outcrops. There are fewer than twenty-five jet pendants found so far in the entire Roman world, but six of these come from Eboracum and are held in the Yorkshire Museum.

York has also yielded up a female skeleton, the Ivory Bangle Lady, wearing two jet anklets, a jet bracelet and a bone and silver bracelet. This raises the question as to whether wearing anklets signified a woman of low morals, as actresses, singers and prostitutes were considered by the Romans. Some scholars (for example, Balsdon) suggest that anklets were synonymous with permissiveness, but the discovery of a relief showing a hairdresser with an anklet on her right ankle from Neumagen throws doubt on that particular stereotype.

Being easy to cut and polishing up well, jet was a gift to jewellery makers and to recipients as presents and heirlooms. It also has the advantage of emitting static electricity when rubbed, thus giving the magicians and witches a field day. Fashioning jet into Medusa gorgon faces and the like was popular in the daily struggle against the evil eye and similar superstitions.

Much evidence for the working and manufacture of jet from the second to the fourth century has been unearthed, although the boom in fashionability came with the third century. One of the star finds is the little bear pendant excavated at Bootham in 1845 along with a coin of Constantine dated 312–5. The Yorkshire Museum also has jet dice which would have been tossed from a dice box (*fritillium*). Other dice have been found in many other parts of the empire – some of them are loaded. The popularity is probably due to the proximity of the Whitby deposits and the arrival of Julia Domna, empress to Severus, in the city. York's jet jewellery had an empire-wide market if the many articles exported to and found around Cologne are anything to go by.

In the third century, Solinus (*Collectanea Rerum Memorabilium* 22, 11) notes the good quality of Whitby jet but it is Pliny the Elder (AD 23–79 *Natural History* 36, 34) who details the geological, pseudo-medical and magical properties of *gagates*:

> Gagates is a stone, so called from Gages, the name of a town and river in Lycia. It is said, too, that at Leucolla the sea throws it up, and that it is found over a space twelve stadia inland. It is black, smooth, light, and porous, looks like wood, is of a brittle texture, and gives off a bad smell

when rubbed. You cannot rub off marks made on pottery with this stone. When burnt, it smells of sulphur; and it is a fact that it ignites when in contact with water, while oil quenches it. Its burning fumes repel snakes and dispel hysteria; it can detect symptoms of epilepsy, and is a test of virginity. A decoction of this stone in wine cures tooth-ache; and, in combination with wax, it is good for scrofula. The magicians, it is said, make use of gagates in the practice of what they call axinomancy [divination by axes] assuring us that it will be sure not to burn if the thing the client desires is about to happen.

Roman Dice and Gambling

The Romans played two games with their dice: *tali* and *tesserae*. *Tali* used four dice and the best score came when each die showed a different number. *Tesserae* was played with three dice and the best score was three sixes. Bad scores were called 'dogs' and the high scores were called 'Venus'. Games such as this would have been very popular and, in the case of the military, a weapon in the war against barrack-room boredom. They threw from a cup called a *fritillium* and usually played on a board made of wood, bronze or marble. The well off enjoyed marble boards encrusted with jewels and had their names incised into the back of the boards. Dice, of course, engendered gambling and the ruin of many a Roman through gambling debt. This provoked the authorities to enact numerous laws such as Lex Alearia (204 BC), Lex Cornelia (81 BC), Lex Publicia, and Lex Titia de Aleatoribus which outlawed gambling with dice and in breach of which offenders could be jailed, exiled or fined up to four times the value of the bet. The Lex Talaria prohibited the gambling of dice except at mealtime and during the Saturnalia festival. The laws were policed (ineffectively) by the *aediles*: these laws, as today, were largely ignored. Gambling debts remained unrecoverable until the reign of Justinian when fixed odds were applied on games of skill.

Other Jewellery

After the late second century, amber became popular in Roman Britain, as elsewhere. Pliny tells us (*Natural History* 37, 30) that amber was expensive and had a special appeal to women. Pliny and Artemidorus (*Onorocritica* 2, 5) agree that when a woman dreams of amber it means good things are coming. It was even believed that women only wore amber when they were going to sleep (Artemidorus was a second-century expert on the interpretation of dreams). A grave group from Walmgate has given up a bracelet of amber and pearl beads.

A coral necklace has also been found in Walmgate. When fashioned into the shape of a phallus, coral was considered to be powerful in warding off the evil eye. In the Roman world the phallus was, therefore, a good luck and fertility charm and had none of the sexual connotations it has today in the 'civilised world'. Variscite is a relatively rare phosphate mineral sometimes confused with turquoise; beads of variscite have been found in York.

Industry in Roman York

Excavations in Coppergate show that glass was manufactured in York from the third century: this provided the usual bowls, bottles and jars as well as phials for potions, perfumes and cosmetics. The manufacture of glass in York endured well into the twentieth century.

Smiths too would have been busy, not least in the manufacture of weapons, armour and other materiel. York has yielded a copper alloy helmet cheek piece at the Purey Cust site. Two bronze kettles (essential army equipment then as now) stamped with the century that owned them have been found. Slag, scrap and tools were unearthed on the site of the General Accident building. Scraps of uniforms and an iron sword probably in for repair have also been found there. In 1860, the grounds of the manor house at Dringhouses gave up a fine tomb relief (now in the Yorkshire Museum) showing a smith complete with protective leather apron, hammer and tongs. Bronze pins and wrought iron were worked in a workshop found in Bishophill Senior from the second century. Other craftsmen at work in York included stonemasons and carvers of bone. Nails would have been much in demand for military and civilian construction work; a horde found in Blake Street probably tells us that they were discarded when stone buildings replaced wooden.

Leather offcuts and bits of shoe confirm the presence of leather working – a trade which persisted for many years in this area, hence Tanner Row and Tanner's Moat; a sizeable fragment from an army tent and pieces from others have also been excavated. The VIth legion centurion and graffiti artist, Marcus Sollius Julianus, must have been having a quiet day when he whiled away his time etching his name on one of the fragments; he turns up again on Hadrian's Wall, his name scratched this time onto a stone used by his men in the construction of the wall. If ever we needed tangible evidence of Legio VI's military and civil engineering ties between York and the wall then this is it.

Other industries include weaving and flax spinning, as evidenced by the spindle dug up at Bishophill Senior.

Britannia Inferior (Lower Britain)

> Then the angry emperor [Severus] took vengeance upon Albinus' friends at Rome. He sent the man's head to the city and ordered that it be displayed. When he reported his victory in dispatches, he added a note stating that he had sent Albinus' head to be put on public view so that the people might know the extent of his anger against them. After settling affairs in Britain, he divided this region into two provinces, each under its own governor.
>
> (Herodian, *History of the Empire from the Death of Marcus*, 8, 1)

Severus obviously wanted to put an end to all of the turmoil caused by usurpers throughout the empire, so he made an example of Albinus by savagely desecrating his body. But this was not his only act of severance: at roughly the same time, in an act of momentous political and military significance, he split Britannia into two – another instance of dividing and ruling. At the same time he divested the governors in Londinium of their power over the legions in the north – in order to dilute their power in the wake of Clodius Albinus' recent bid to become emperor. In doing this he focused the power on the legions stationed in the trouble spots, not least Hadrian's Wall. Severus had set a precedent for this in Syria. The new Britannia was probably formalised around 214 by Severus' surviving son Caracalla.

Britannia Inferior takes in much of modern northern England. Its capital, of course, was Eboracum, under the leadership of a Praetorian legate in command of a single legion and numerous auxiliaries stationed in the city. This subdivision lasted throughout the Severan dynasty until the reorganisation of the empire under Diocletian in 296 when he established the newly named Diocese of Britannia which was subdivided into four provinces, Britannia Prima (capital Cirencester) and Maxima Caesariensis (capital London) from Britannia Superior and Britannia Secunda (capital in Eboracum) and Flavia Caesariensis (capital in Lindum) from Britannia Inferior.

Eboracum as an Urban Settlement: *Coloniae, Municipia, Civitates, Canabae* and *Vici*

The Roman fortress would have exerted many varied influences on the local community and environment: at once a source of local labour and of women for conjugal relationships and prostitution, and at the same time a golden opportunity for the more enterprising and venal elements in the local population to enrich themselves by running ancillary businesses in support of the garrison, or to enhance their standing in the community with a career in local government. The spiv has always been with us. Away from the fortress, other tribes and local communities became self-governing: the Brigantes had Aldborough, the Parisi Brough-on-Humber.

The first thing the military authorities would have done after selecting their fortress site back in AD 71 would have been to requisition a tract of land on which they would construct the fortress and reserve for other military related activities. Such land was called *prata* or *territorium* and could be up to 125,000 acres. Inevitably, this would have entailed the compulsory requisitioning of native settlements (such as at Rawcliffe Moor) by the authorities. The *territorium* would have included an area for soldiers' families (when these were officially permitted) in much the same way as modern barracks have a 'patch' for family quarters on site or nearby.

Coloniae

By 237 Eboracum was accorded the privilege and status of a *colonia*, the Roman urban settlement at the top of the hierarchy when it came to the status and importance of settlements under Rome. York was now self-governing, administratively, as with other *coloniae*, a mirror image of Rome itself with a council or senate (*ordo*) made up of up to 100 rich locals, merchants, and veteran soldiers (decurions). The honour did not come cheap: the decurions were obliged to contribute to the costs of baths and other public buildings fitting for a *colonia*, as well as chipping in to the treasury. What the locals lost in money they made up with in the kudos implicit in ingratiating oneself with the Romans. AD 237 was the date when Marcus Aurelius Lunaris, as *Sevir Augustalis* at the *coloniae* of both Lindum and Eboracum, dedicated his temple to the local deity Tutela Boudiga at Bordeaux. From now on this is where the governor of that province would sit. Marcus Antonius Gordianus was the first to fill that post, but he had higher honours to come when he was made emperor at the age of 81 in 238. One year later he died, not through illness or natural causes, but by taking his own life.

A Roman *colonia* was originally an outpost established in conquered territory as a security measure, as a kind of garrison, as a piece of Rome in a foreign land. Initially the *coloniae* would consist partly of Roman citizens, usually about 300, but after Augustus the number was increased and many thousands of Roman veterans were gifted lands in *coloniae* throughout the empire, often in recognition of military service. Augustus needed to settle over 100,000 of his veterans at the end of the civil wars, and so began a massive *colonia* creation programme throughout the empire.

All citizens of a *colonia* were automatically accorded Roman citizenship with all the apparent freedoms and benefits that brought. So, when a place became a *colonia,* and when land was granted nearby to veterans who had retired, the idea was that these legionnaires would start families and provide future recruits to the legions, which, in the earlier years of the empire, were only open to Roman citizens. The veterans were also responsible for the Romanisation of many territories, mainly through the spread of Latin and of Roman laws, culture and customs.

According to Livy (1, 11), Rome's first colonies were established in about 752 BC (just after the very founding of Rome in 753 BC) at Antemnae and Crustumerium – both very close to Rome. Colonies then were always a part of Roman life and foreign policy. The first *colonia* in Britain was at Colonia Claudia Victricensis Camulodunum (Colchester), established around AD 49, followed by Lindum Colonia or Colonia Domitiana Lindensium (Lincoln) in AD 71 and Colonia Nervia Glevensium (Gloucester), founded in AD 97 by Nerva. As noted, each *colonia* was governed by an *ordo* (council), under the control of four *quattuoviri*, annually appointed magistrates. These in turn oversaw 100 decurions aged over 30 who satisfied the property qualifications. The following random list shows the spread of *coloniae* in place and time:

Arles	Colonia Iulia Paterna Arelatensis Sextanorum; province: Gallia Narbonensis, 45 BC established by Julius Caesar
Belgrade	Singidunum; province: Moesia Superior, AD 239 founded by Celts c. 279 BC, conquered by Romans in 15 BC
Budapest	Aquincum; province: Pannonia, AD 41 54
Köln	Colonia Claudia Ara Agrippinensium; province: Germania Inferior, AD 50

Jerusalem (site of) Colonia Aelia Capitolina Hierosoloma; province: Judaea after Bar Kokhba's revolt, by Hadrian

| *Narbonne* | Colonia Iulia Paterna Claudius Narbo Martius Decumanorum; province: Gallia/Gallia Narbonensis 118 BC by Gnaeus Domitius Ahenobarbus; refounded by Caesar in 45 BC |

Municipia

These were also often inhabited by Roman citizens but the populations were more mixed – in some respects the difference between *coloniae* and *municipia* was blurred and insignificant. Whereas the *coloniae* were based on the city of Rome as a template for town planning and organisation, *municipia* could also enjoy local laws and practices. *Municipia* were often settlements that may once have been tribal towns or *vici*. Examples of *municipia* include Verulamium, Leicester, Dorchester and Canterbury. It is possible that both York (if Aurelius Victor is to be believed) and London were initially *municipia* before becoming *coloniae,* York to reflect its status as capital of Britannia Inferior and to posh it up for Severus' visit.

Civitas Capitals (civitates)

The lowest rank of town serving as administration centres for local-level government. Again, these may have originated as pre-existing Iron Age settlements or have been newly sited, but there is a suggestion that the local populace might have had some involvement in their development. They show signs of being planned and organised but not standardised across the country. Examples of *civitas* capitals in Britain include Wroxeter, Chichester, Carlisle, Silchester, Exeter, Ilchester and Aldborough. Most of the inhabitants would not have enjoyed Roman citizen status; the Romans called them, somewhat disparagingly, *peregrini* (aliens).

Canaba

A *canaba* was originally a hut or hovel but from the time of Hadrian denoted a town that emerged as a civilian settlement (*canaba legionis*) in the vicinity of a Roman legionary fortress (*castrum*). A settlement that grew up outside a smaller Roman fort was a *vicus* (village). *Canabae* were also often divided into *vici*.

Permanent forts naturally were a magnet for anyone and everyone dependant on the military garrison and civilian contractors who serviced the base; these all needed housing and feeding. They included traders, artisans, sellers of food and drink, prostitutes, and also unofficial wives of soldiers and their children; hence most forts had *vici* or *canabae*. Many of these communities became towns through synoecism with other communities, some are still towns today.

Canabae at legionary fortresses include:

> Deva Victrix, Chester
> Isca Silurium, later Caerleon
> Vindobona, later Vienna
> Argentoratum, later Strasbourg
> Nijmegen

Vicus

The fortress was strictly military. So what about the commercial, cultural, spiritual and social needs of the fortress soldiery when they were having a spot of rest and recuperation? On the other side of the fortress wall, civilians, as noted, from near and far were eager to take advantage of the extensive commercial opportunities brought by the garrison of usually more than 5,000 men, be they selling bread, arena tickets (*panem et circenses*) or their bodies. The fort was a magnet drawing in artisans, labourers, traders, wives, actors, dancers, musicians slaves, camp followers and sex workers.

A *vicus* could and often did, over the years, flourish and grow until it attained the status of an independent *municipium* in its own right; it may then even graduate to *colonia* status, as is the case with Eboracum. Here the ever-burgeoning civilian settlement followed the line of some of the roads leading in and out the fortress, for example at the south-west gate where the road crossed the Ouse Bridge, then on up the hill to enter the walls near Micklegate Bar. There is also *vicus* evidence on the north-east side of the river around Spurriergate and Nessgate. A replica of the dedication stone from a temple of Hercules is set into the wall of a building in Nessgate where the original was found; wharves have been discovered along the Foss which may have been a harbour, and a mosaic has been unearthed south of the fortress east angle. Burials have been excavated along a road along the line of Toft Green and Tanner Row; around AD 200 there was a bronze workshop at Bishophill, later replaced by two stone buildings. Clementhorpe is the site of a grand house typical of those which came complete with underfloor heating, some mosaics and frescoed walls.

Each *vicus* had its own board of officials who oversaw local matters.

The Imperial Crisis (AD 235–AD 284)

The Imperial Crisis exploded when the Roman Empire was rocked by a seemingly endless series of barbarian invasions, rebellions and imperial pretenders queuing up to wrestle power from the man in charge. The effect on Britain, and York, probably varied over time but essentially the province was largely immune from the turbulence.

It all began with the assassination of Severus Alexander by his own troops in 235 who then proclaimed Maximinus Thrax, commander of one of the legions, the new emperor. Maximinus (regarded as a bit of a peasant by the senate) was the first of the so-called barrack-room emperors – rulers who were elevated by their troops even though they lacked any of the traditional aristocratic Roman qualifications for the job: political experience, a supporting faction, distinguished ancestors, or a hereditary claim to the imperial throne. The assassination ignited a fifty-year period during which there were at least twenty-six claimants to the title of emperor, mostly prominent Roman army generals, who assumed imperial power over all or part of the empire.

At the heart of it all was the remuneration of the legions. The army demanded increasingly large retainers or bribes to remain loyal. Severus had raised the pay of legionaries, and gave substantial *donativum* (gifts of money doled out to the soldiers of the Roman legions or to the Praetorian Guard) to the soldiery. This was to cause major problems for all of his successors. His son Caracalla also raised the annual pay and lavished many benefits on the army in accordance with the death-bed advice of his father to keep them on side.

The catastrophic Year of the Six Emperors followed in 238 during which all of the original claimants (Maximinus Thrax; Gordian I; Gordian II; Pupienus, half-British Balbinus and Gordian III) were killed. Here is a summary of the imperial carnage: in 238 a revolt broke out in Africa led by Gordian I and Gordian II, supported by the senate; this was soon put down with Gordian II killed and Gordian I committing suicide. The senate raised two of their own as co-emperors, Pupienus and Balbinus with Gordian I's grandson Gordian III as *Caesar* (junior emperor). Maximinus marched on Rome but was assassinated by his Legio II *Parthica*, and subsequently Pupienus and Balbinus were murdered by the Praetorian Guard.

By 268 the empire had splintered into three competing states: the Gallic Empire, the Palmyrene Empire (including the eastern provinces of Syria Palaestina and Aegyptus); and the Italian-centred independent Roman Empire proper. Later, Aurelian (r. 270–275) reunited the empire. The crisis ended with Diocletian and the implementation of his reforms in 284.

The Gallic Empire was a breakaway part of the Roman Empire that functioned *de facto* as a separate state from 260 to 274. It seemed that everything that could go wrong for the Roman Empire was going wrong: there were frequent raids across the Rhine and Danube frontiers by foreign tribes, including the Carpians, Goths, Vandals, and Alamanni, and attacks from Sassanids in the east. Climate change and a sea level rise destroyed the harvests of what is now the Low Countries, forcing tribes to pour into Roman territory. The Plague of Cyprian (probably smallpox), as already mentioned, erupted with a vengeance, causing high levels of mortality and severely weakening the empire. To make matters worse, in 260 the emperor Valerian was captured in battle by the Sassanids and later died in captivity. The civil wars continued, there were peasant revolts, political instability with multiple usurpers jousting for power, Roman dependence on and growing influence of barbarian mercenaries (*foederati*) and commanders nominally working for Rome but increasingly acting independently, debasement of currency, and economic depression.

The Gallic Empire was set up by Postumus in 260 in the wake of these barbarian invasions and instability in Rome; at its height it included the territories of Germania, Gaul, Britannia, and (temporarily) Hispania. After Postumus was assassinated in 268, it lost much of its territory, but continued under a number of emperors and usurpers. It was retaken by Aurelian after the Battle of Châlons in 274.

The turning point came when an invasion of Macedonia and Greece by Goths, who had been displaced from their lands on the Black Sea, was defeated by emperor Claudius II Gothicus at the Battle of Naissus in 268. Further victories by Claudius Gothicus repulsed the Alamanni and recovered Hispania from the Gallic Empire. He died of the plague in 270 and was succeeded by Aurelian, who had commanded the cavalry at Naissus. Aurelian held power through the worst of the crisis, gradually restoring the empire. He defeated the Vandals, Visigoths, Palmyrene Empire, and finally the remainder of the Gallic Empire. By late 274, the Roman Empire had been reunited into a single entity. However, Aurelian was assassinated in 275, spawning a further series of competing emperors. The situation was not to stabilise until Diocletian, himself a barrack-room emperor, took power in 284.

The Carausian Revolt

The Carausian Revolt (286–296) occurred when a somewhat dubious Roman naval commander, Carausius, declared himself emperor over Britain and northern Gaul, thus creating the Britannic Empire. In the end, his Gallic territories were retaken by Constantius Chlorus in 293 (*Caesar* of the West then *Augustus*; r. 293–306) after which Carausius was assassinated by his treasurer (*rationalis*) Allectus. Britain was brought back into the fold by Constantius and Asclepiodotus in 296.

Carausius, a Menapian of low birth, rose through the ranks of the Roman military and was appointed to a naval command in the Britannic fleet at Bononia-Gesoriacum (Boulogne), tasked with eradicating Frankish and Saxon raiders and pirates from the English Channel. When he got wind of the death sentence decreed on him by the emperor Maximian on charges of colluding with Frankish and Saxon pirates and embezzling recovered treasure, he responded by organising a coup, declaring himself emperor in Britain and taking control over the provinces of Britain and some in northern Gaul while Maximian was distracted with uprisings elsewhere. His not inconsiderable force comprised not only the fleet, augmented by new ships he had built, and the three legions stationed in Britain, but a legion he had appropriated in Gaul, a number of foreign auxiliary units, a levy of Gaulish merchant ships, and barbarian mercenaries attracted by the chance of booty.

An invasion in 288 to depose him failed due to bad weather, although Carausius claimed it as a military victory (*Panegyrici Latini* 10, 12,1; 8, 12, 2); Eutropius (*Abridgement of Roman History* 22) says that hostilities were in vain, thanks to Carausius' military skill; a ceasefire was agreed and an uneasy peace ensued, with Carausius obviously warming to his new status – minting coins and bringing their value into line with Roman issues as well as acknowledging and honouring Maximian and then Diocletian. Legends on the coins included *Restitutor Britanniae* (Restorer of Britain) and *Genius Britanniae* (Spirit of Britain) to win British support. Constantius responded with a medal struck after his victory, in which he described himself as *redditor lucis aeternae*, 'restorer of the eternal light' (i.e. of Rome).

In 293 Constantius, now the western *Caesar*, cut Carausius off by retaking the territory he had seized in Gaul. He besieged Bononia and invaded Batavia in the Rhine delta. After seven years of power Carausius was assassinated by Allectus, who took on the command.

In 296 the reconquest of Britain began. With Maximian holding the Rhine frontier, Constantius divided his fleet into several divisions. He led one division himself from Bononia; another, sailing from Le Havre, was commanded by Asclepiodotus, prefect of the Praetorian Guard. Asclepiodotus' ships slipped past Allectus' fleet, stationed off the Isle of Wight, in the fog. They landed near Southampton and burned their boats. The rebels were routed at Calleva Atrebatum (Silchester); Allectus himself was killed in the battle. Constantius, it seems, did not reach Britain until it was all over but he was welcomed by the Britons as a liberator (*Panegyrici Latini* 8, 19).

The Diocletian reforms were introduced: Britain as a whole became the Diocese of the Britains under the administration of the Prefecture of the Gauls based in Augusta Treverorum (Trier) and was divided from two provinces into four or five.

Constantius Chlorus (c. AD 250–AD 306)

Constantius Chlorus rose from virtually nowhere to become the emperor of the western Roman Empire. Like, Carausias, his adversary, he was a soldier who had worked his way up through the ranks, but his shrewdest act came in 289 when he married Theodora, the stepdaughter

Drawing of two Ancient Britons; one with tattoos carrying a spear and shield; the other painted with woad, and carrying a sword and round shield. C. 1574. (*Provided by the British Library from its digital collections. Catalogue entry: Add MS 28330*)

Above left: 'Io Saturnalia!' The Standard bearer (*signifer*) of the Xth Legion jumps from his ship and wades up the shores of England, leading the Roman invasion, James William Edmund Doyle, 1822–1892. ('The Britons' in *A Chronicle of England BC 55–AD 1485, London 1864*)

Above right: An eighteenth-century illustration of a wicker man, the form of execution that Caesar claimed the druids used for human sacrifice. From the 'Duncan Caesar', Tonson, Draper, and Dodsley edition of the *Commentaries of Caesar* translated by William Duncan and published in 1753. An image from a set of eight extra-illustrated volumes of *A Tour in Wales* by Thomas Pennant (1726–1798) that chronicle the three journeys he made through Wales between 1773 and 1776. These volumes are unique because they were compiled for Pennant's own library at Downing. This edition was produced in 1781.

Andrew Birrell (after Henry Fuseli), *Caractacus at the Tribunal of Claudius at Rome*, (1792). A defiant Caractacus in captivity having been sold down the river by Queen Cartimandua, puppet queen of the Brigantes from around AD 43 to 69, when he sought refuge with the Brigantes after his opposition to the Romans. (*Public domain: Wikimedia Commons*)

The last definite attestation of the IXth legion: a stone inscription at York dated AD 108, on display in the Yorkshire Museum. The inscription has well-formed Roman letters and numbers. Described in *Eboracum* as: 'Commemorative Tablet fragment in magnesian limestone, comprising the middle part – 3 and 1/3ft by 3 and 3/4ft – of an inscription recording the building in stone of the SE gate of the fortress under Trajan. The fine lettering decreases in height from 6 ins in the first line to 3 and 1/2 ins in the last.

"IM]P(ERATOR) CAESAR DIVI N]ERVAE FIL(IVS) N[ERVA TRAI] ANVS AVG(VSTVS) GER[M(ANICVS DAC ICVS PO]NTIFEX MAXMV[S TRIBV NICIAE PO]TESTATIS XII IMP(ERATOR) V [CO(N)S(VL) v P(ATER) P(ATRIAE) PORTAM] PER LEG(IONEM) VIIII HI[SP(ANAM) FECIT": "The Emperor Caesar, son of the divine Nerva, Nerva Traianus Augustus, Germanicus, Dacicus, pontifex maximus, in his twelfth year of tribunician power, five times acclaimed Imperator, five times consul, father of his country, made this gateway by agency of the Ninth Legion Hispana."

'This stone is dated by Trajan's twelfth tribunician power to the year 10 Dec 107–9 Dec 108. The lettering is of very great elegance and its form suggests a draft written with pen or brush, faithfully copied by the mason and thus affording a glimpse of the official style used by clerks or draughtsmen of the IXth legion.

'Found in 1854 at a depth of 26ft to 28ft in King's Square near the house at the corner of Goodramgate and King's Square while making a drain along Goodramgate and Church Street.'

Inset: Roof tile bearing the IXth legion stamp.
(*Images courtesy of York Museums Trust*)

Above left: A dignified Boudica and her daughters; she, a queen, was flogged and they were raped by the Romans. (*Courtesy of Geoff Cook at Cardiff City Hall*)

Above right: Relief carving in Aphrodisias Museum, Turkey. Originally sited on the Sebasteion in Aphrodisias. A victorious Claudius stamping out Britannia. Claudius is on the point of delivering a death blow to the slumped figure of Britannia. He wears helmet, cloak, and sword belt with scabbard. Britannia wears a tunic with one breast bare – like the Amazon figures on which she was based. The inscription reads 'Tiberios Klaudios Kaisar – Bretannia'. (*Public domain: Wikimedia Commons*)

Roman generals and emperors in the frieze of the Great Hall of the National Galleries Scotland, by William Brassey Hole 1897. Agricola is second from the right, Tacitus far right with the scroll. (*www.nationalgalleries.org/art-and-artists/159703/processional-frieze-great-hall-scottish-national-portrait-gallery*)

The Multangular Tower in York's Museum Gardens. The magnificent Multangular Tower forms the west corner of the Roman fortress. One of its stones is 21ft by 11ft wide and bears the legible inscription '*Genio loci feliciter*': '*good luck to the guardian spirit of this place*' – (*RIB* 647). It was uncovered in 1702 when digging a cellar below the Black Swan Inn in Coney Street outside the south angle of the fortress and is now in the Yorkshire Museum YORYM: 2007.6197. (*Author's Own*)

On 13 March 2010, to commemorate the 1600th anniversary of the end of Roman rule in Britain, a series of 500 beacons were lit along the length of Hadrian's Wall. This monumental barrier extended seventy-three miles comprising ditch, a thicket of spikes, a stone wall, a sequence of forts, mile castles and observation turrets, and a permanent garrison of up to 8,000 men. (*From www.geograph.org.uk. Author Gary Dickson*)

The Antonine Wall near Bar Hill. Work on the Antonine Wall began in AD 142, extending from the Firth of Forth to the Firth of Clyde. This was abandoned after twenty years and only occasionally re-occupied. (*Public domain: Wikimedia Commons*)

Constantine outside York Minster, which was built on his fortress. This powerful bronze statue was commissioned by York Civic Trust and designed by the sculptor Philip Jackson. It was unveiled in 1998 to commemorate the accession of Constantine as Roman Emperor in AD 306 on this site, after the death, in York, of his father Constantius Chlorus. The statue depicts a seated Constantine wearing military dress. His right arm is outstretched behind him and his left holds the pommel of a sword, the tip of which is shown to be broken. A legend inscribed on the base reads 'Constantine by this sign conquer': a translation of the Latin '*in hoc signo vinces*' from Eusebius of Caesaria, who recounts how Constantine was marching with his army and looked up to the sun and saw a cross of light above it, and with it the Greek words '(ἐν) τούτῳ νίκα' ('In this sign, you conquer'). Inevitably, the statue was given a protective face mask during the COVID-19 pandemic in 2020. (*Author's Own*)

Above left: Blowing the *cornu*. A *cornicen* (hornblower) photographed during a re-enactment of Legio XV from Pram, Austria. The *cornu* was carried by the *cornicen* who 'translated' his commander's orders into signals and broadcast them over the field during battles. Every legion had their cornicens. (*This file is licensed under the Creative Commons Attribution-Share Alike 3.0 Unported license*)

Above right: Obols have been found in Roman graves in York so that the deceased could pay the surly ferryman, Charon, and cross the River Styx. This is a nineteenth-century interpretation of Charon's perilous crossing by Alexander Dmitrievich Litovchenko (1835–1890). *Charon Carries Souls across the River Styx* (1861) is now in the Russian Museum, St Petersburg. (*Public domain: Wikimedia Commons*)

Above left: Marble bust of the Emperor Constantine I, found before 1823, in Stonegate. Here he is clean-shaven and wearing an imperial oak wreath; weathering suggests that he originally stood in the open, perhaps in front of the headquarters building of the legionary fortress. Date c. AD 306–AD 337. In the Yorkshire Museum, YORYM: 1998.23. (*Courtesy of York Museums Trust*)

Above right: Constantine regally surveying his fortress from outside York Minster with the impressive column in the foreground salvaged from the basilica where it fell in the ninth century.

Above: The Course of Empire 4 – *Destruction* by Thomas Cole (1836). End of Empire – one of Rome's final disasters. (*New York Historical Society*)

Left: The stunning life-size statue of Mars, god of war, confronts you as you enter the Yorkshire Museum. He is wearing full armour and is carrying a shield. He has a sword on his hip and in his other hand he was probably carrying a metal spear. The statue would have been painted in bright colours. Mars was dug up in 1880 along with three altars in the grounds of the Bar Convent next to Micklegate Bar. (*Image courtesy of and © York Museums Trust*)

Right: Complete 'Julia Domna style' female head pot. (*Image courtesy of and © York Museums Trust*)

Below: The magnificent 'Four Seasons Mosaic' was uncovered in 1853 during drainage work at Tanner Row. Three other mosaics were also found in the same house, suggesting someone very wealthy lived there. A coin of the emperor Claudius Gothicus was discovered underneath it, thereby telling us that the mosaic must have been laid down during or after his reign (AD 268–270). (*Image courtesy of and © York Museums Trust*)

The mosaic depicts the head and shoulders of Medusa who is surrounded by the four seasons. Medusa was a popular image in Roman homes: her petrifying ability to turn people to stone was thought to ward off evil. The four seasons were each shown with items associated with their particular season. Spring is depicted with a bird, summer with a bunch of grapes, autumn with a rake and winter with a bare branch. (*Image courtesy of and © York Museums Trust*)

Stone statue of a winged deity (*RIB* 641). Dressed in a fringed skirt, this winged figure holds two keys in his left hand, while a serpent acts as a belt and rests its head above his right knee. The right hand and the head are lost. Found under the City Wall while building the railway station in 1874. Now in the Yorkshire Museum YORYM : 2007.6162. The dedication reads:

'VOL(VSIVS) IRE[NAEVS D(ONVM) [D(EDIT) ARIMANI V(OTVM) [S(OLVENS L(IBENS) M(ERITO)]': 'Volusius Irenaeus, paying his vow willingly and deservedly to Arimanes, gave (this) gift.'

Eboracum tells us that the dedication is 'to Arimanius, the Mithraic god of Evil. The missing head was most probably that of a lion, symbolic of all-devouring Death. The snake girdle represents the tortuous course of the sun though the sky; the wings signify the winds; while the keys are those of the heavens and the sceptre is the sign of dominion.'

(*Image courtesy of and © York Museums Trust*)

Perhaps the exhibit in the Yorkshire Museum with the most impact is a preserved head of hair, with jet hairpins and cantharus-shaped heads in situ, from a fourth-century inhumation burial found at the railway station booking office site. The hair is fashioned into a loose bun. It is exhibits like this which bring Roman York to life, allowing you to experience day-to-day living and get inside the lives of the Romans. (*Image courtesy of and © York Museums Trust*)

An unusual roofed coffin using roof tiles.
(*Image courtesy of and © York Museums Trust*)

The Serapis dedication-slab (*RIB* 658) was found in 1770 and is now in the Yorkshire Museum: YORYM 1998.27. It reads

'To the holy god Serapis Claudius Hieronymianus, legate of the VIth Legion Victrix, built this temple from the ground up.' (*Image courtesy of and © York Museums Trust*)

Top left: A third or fourth-century oval jet pendant showing what is probably a man and wife. This is the only jet pendant excavated in Britain showing a posed couple. *Top right*: Jet woman; *Left*: Jet family group.
(*Images courtesy and © York Museums Trust*)

The Corellia Inscription: 'To the spirits of the departed: Corellia Optata, aged 13. You mysterious spirits who dwell in Pluto's Acherusian realms, and whom the meagre ashes and the shade, empty semblance of the body, seek, following the brief light of life; father of an innocent daughter, I, a pitiable victim of unfair hope, bewail her final end. Quintus Corellius Fortis, her father, had this set up.'

A large glass vessel inside the coffin, sealed with lead, contained Corellia's ashes. The reference to Dis – god of the underworld – and Acheron – one of the rivers of the underworld – make this epitaph particularly vivid and pathetic. (*Image courtesy of and © York Museums Trust*)

Julia Fortunata, celebrated in *RIB* 687, was from Sardinia. Her husband, Verecundius Diogenes, set up the tomb, perhaps quoting a hexameter written by Catullus (lxii, 54) in his last line. It was unearthed during the building of the railway station. Verecundius Diogenes was a *sevir augustalis*; these magistrates looked after the cult of the emperor's divinity – a symbol of loyalty – ceremony and entertainment. Diogenes hailed from Bourges, southern France. The sarcophagus was found near Scarborough Bridge – but it contained the skeleton of a man. A good example of the recycling of sarcophagi which, if anything would have been cheaper when second hand – sold as having one careful owner? (*Image courtesy of and © York Museums Trust*)

A model of the *principium* in the Minster Undercroft Museum featuring structural remains of the Roman fortress headquarters and parts of the First Cohort centurions' quarters, along with one of the sewers serving the fortress. Remains of the Roman *basilica* building, at the north side of the *principia,* are visible in the undercroft. (*Author's Own*)

Julia Velva's tomb and inscription (*RIB* 688). Funeral feasts are depicted on the tombstones of Julia Velva, Mantinia Maercia and Aelia Aeliana to cater for their culinary needs in the afterlife; here Julia's family are shown reclining on a couch and being served food and wine. Julia Velva is depicted holding a wine jar with her daughter, the wife of Aurelius Mercurialis, who can be seen holding a scroll – possibly Julia's will. Julia lived a good life – fifty years – and was believed by the family to participate in the annual celebration. (*Image courtesy of and © York Museums Trust*)

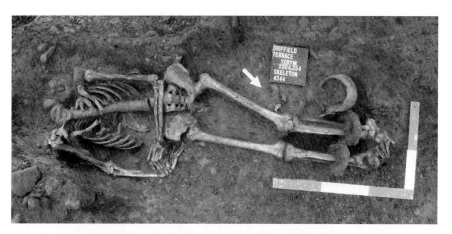

Decapitated skeletons from Trentholme Drive cemetery thought to be gladiators. This shows the decapitated skeleton with shackles round his ankles; detail of the iron rings; a typical decapitation with the head beside the torso.
(*All courtesy and © York Archaeological Trust*)

The Ophiotaurus mosaic. A fantastic sea creature from a mosaic found in Toft Green. According to its sole classical reference in Ovid's *Fasti* (3.793 ff), the Ophiotaurus (Οφιόταυρος Serpent Bull) was powerful enough to enable whoever slew it and then burnt its entrails to bring down the gods. The monster was killed by an ally of the Titans during the Titanomachy, but the entrails were retrieved by an eagle sent by Zeus before they could be burned. The creature had emerged from Chaos with Gaia and Ouranos. (*Courtesy and © York Museums Trust*)

The Severan Tondo, from c. AD 200, is one of the few preserved examples of panel painting from classical antiquity. It is a tempera or egg-based painting on a circular wooden panel (tondo), with a diameter of 30.5 cm. It is currently on display at the Antikensammlung Berlin (inventory number 31329).

The panel depicts Septimius Severus with his family: to the left his wife Julia Domna, in front of them their sons Geta and Caracalla. All are wearing sumptuous ceremonial garments; Septimius Severus and his sons are also holding sceptres and wearing gold wreaths decorated with precious stones. Geta's face has been erased after his murder by his brother Caracalla and the ensuing *damnatio memoriae*.
(*Image courtesy of and © York Museums Trust*)

of the emperor Maximian. By this time Constantius already had a son, Constantine, by Helena his first wife.

In 293 the Roman Empire had become a 'tetrarchy' – it was ruled by four emperors. Constantius Chlorus was elected by Maximian to be one of them – he became *Caesar* of the north west. This was something of a poison chalice because much of his territory had been grabbed by Carausius. Nevertheless, as noted above, Constantius won it all back ushering in nine years of relative peace which only came to an end in 305 when the Picts attacked the northern limits of the empire in Britain. York became an important strategic centre in the ensuing battle for the north of England.

Constantius was by now elevated to *Augustus*, the senior emperor of the west. He had his son Constantine join him in Gaul and together they made for York, winning a series of victories over the Picts but then, on 25 July 306, everything changed: Constantius became the second emperor to die in York.

Constantius' first wife Helena was elevated to the sainthood after being credited with finding the relics of the True Cross. St Helen's Church and St Helen's Square in York are named after her. Their son became the next Roman emperor: Constantine the Great.

Empress Helena

Helena, Helena Augusta, and Saint Helena (c. 246–c. 330), was born of a humble background; she became the consort of Constantius Chlorus and was the mother of the future emperor Constantine the Great. She is an important figure in the history of Christianity due to her influence on her son. In her final years, she made a religious tour of Syria, Palaestina and Jerusalem, during which ancient tradition claims that she discovered the True Cross about 326. The True Cross is a significant Christian relic, reputedly the wood of the cross on which Jesus Christ was crucified. Tradition holds that when Helena met Constantius they were wearing identical silver bracelets; Constantius saw her as his soulmate sent by God.

But it did not last. Constantius divorced Helena some time before 289, when he married Theodora, Maximian's daughter. Helena never remarried and lived for a time in obscurity, though she always remained close to her only son. After his elevation, Helena returned to public life and the imperial court in 312. She features in the *Eagle Cameo* portraying Constantine's family, probably commemorating the birth of Constantine's son Constantine II in the summer of 316. She received the title of *Augusta* in 325. According to Eusebius, Helena converted to Christianity when her son became emperor. Constantine awarded his mother the title of *Augusta Imperatrix*, and gave her unlimited access to the imperial treasury in order to locate the relics of the Christian tradition. Constantine ordered the building of the Church of the Holy Sepulchre in Jerusalem on the site where Helena discovered the True Cross.

What is reputed to be her skull is displayed in the cathedral at Trier. Bits of her relics are found at the Basilica of Santa Maria in Ara Coeli in Rome, the Église Saint-Leu-Saint-Gilles in Paris, and at the Abbaye Saint-Pierre d'Hautvillers. The Church of Sant'Elena in Venice claims to have the complete body of the saint enshrined under the main altar.

Both Geoffrey of Monmouth and Henry of Huntingdon promoted a popular, but erroneous, tradition that Helena was a British princess and the daughter of 'Old King Cole', King of Britain. This led to the dedication of 135 churches in England to her, many in Yorkshire. She is the hero in Evelyn Waugh's *Helena* (1950).

The Roman Emperor

By the end of the third century, the arrangement of emperors in the Roman Empire had become somewhat more complicated than the previous and original one empire one emperor. Octavius assumed the title of emperor in 27 BC, changed his name to Augustus, and closed the door on the republic taking sole command of the Roman world. This straightforward arrangement, in which there was one and only one emperor, lasted right up to the reign of Diocletian in AD 284. Augustus established the principate, which combined elements from the republican constitution with the traditional powers of a monarchy. The senate still functioned, though Augustus, as *princeps*, or first citizen, was in control of the government. Under Augustus, the emperor came to be looked upon as a god. Thereafter, all 'good' emperors were worshipped as gods after death. From Diocletian things got more complicated with emperors of the east and emperors of the west sharing the stage.

In the early days the Roman Emperor was best known simply by his name: Nero or Hadrian, for example. Later they assumed the title of *Augustus* or *Caesar*. Another title was *imperator*, originally a military honorific. Early emperors also used the title *Princeps Civitatis* ('first citizen').

For the life of the empire, emperors ruled in a relatively monarchic style; although the imperial succession was generally hereditary, it was only hereditary if there was a suitable candidate acceptable to the army and the state. Nevertheless, elements of the republican framework (senate, consuls, and magistrates) were preserved even after the end of the Western Empire.

The reign of Constantine the Great saw the replacement of the *Caput Mundi* from Rome to Constantinople. The Western Roman Empire crumbled in the late fifth century following wave after wave of invasions of imperial lands by Germanic barbarian tribes. Romulus Augustulus is often said to be the last emperor of the West after his forced abdication in 476, although Julius Nepos maintained a claim recognised by the Eastern Empire to the title until his death in 480. Following Nepos' demise, the Eastern Emperor Zeno abolished the division of the position and proclaimed himself as the sole emperor of a reunited Roman Empire. The Eastern imperial lineage continued to rule from Constantinople ('New Rome'); they continued to style themselves as Emperor of the Romans (later βασιλεύς Ῥωμαίων), but are often referred to as Byzantine emperors. Constantine XI Palaiologos was the last Roman emperor in Constantinople, dying in the Fall of Constantinople to the Ottoman Empire's Mehmed II in 1453. The Muslim rulers then claimed the title of *Caesar* of Rome.

Diocletian and the Tetrarchy

Gaius Aurelius Valerius Diocletianus Augustus; born Diocles (AD 244) was Roman Emperor from 284 to 305. Born to a lowly family in Dalmatia, Diocletian rose through the ranks to a cavalry commander of Emperor Carus' army. After the deaths of Carus and his son Numerian on campaign in Persia, Diocletian was proclaimed emperor. The title was also claimed by Carus' surviving son, Carinus, but Diocletian saw him off in the battle of the Margus.

Diocletian regarded his life work to be that of a restorer dedicated to returning the empire to peace, to recreate stability and justice where barbarian hordes and wayward pretenders had wrecked it. Diocletian literally rewrote history when he pedalled a version of the empire before the tetrarchy as a time of civil war, despotism, and as an empire collapsing in on itself. Inscriptions of the time describe Diocletian and his colleagues as 'restorers of the whole world', (*Inscriptiones Latinae Selectae* 617), and men who succeeded in 'defeating the nations of the barbarians, and confirming the tranquillity of their world' (*Inscriptiones Latinae Selectae* 641). Diocletian was nothing less than the 'founder of eternal peace' (*Inscriptiones Latinae Selectae* 618).

A new normal was cultivated, one which highlighted the distinction of the emperor from everyone else. The pseudo-republican ideals of Augustus' *primus inter pares* were abandoned for all but the tetrarchs themselves. Diocletian took to wearing a gold crown and jewels, and forbade the use of purple cloth to everyone except the emperors. His subjects were required to prostrate themselves in his presence (*adoratio*); only the most privileged were allowed to kiss the hem of his robe (*proskynesis*, προσκύνησις). Circuses and *basilicas* were designed to keep the face of the emperor perpetually in view, and always in a prominent seat. Around 286 or 287, a new feature of the imperial collegiality emerged: Diocletian and Maximian began to use the epithets 'Iovius' and 'Herculius', thus linking themselves with Jupiter and Hercules. Shades of Caligula and Nero come to mind.

What effect did Diocletian's 'reforms' have in York?

Obviously the move away from anything resembling republicanism to this autocracy would have been keenly felt around the empire: imperial government was no longer a synergistic affair between emperor, army, and senate. Diocletian's new autocratic structure replaced the *consilium principis* and was known as a *consistorium*, the emperor's cabinet, no more a council. To run it all Diocletian introduced a number of high-level official posts and a prodigious increase in the number of civil servants and bureaucrats. Lactantius observed that there were now more men spending tax revenue than there were paying it (*De Mortibus Persecutorum* 7, 3). Some historians estimate that the number of civil servants doubled from 15,000 to 30,000 or that there was 30,000 bureaucrats for an empire of 50–65 million inhabitants, which works out at approximately 1,667 or 2,167 inhabitants per imperial official. York, as everywhere else, would have been swamped by this influx of bureaucrats, physically and financially.

No one could deny that running an empire the size of Rome's must have been a stressful job. So, to lessen and share the burdens of state, and to introduce a less painful succession, Diocletian introduced a tetrarchy – four-man rule. Also, local rebellions, be they orchestrated by truculent natives or by ambitious generals or governors, were a constant threat to all provincial administrations. To that end, in 286, Diocletian appointed Maximian, an Illyrian, the son of a peasant from around Sirmium as co-emperor. Maximian would rule from the west, Diocletian the east; Maximian would look after military matters, Diocletian administration. The two emperors would take the title *Augustus*. To facilitate a more streamlined system of tax collection, and to benefit from more efficient logistics and to improve law enforcement, Diocletian doubled the number of provinces from fifty to almost 100 (see the *Laterculus Veronensis* or *Verona List,*). This was effected by the appointment of two *Caesares* (junior emperors – one reporting to Diocletian, one to Maximian); they were Galerius and Constantius Chlorus respectively.

In addition to these 'efficiencies', Diocletian's intention was that the tetrarchy – the gang of four, a quadvirate – would reduce the usurpations and incursions that a single emperor had to put up with. On the retirement or death of an *Augustus*, the *Caesar* who supported that *Augustus* would automatically step into his sandals to replace him. A new *Caesar* would then be chosen by the new *Augustus* with the approval of his colleague. The prospect of promotion, elevation and the binding of the relationship between the emperors with marital ties would dissuade the *Caesares* from rebellion, offering the *Augusti* a degree of security and freedom from the threat of assassination: the four emperors could, theoretically at least, between them deal with both foreign and domestic threats throughout the empire.

In 305, the senior emperors did abdicate and retire, allowing Constantius and Galerius to be elevated to *Augusti*. They in turn appointed two new *Caesars* – Flavius Valerius Severus Caesar – in the west under Constantius, and Maximinus in the east under Galerius – the second tetrarchy was thus born.

The four tetrarchs were not based at Rome but, significantly, in other cities, known as the tetrarchic capitals, strategically closer to the frontiers, intended as control headquarters for the defence of the empire against troublesome neighbours, notably Sassanian Persia. Other barbarians were mainly Germanic, swelled by an endless stream of nomadic or displaced tribes from the Eastern Steppes, at the Rhine and Danube frontiers. From this time, Rome ceased to be a functioning capital, although she continued to be nominal capital of the entire Roman Empire under its own, unique prefect of the city, *praefectus urbi*.

The four tetrarchic capitals were:

> *Nicomedia* in northwestern Asia Minor (modern Izmit in Turkey), to defend against invasion from the Balkans and Persia's Sassanids; it was Diocletian's capital.

> *Sirmium* (in modern Serbia, near Belgrade, on the Danube border) was the capital of Galerius, the eastern *Caesar*; this was to become the Balkans-Danube prefecture Illyricum.

> *Mediolanum* (modern Milan) was the capital of Maximian Daia, the western *Augustus*; his remit became Italia et Africa.

> *Augusta Treverorum* (modern Trier) was the capital of Constantius Chlorus, the western *Caesar*, near the strategic Rhine border; this became the prefecture Galliae.

> *Aquileia*, a port on the Adriatic coast, and *Eboracum* were also significant places for Maximian and Constantius respectively.

The provinces were now grouped into twelve dioceses, a new layer of administration, each governed by an appointed official called a *vicarius*, or 'deputy of the Praetorian prefects'. In Britannia, the senior *vicarius* was the Vicar of Britain headquartered in London (Augusta) and reporting to the prefect of the Gauls in Trier. By 314, Diocletian *vicarii* and governors were divested of their military responsibilities and put in charge of justice and taxation; a new class of *duces* (dukes), acting independently of the civil service, took over the military commands. These dukes sometimes administered two or three of the new provinces, and had forces ranging from 2,000 to more than 20,000 men. In addition to their roles as judges and tax collectors, the somewhat reduced governors were now expected to maintain the all-important postal service (*cursus publicus*) and ensure that town councils discharged their duties. More bureaucratic it certainly was, but it helped keep the Western Empire going for another century or so.

Civilian and military authority would no longer be exercised by one official, with rare exceptions until the mid-fifth century, when a *dux* (governor) was appointed for Upper Egypt. The responsibilities of the *vicarii* were to control and coordinate the activities of governors; monitor but not interfere with the daily functioning of the Treasury and Crown Estates, which had their own administrative infrastructure; and act as the regional quartermaster-general of the armed forces. In short, as the sole civilian official with superior authority, he had general oversight of the administration, as well as direct control, while not absolute, over governors who were part of the prefecture; the other two fiscal departments were not.

Constantius I (Chlorus)

Marcus Flavius Valerius Constantius (c. AD 250–306), ruled as *Caesar* from 293 to 305 and as *Augustus* from 305 to 306. He was the junior colleague of the *Augustus* Maximian under the tetrarchy and succeeded him as senior co-emperor of the western part of the empire. Constantius ruled the West while Galerius was *Augustus* in the East. He was the father of Constantine the Great and founder of the Constantinian dynasty.

As we have seen, in late 293, Constantius overcame Carausius in Gaul, capturing Bononia and this triggered the assassination of Carausius by his *rationalis* (finance officer) Allectus, who assumed command of the British provinces until his death in 296.

Constantius spent 294–295 extinguishing the threat posed by the Franks, allies of Allectus, as northern Gaul remained under the control of the British usurper until at least 295. As noted, when Maximian relieved him at the Rhine frontier he assembled two invasion fleets to cross the English Channel. The first was delegated to Asclepiodotus, Constantius' long-serving Praetorian prefect, who sailed from the mouth of the Seine, while the other, under Constantius himself, was launched from his base at Bononia. The fleet under Asclepiodotus landed near the Isle of Wight where his army encountered the forces of Allectus, resulting in the defeat and death of the usurper. Constantius in the meantime occupied London, saving the city from an attack by Frankish mercenaries who were now roaming at liberty around the province. Constantius massacred all of them. He remained in Britannia for a few months and replaced most of Allectus' officers while the British provinces were subdivided along the lines of Diocletian's tetrarchy.

In 303, Constantius had to decide how to deal with the imperial edicts instituted by Diocletian relating to the persecution of Christians. The campaign against them was zealously pursued by Galerius. It had not escaped his notice that Constantius was well-disposed towards the Christians and reluctant to persecute them: Galerius thus saw an opportunity to drive a wedge between Constantius and Diocletian, seeing it as a way of advancing his career prospects with the aging Diocletian. Of the four tetrarchs, Constantius made the least effort to implement the decrees in his western provinces, limiting himself to knocking down a few churches.

Between 303 and 305, Galerius was all the while positioning himself to ensure that he succeeded Constantius after the death of Diocletian. In 304, Maximian and Galerius met to discuss the succession issue; Constantius either was not invited or was detained on the Rhine. Before 303 there was a tacit agreement among the tetrarchs that Constantius' son Constantine and Maximian's son Maxentius would be promoted to *Caesar* once Diocletian and Maximian had resigned the purple. But by the end of 304, the wheedling Galerius had convinced Diocletian, who in turn convinced Maximian, to appoint Galerius' nominees Flavius Valerius Severus and Maximinus Daia as *Caesars*.

Diocletian and Maximian duly stepped down as co-emperors on 1 May 305, possibly due to Diocletian's ever declining health. In front of the assembled armies at Milan, Maximian removed his purple cloak and handed it to Valerius Severus, the new *Caesar*, and proclaimed Constantius as *Augustus*. The same scene was played out in Nicomedia under the authority of Diocletian. Constantius, notionally the senior emperor, ruled the western provinces, while Galerius took the eastern provinces. This left a very disappointed Constantine – his hopes to become a *Caesar* dashed – so he fled the court of Galerius after Constantius had asked Galerius to release his son on compassionate grounds as Constantius was ill. Constantine made his way through the territories of the hostile Severus to join his father at Gesoriacum (modern Boulogne). They crossed over to Britain together.

In 305, Constantius and Constantine travelled to the north of Britannia and launched a military expedition against the Picts, claiming a victory against them and the title Britannicus Maximus II by 7 January 306. After wintering in Eboracum, Constantius had planned to continue the campaign, but on 25 July 306 he died. As he was dying, Constantius recommended his son to the army as his successor; Constantine was declared emperor by the legions at York.

146

York and the Tetrarchy: Britannia Secunda and the Elevation of Constantine

Britannia Secunda was one of the provinces of the Diocese of the Britains created after the defeat of the usurper Allectus by Constantius Chlorus in 296 and featured in the 312 *Verona List* of the Roman provinces. After the Carausian Revolt, Britain was retaken by Constantius Chlorus and the newly formed Diocese of the Britains with its *vicarius* at Londinium was made a part of the prefecture of Gaul. The Britains were divided among four provinces, which were called Prima, Secunda, Maxima Caesariensis (Londinium and southeastern England), and Flavia Caesariensis (southern Pennines and including the lands of the Iceni with its capital at Lindum), Colonia (Lincoln), and Valentia. All of these seem to have initially been under the control of a governor (*praeses*) of equestrian rank.

The untimely death of Constantius at Eboracum was the first crack in the framework of the tetrarchy. As we have just noted, rather than obligingly accept the elevation of Flavius Valerius Severus from *Caesar* to *Augustus*, the garrison at Eboracum unilaterally backed Constantius' son, Constantine, for *Augustus*. They were supported in this mutiny of sorts by Crocus (fl. AD 260–306), a king of the Alamanni attached to the Roman army in Britain. Crocus' reputation preceded him: he had something of a predilection for destruction on a grand scale and may have sent out loaded messages which deterred people from crossing him. In 260, he led an uprising of the Alamanni against the Romans, crossing the Upper Germanic Limes and advancing as far as Clermont-Ferrand and Ravenna, and he may have been present at the Alamannic conquest of the French town of Mende.

Galerius, the senior emperor, was sent a portrait of Constantine wearing a crown of laurels; by accepting this inflammatory representation, Galerius would be acknowledging Constantine's right to be heir to his father's throne (Lactantius, *De Mortibus Persecutorum* 25). Constantine was constitutionally not eligible and blamed his unlawful elevation on his army, claiming they had 'forced it upon him'. Galerius was, predictably, apoplectic and intent on burning the portrait. His advisors, however, advised caution as a denial of Constantine's claims would mean certain civil war. Galerius was compelled to compromise: he grudgingly granted Constantine the title *Caesar* rather than *Augustus* which went to Severus

147

instead. Wishing to make it clear that he alone underwrote Constantine's legitimacy, Galerius personally sent Constantine the emperor's purple robes. Constantine accepted the decision, happy that it would eradicate further doubts about his legitimacy to the throne.

Despite all the carnage and chaos, however, these were not bad years for York. Salway (1981) records that:

> the reconstruction carried out in the time of Constantius and Constantine, however, ushered in an era of spectacular prosperity, at least in so far as that can be judged by the private and public architecture of the age. Among the signs of military reconstruction pride of place must surely go to York.

Much of Salway's enthusiasm is predicated on the erroneous belief that the walls and particularly the Multangular Tower were constructed at this time, when most of the stone tower was built between 209 and 211 by Septimius Severus. Nevertheless, other infrastructure and defence projects no doubt benefitted and beautified the city.

The *Verona List*

The *Laterculus Veronensis* or *Verona List* is a list of Roman provinces during the reigns of Diocletian and Constantine I. The list comes to us only in a seventh-century manuscript now in the Chapter House Library (Biblioteca Capitolare) in Verona. It is a list of the names of the 100 or so provinces of the empire as organised in the twelve newly created regional dioceses in two separate eastern and western groups, the eastern group (Oriens, Pontica, Asiana, Thraciae, Moesiae, Pannoniae) preceding the western (Britannia, Galliae, Viennensis, Italiae, Hispaniae, Africa).

The dates of the listings are currently thought to be 314–324 for the eastern half and 303–314 for the western half of the empire. As noted, Britannia's four provinces were Britannia Prima; Britannia Secunda; Maxima Caesariensis; and Flavia Caesariensis.

The *Notitia Dignitatum*: the British Section

The *Notitia Dignitatum* (List of Offices) details the administrative organisation of the Eastern and Western empires. As one of very few surviving documents of Roman government it is unique, and describes several thousand offices from the imperial court to provincial governments, diplomatic missions, and army units, military commanders, *comites rei militaris*, and *duces*, providing the full titles and stations of their regiments. It is probably accurate for the Western Roman Empire in the 420s and for the Eastern or Byzantine Empire in the 390s. However, the text itself is without date or author.

For Britannia, we get lists for three military commands: the *Dux Britanniarum*, the *Comes litoris Saxonici per Britannias*, and the *Comes Britanniarum*, the governors of the four British provinces and the staff of the *vicarius* in London. *Dux Britanniarum* was a *limitaneus* or frontier command which comprised the region along Hadrian's Wall and the coast from Cumbria, perhaps as far south as today's Welsh border. It presumably consisted of three parts: one containing the forts of the wall (*per lineam valli*) and the Cumbrian coast, the other the units in Yorkshire and the third, presumably the units and forts in Wales, but this is now lost.

The *Notitia* is the only historical source for the Saxon Shore, *Comes litoris Saxonici per Britannias*: nine forts– including Dubris (Dover), Lemannis (Lympne), Regulbium (Reculver), Rutupiae (Richborough) and Anderida (Pevensey) – built around south-east Britain in the later third and fourth centuries, possibly to defend against the Saxons, or be defended by the Saxons.

The Revolts of Maxentius and Maximian

Soon after Constantine became *Caesar*, Maxentius, son of Maximian, usurped power in Rome. When Severus set out to defeat the usurper, his troops defected and he was imprisoned by Maxentius. Maximian, brought out of retirement to support his son, tried to buy Constantine's support with his daughter's hand and the title of *Augustus*. Constantine accepted the title but continued to spend his time defending the borders rather than becoming embroiled in the usurpation. Not unsurprisingly, Galerius rejected the claims of Maximian, Maxentius and Constantine and convened a council at Carnuntum to resolve the crisis. There, with the support of his predecessor Diocletian, he appointed another *Augustus*, Licinius, demoted Constantine to *Caesar* of the West and stripped Maxentius and Maximian of their titles. However, by 310,

Maximian had returned once more and Galerius was willing to refer and defer to both Maxentius and Constantine as *Augusti*.

In 310, Maximian rebelled against Constantine while the emperor was campaigning against the Franks. Maximian had been sent south to Arles with part of Constantine's army to defend against attacks by Maxentius in southern Gaul. In Arles, Maximian resorted to fake news: outrageously he announced that Constantine was dead and took up the imperial purple. Despite offering bribes to any who would support him as emperor, Maximian would have been disappointed to find that most of Constantine's army remained loyal; Maximian was compelled to flee. When Constantine heard of the rebellion, he abandoned his campaign against the Franks, and moved quickly to southern Gaul, where he confronted the fleeing Maximian at Massilia (Marseille). The town was better able to withstand a longer siege than Arles, but it made little difference as loyal citizens opened the back gates to Constantine. Maximian was captured, reproved for his crimes, and stripped of his title for the third and last time. Constantine granted Maximian some clemency but strongly encouraged his suicide. In July 310, Maximian hanged himself.

Maxentius was now prepared to go to war to avenge his father. Both men looked to the east for support: here they found a situation no less fraught: following Galerius' death in 311, his *Caesar*, Maximinus, and Licinius were at each other's throats whilst dividing his provinces between themselves. Licinius and Constantine found common ground and supported one another with the promise of a marriage between Constantia (half-sister of Constantine) and Licinius. This happened in 313.

However, before that, Constantine made his move against Maxentius. In 312 he pushed forward through Italy, sweeping aside opposing forces in the north before heading for Rome. Faced with the prospect of a siege and the slow erosion of his rule, Maxentius made his stand near Saxa Rubra at the Milvian Bridge.

The tetrarchy was turning out to be something of a poison chalice. Between 309 and 313, most of the imperial college died or were killed in various civil wars. Constantine forced Maximian's suicide in 310. Galerius died naturally in 311. Maxentius was defeated by Constantine at the battle of the Milvian Bridge in 312 and subsequently slaughtered. Maximinus committed suicide at Tarsus in 313 after being defeated in battle by Licinius. So, by 313, there were only two emperors left:

Constantine in the west and Licinius in the east. The tetrarchic system had run its course, although it took until 324 for Constantine to finally defeat Licinius, reunite the two halves of the Roman Empire and declare himself sole *Augustus*.

Setting aside his momentous reversal of Diocletian's policy of persecution against the Christians, his world-changing contribution to the acceptance of the Christian faith and his own conversion, Constantine's other achievements are of enormous importance: in his reign (306–337), the second-longest of any Roman emperor, Constantine succeeded in becoming the sole ruler of Rome, he made Byzantium (Constantinople, then Istanbul) his capital, and shifted imperial power away from Rome itself ensuring its long endurance in the east.

The View from the Bridge: the Vision of Constantine

The decisive Battle of the Milvian Bridge took place between Constantine I and Maxentius in 312. It takes its name from the Milvian Bridge, an important strategic crossing over the Tiber north of Rome. Constantine was victorious: the battle enabled him to become the sole ruler of the Roman Empire. Maxentius drowned in the Tiber during the battle; his body was later fished out and decapitated, and his head was paraded through the streets of Rome the day after the battle and, for good measure, carried to Carthage as a warning to the Carthaginians to keep the corn supply coming to Rome.

Constantine's army came to the battle with strange symbols depicted on their standards and their shields. Lactantius states that, on the eve of the battle, Constantine was told in a dream to 'depict the heavenly sign on the shields of his soldiers.' So, 'he marked on their shields the letter X, with a perpendicular line drawn through it and turned round thus at the top, being the cipher of Christ.' This was the 'heavenly divine symbol' (*coeleste signum dei*). Eusebius of Caesarea (d. 339) says that Constantine was marching somewhere when he looked up to the sun and saw a cross of light above it, and with it the Greek words Ἐν Τούτῳ Νίκα. The Latin translation is *in hoc signo vinces* – literally 'In this sign, you will conquer' or 'By this, conquer!' (*Historia Ecclesiastica* lines 28-32).

At first Constantine was baffled, unsure of the meaning of the apparition, but the following night he had a dream in which Christ explained to him that he should use the sign (the *labarum*) against his enemies.

The *labarum* (λάβαρον) was a *vexillum* or military standard that displayed the 'Chi-Rho' symbol ☧, a christogram formed from the first two Greek letters of the word 'Christ' (ΧΡΙΣΤΟΣ, or Χριστός) – Chi (χ) and Rho (ρ). Since the *vexillum* consisted of a flag suspended from the crossbar of a cross, it was ideally suited to symbolise the crucifixion of Christ .

Throughout his later life, Constantine ascribed his success to this new religious allegiance, his conversion to Christianity and the support of the Christian god. The famous triumphal arch erected in his honour at Rome after the defeat of Maxentius ascribed the victory to the 'inspiration of the Divinity' as well as to Constantine's own genius (although it does not feature the powerful chi rho symbol). A contemporary statue showed Constantine himself holding aloft a cross and the legend, 'By this saving sign I have delivered your city from the tyrant and restored liberty to the Senate and people of Rome.'

As he entered Rome as sole ruler of the West, Constantine was once again hailed as *Augustus*, but one man still stood between him and control over the entire Roman Empire. Licinius defeated Maximinus the following year and peace was to reign within the empire for two years before the inevitable conflict broke out in 316. After a brief war, Constantine was content to allow his rival to remain as emperor as long as two of his sons were made *Caesares*. However, seven years later, a dispute over boundaries and the authority of each *Augustus* once again led to war. This time, Licinius was not to retain his power and in 324 Constantine established his rule over the entire empire.

After his victory over Licinius, Constantine wrote that he had come from the farthest shores of Britannia as God's chosen instrument for the suppression of impiety, and in a letter to the Persian king Shāpūr II he proclaimed that, aided by the divine power of God, he had come to bring peace and prosperity to all lands.

Constantine's victory gave him total control of the Western Roman Empire paving the way for Christianity to become the dominant religion for the Roman Empire and ultimately for Europe.

The Diocletian Persecution, AD 303, and the Edict of Milan, AD 313

The Edict of Milan of AD 313 or *Edictum Mediolanense*, one year after the Milvian Bridge battle, is attributed to Constantine and Licinius; it was the agreement to treat Christians benevolently within the Roman Empire. The two emperors agreed to change radically Roman policy towards Christians following the Edict of Toleration issued by Galerius, as *Caesar*, two years earlier in Serdica. The Edict of Milan gave Christianity a legal status, but did not make Christianity the state church of the Roman Empire; this only took place under Theodosius I in 380 with the Edict of Thessalonica. The document survives in Lactantius' *De Mortibus Persecutorum* and in Eusebius of Caesarea's *History of the Church* with significant differences between the two, prompting some to question whether or not there was a formal 'Edict of Milan'.

On 23 February 303, on the Terminalia feast, Diocletian issued a persecutory edict. It prescribed 'destroying of churches and burning of the Holy Scriptures; confiscation of church property; banning Christians from undertaking collective legal action; loss of privileges for Christians of high rank who refused to recant; the arrest of some Christian state officials.'

In 305 Diocletian abdicated; Galerius, his successor, carried on with the persecution in the East until 311 when the Edict of Serdica, the Edict of Toleration, was issued in Serdica (modern Sofia), officially ending the Diocletianic persecution of Christianity. It implicitly granted Christianity the status of *religio licita*, a worship recognised and accepted by the Roman Empire. It was the first edict legalising Christianity.

In any event it is an important document which guaranteed freedom of religion in the Roman world and particularly liberated Christians from the systematic oppression that Diocletian and some of his predecessors had presided over. The Edict of Milan required that the wrong done to the Christians be righted as speedily and thoroughly as possible; it claimed 'it has pleased us to remove all conditions whatsoever.' The edict further demanded that individual Romans right any wrongs towards Christians, claiming that 'the same shall be restored to the Christians without payment or any claim of recompense and without any kind of fraud or deception.' It was never just an act or expression of religious tolerance and understanding though. The edict states that righting the wrongs should be done so that 'public order may be secured'. It was not implemented for the intrinsic value of justice or the glory of God, reflecting the leaders' anxiety to avoid unfavourable consequences, which in this case included social unrest and further conquests; the sooner this balance was restored by the Romans, the sooner the state would become stable. Nevertheless, religious tolerance, of a sort, had arrived.

At the time only around ten per cent of the Roman Empire's population was Christian. The majority of the ruling elite worshipped the old Olympian gods of ancient Rome and, from time to time, followed a number of oriental and mystery religions imported from Egypt and other points east. Constantine was the first emperor to allow Christians and others to worship freely, helping to unite and promote the faith. He went on to instigate the celebration of the birth of Christ we call Christmas.

The Council of Arles, AD 315

Constantine called this meeting of thirty to forty Catholic bishops in order to settle a divisive spat that had been running for three years: namely the question of the Bishopric of Carthage, disputed between Cyprian and Donatus. According to Constantine's own letter, the bishops came from 'a great many different places' to the palace in Arles. Among the bishops from 'the Gauls' present at the council was *Eborius episcopus de civitate Eboracensi, provincia Britanniæ* – Eborius, bishop of the city of York in the province of Britannia. Eborius was a bishop and a deacon who had assumed a name homonymous with his see. This, of course, proves that Christianity had a following in the city in the fourth century.

The other two British bishops at Arles were *Restitutus, episcopus de civitate Londinensi* (London) and *Adelfius episcopus de civitate colonia Londinensium* – a mistake for Lindumensium so Lindum (Lincoln). A presbyter and a deacon, *Sacerdos presbyter* and *Arminius diaconus*, also attended the council with Adelfius.

The council settled the dispute by confirming the appointment of the Bishop of Carthage. The assembled bishops affirmed a number of other miscellaneous new church laws, or canons, including:

Actors were to be excluded if they continued to act; young women who married unbelievers should be excluded; deacons should be discouraged from conducting services in too many places; conscientious objectors would be excommunicated; Easter should be held on the same day throughout the world, rather than being set by each local church.

Donatism (a schism which argued that Christian clergy must be faultless for their ministry to be effective and their prayers and sacraments to be valid) was condemned as a heresy and Donatus Magnus was excommunicated. This had begun as an appeal by the Donatists to Constantine the Great against the decision of the Council of Rome in 313 at the Lateran under Pope Miltiades. The appeal had turned out unfavourably to the Donatists who afterwards became enemies of the Roman authorities.

In addition, those who participated in races and gladiatorial fights were to be excommunicated; the rebaptism of heretics to be forbidden; clergymen proven to have handed over copies of the scriptures to be destroyed by the authorities during persecution, (the *traditores*), should be deposed, but their official acts were to be held valid. Ordination required the assistance of at least three bishops.

The Council of Nicaea, AD 325

The First Council of Nicaea was held in Nicaea in Bithynia (Iznik in modern Turkey); it was the first ecumenical conference of bishops of the Christian Church, and most significantly resulted in the Nicene Creed – the first uniform Christian doctrine. By 325, Arianism, a school of Christology which contended that Christ did not possess the divine essence of the Father but was rather a primordial creation and an entity subordinate to God, had become sufficiently widespread and controversial in early Christianity that Constantine called the Council of Nicaea in an attempt to end the controversy by establishing an empire-wide, or ecumenical, orthodoxy. The council came up with the original text of the Nicene Creed, which rejected the Arian confession and upheld that Christ is 'true God' and 'of one essence with the Father'.

Additionally, the council promulgated twenty new church laws (canons), that is, unchanging rules of discipline. Here are some of them.

Prohibition of self-castration; establishment of a minimum term for catechumen (a young Christian preparing for confirmation); prohibition of the presence in the house of a cleric of a younger woman who might bring him under suspicion; prohibition of usury among the clergy; prohibition of kneeling during the liturgy, on Sundays and in the fifty days of Eastertide (the Pentecost).

Standing was the usual posture for prayer at this time, as it still is among the Eastern Orthodox. Eventually, Western Christianity adopted the term Pentecost to refer to the last Sunday of Eastertide, the fiftieth day.

For the first time, the emperor played a role, by convening the bishops under his authority, and using the power of the state to give the council's orders effect. This was the start of the Constantinian shift.

The Edict of Thessalonica (also known as *Cunctos populos),* jointly issued on 27 February 380 by emperors Theodosius I, Gratian, and Valentinian II, made Nicene Christianity the state religion of the Roman Empire. It condemned other Christian creeds such as Arianism as heresies of madmen, and authorised their persecution. It re-affirmed a single expression of the Apostolic faith as legitimate in the Roman Empire, 'catholic' (that is, universal) and 'orthodox' (that is, correct in teaching).

Constantine died in York in 337 – he was the first emperor to embrace the Christian faith, beginning the ending of the persecution of Christians in the Roman Empire in what was later known as the Triumph of the Church, the Peace of the Church or the Constantinian Shift.

Goodbye to All That

Constans, Magnentius and Magnus Maximus

The latter part of the fourth century is characterised by more turmoil. Britannia was briefly loyal to the usurper Magnentius (r. 350–353) commander of the Herculians and Jovians, the Imperial Guard units. Magnentius succeeded Constans (r. 337–350) at Augustodunum (Autun in the Saône-et-Loire department) after he had him murdered in response to the army's homophobic disaffection caused by the emperor's homosexuality and by the favouritism he showed towards his barbarian bodyguards. Eutropius (*Breviarium ab urbe condita*) euphemistically says Constans 'indulged in great vices'; Aurelius Victor (*Epitome de Caesaribus*) relates that Constans had a reputation for scandalous behaviour with 'handsome barbarian hostages'. Interestingly, Constans sponsored a decree with Constantius II that ruled that marriage based on 'unnatural' sex should be punished ruthlessly.

In 341–342, Constans fought a successful campaign against the Franks, and in early 343 he visited Britain, according to Julius Firmicus Maternus who does not give us a reason. However, the urgency of the crossing and the inherent danger in crossing the Channel in the winter months suggests it was in response to a military emergency, possibly to repel the Picts and Scots.

In the Battle of Mursa Major in 351, in Pannonia (modern Osijek, Croatia), Magnentius led his troops into battle, while Constantius spent the day of battle praying in a nearby church. Despite Magnentius' heroism, his troops were defeated and forced to retreat back to Gaul. Magnentius was again defeated and subsequently fell on his sword in the Battle of Mons Seleucus (now La Bâtie-Montsaléon in Hautes-Alpes, southeastern France) in 353 after which Constantius II dispatched his chief imperial notary, Paulus Catena, to hunt down Magnentius' supporters. Catena's serial cruelty was notorious throughout the Roman world and the mission was nothing short of a witch-hunt with trumped-up charges devoid of any evidence. This forced the *vicarius,* Flavius Martinus, to get involved. Paulus' nickname means 'the chain' – awarded because he habitually chained people up and dragged them by their chains through the streets. When Paulus retaliated by accusing Martinus of treason, the *vicarius* attacked Paulus with a sword, with the aim of assassinating him, but in the end Martinus committed suicide. According to Ammianus Marcellinus (*Res Gestae*), Paulus was condemned to death by Arbitio at the Chalcedon tribunal under Constantius' successor, Julian the Apostate, in late 361. He was burned alive.

Some contend that Magnentius' father was a Briton and his mother a Frank. His wife, Justina, later married Valentinian I.

As the fourth century went on, attacks from the Saxons in the east and the Scoti (Irish) in the west kept on coming in wave after wave. A series of forts was built, starting from 280, to defend the coasts, but these failed to cope when a massed assault of Saxons, Scoti and Attacotti, combined with dissension in the garrison on Hadrian's Wall, left Roman Britain on its knees in 367. This crisis, the Barbarian Conspiracy or the Great Conspiracy, was settled by Count Theodosius with a series of military and civil reforms.

To make matters much worse the empire was in the hands of a dynasty that included the emperor Theodosius I. This family kept political power firmly within the family, Mafia-like, and formed alliances by intermarriage with other dynasties. Simultaneously, they were all the while engaging in internecine power struggles and fending off outside contenders or usurpers attempting to replace their dynasty with one of their own. The effect of these machinations was to starve the empire of both military and civilian resources. Many thousands of soldiers were lost in battling attempted coups by usurpers such as Firmus, Magnus Maximus and Eugenius.

The German tribes were always a problem; relations were sometimes hostile, sometimes supportive, but in the end they were to prove terminal for Rome. By the early fifth century, as a result of severe losses and depleted tax income, the Western Roman Empire's military forces were dominated by Germanic troops, and Romanised Germans were playing an influential role in the empire's internal politics. Various Germanic and other tribes beyond the frontiers were able to take advantage of the empire's weakened state, both to expand into Roman territory and, in some cases, to move their entire populations into lands once considered exclusively Roman, culminating in various successful migrations from 406 onwards. The crossing of the Rhine terrified authorities in Britannia, fearing they might be cut off from the empire by raids on the primary communications route from Italy to the Channel ports.

Another imperial usurper, Magnus Maximus (r. in the Western Empire 383–388), emerged at Segontium (Caernarfon) in North Wales in 383; he fought a successful campaign against the Picts and Scots the following year. As commander of Britain, he usurped the throne of Emperor Gratian, and by negotiation with Emperor Theodosius I, he was made emperor in Britannia, Gaul and Spain while Gratian's brother Valentinian II retained Italy, Pannonia, Hispania, and Africa. Maximus made his capital at Augusta Treverorum (Treves, Trier) in Gaul. However, his campaigns on the mainland required troops from Britain, and forts at Chester and elsewhere were abandoned to reinforce Maximus. The inevitable opportunist raids by the Irish followed. In 387, Maximus' ambitions provoked an invasion of Italy, resulting in his defeat in 388 by Theodosius I in Pannonia at the Battle of the Save (in modern Croatia) and at the Battle of Poetovio (Ptuj in modern Slovenia). He was then executed by Theodosius. His death marked the end of direct imperial presence in northern Gaul and Britain, but it is unlikely that all of the British troops came back given that the military was stretched to the limit along the Rhine and Danube. Some historians believe Maximus may have founded the office of the *Comes Britanniarum*.

The *Comes Britanniarum*

The *Comes Britanniarum* (Count of the Britains) was a military post with command over the mobile field army from the mid-fourth century onwards. It is named in the List of Offices as being one of the three commands in Britain, along with the Duke of the Britains and the Count of the Saxon Shore. His troops were the main field army (*comitatenses*) in Britain and not the frontier guards (*limitanei*) commanded by his two colleagues.

The first count in Britain was Gratian the Elder, the father of emperor Valentinian I. A permanent office was created later in the fourth or early fifth century, perhaps by Stilicho who withdrew troops from Britain to defend Italy in 402. The title was transitory and certainly did not have the permanence of the *Dux Britanniarum* and the *Comes Litoris Saxonici*.

According to the *Notitia Dignitatum*, the count commanded six cavalry and three infantry units, probably a force of no more than 6,000 troops. This tiny detachment was charged with supporting the frontier troops in fending off the increasing number of barbarian raids in the period. Some units seem to have been transferred from the Duke of the Britains' or Count of the Saxon Shore's armies.

In the *De Excidio et Conquestu Britanniae* written c. 540 by Gildas, we learn that Maximus 'deprived' Britain not only of its Roman troops, but also of its 'armed bands ... governors and of the flower of her youth', never to return.

With Maximus' death, Britain came back under the rule of Emperor Theodosius I until 392, when the usurper Eugenius would successfully bid for imperial power in the Western Roman Empire, surviving until 394 when he was defeated and slain by Theodosius. When Theodosius died in 395, his 10-year-old son Honorius succeeded him as Western Roman Emperor. The real power behind the throne, however, was Stilicho, the son-in-law of Theodosius' brother and the father-in-law of Honorius.

Around 396, there were more barbarian incursions into Britain against which Stilicho led a punitive expedition. In 401, Stilicho had to deal with wars with Alaric and the Ostrogothic king Radagaisus. Needing military manpower, he withdrew troops from Hadrian's Wall for the final time. AD 402 is the last date of any Roman coinage found in significant numbers in Britain, suggesting either that Stilicho also stripped the remaining troops from Britain, or that the empire could no longer afford to pay the troops who were still there. Meanwhile, the Picts, Saxons and Scoti persisted with their raids, which presumably were increasing all the time.

Honorius and the Withdrawal from Eboracum

Child emperor Honorius had a lot on his mind when, in around 410, he recalled the VIth Legion from Britannia to protect Rome and bluntly told the Britons to look after their own defence from now on (Zosimus 10, 2). Honorius replied to a request for assistance in defending Britannia with the *Rescript of Honorius*.

The early life of Flavius Honorius (r. 393–423) has something of the Caligulan about it: he was Western Roman Emperor from age 10 (having been consul at age 2) and it was on his watch that the empire in the west fell to the barbarians and Rome was sacked.

The date 31 December AD 406 was significant for the Roman Empire, for Roman Britain and for Eburacum: this was when the Alans, Vandals and Suebi living to the east of Gaul crossed the Rhine and began a programme of widespread devastation. The Romans failed to respond so when the remaining Roman military in Britain heard of this they naturally feared that a Germanic crossing of the Channel into Britain was next. Accordingly, they shrugged off and dispensed with imperial authority – an action made easier since it is likely that the troops had not been paid for some time. The British plan was to elect a commander who would lead them out of their predicament: their first two choices, Marcus and Gratian, failed to impress and were butchered (Zosimus 612). Their third choice was Constantine III.

Flavius Claudius Constantinus, Constantine III, (d. 411) was co-emperor with Honorius from 409 until 411. He surged to power during a bloody power struggle in Britain and was acclaimed emperor by the local legions in 407. He promptly crossed over to Gaul where the legions declared for him, taking with him all of the troops from Britain, to confront the various Germanic invaders – the Vandals, the Burgundians, the Alans and the Sueves – who had crossed the Rhine the previous winter, near Mainz, and overran the Roman defensive works in a successful invasion of the Western Roman Empire.

Constantine won several engagements with the Vandals and quickly secured the Rhine. An increasingly nervous Honorius ordered Stilicho, his *magister militum*, to dispense with Constantine. Sarus the Goth, a commander of Honorius, defeated two of Constantine's generals, Iustinianus and the Frank Nebiogastes, who were in the vanguard of his forces. Nebiogastes was first trapped in, then killed outside, Valence (Zosimus 6,2,3). Constantine dispatched another army headed by Edobichus and Gerontius, and Sarus retreated into Italy, needing to buy his passage through the Alpine passes from the brigand Bagaudae, who controlled them. With these advances, Constantine commanded all of Gaul and garrisoned the Alpine passes into Italy. By May 408 he had made Arles his capital, where he appointed Apollinaris, the grandfather of Sidonius Apollinaris (the poet, diplomat and bishop), as prefect.

By the summer of 408 the Roman forces in Italy had regrouped to face Constantine. Constantine struck first at Hispania having summoned his eldest son, Constans, from the monastery where he was living, elevated him to *Caesar*, and sent him with the general Gerontius to Hispania where they easily defeated the cousins of Honorius (Zosimus 6, 2, 5). Constans returned to Arles to report to his father while the loyalist Roman army mutinied at Ticinum (Pavia) followed by the execution of Stilicho. Sarus and his men abandoned the western army. This left Honorius in Ravenna without any viable military power, and facing a Gothic army under Alaric that roamed unchecked in northern Italy. So, when Constantine's envoys arrived to parley, an anxious Honorius recognised Constantine as co-emperor: the two were joint consuls for the year 409.

Things could only go downhill for Constantine; some of his forces were tied up in Hispania, disqualifying them for action in Gaul, and some of those in Gaul were persuaded against him by loyalist Roman generals.

While he had been fighting Honorius' armies, some of the Vandal tribes had overrun Constantine's Rhine defences and spent two years and eight months burning and plundering their way through Gaul. The tribes reached the Pyrenees, where they broke through Constantine's garrisons and invaded Hispania. Constantine prepared to send Constans back to deal with this crisis when word came that his general, Gerontius, had rebelled, raising his relative, Maximus of Hispania, as co-emperor. Despite Constantine's best efforts, the feared attack from Hispania came the following year, when Gerontius advanced with the support of his barbarian allies.

Constantine took a final desperate gamble: he marched on Italy with what troops he had left; they wanted to replace Honorius with a more capable ruler. Constantine, though, had insufficient forces and retreated back into Gaul in the late spring of 410. His position became untenable; Gerontius defeated his forces at Vienne in 411 where his son Constans was captured and executed. Constantine's Praetorian prefect Decimus Rusticus, who had replaced Apollinaris a year earlier, abandoned Constantine to be caught up in the new rebellion of Jovinus in the Rhineland. Gerontius trapped Constantine inside Arles and besieged him.

Britain, now without any troops for protection and having suffered particularly severe Saxon raids in 408 and 409, viewed the deteriorating situation in Gaul with renewed alarm. Feeling helpless and hopeless under Constantine, both the Romano-Britons and some of the Gauls expelled Constantine's magistrates in 409 or 410. In the opinion of Zosimus, the Britons blamed Constantine for the expulsion, saying that his inertia had allowed the Saxons to raid, and that the Britons and Gauls were reduced to such straits that they had no choice but to secede from the Roman

Empire, and they 'rejected Roman law, reverted to their native customs, and armed themselves to ensure their own safety.'

Meanwhile Honorius enlisted a new general, the future Constantius III, who arrived at Arles and put Gerontius to flight. Gerontius committed suicide and many of his troops deserted to Constantius, who took over the siege. Constantine held out, hoping for the return of Edobichus, who was raising troops in northern Gaul amongst the Franks. But Edobichus was defeated in an ambush. Constantine, his hopes ever fading after his troops guarding the Rhine abandoned him to support Jovinus, surrendered to Constantius who had him beheaded on his way to Ravenna in September 411. His head was presented to Honorius on a pole and was later displayed outside Carthage.

A later appeal for help by the British was, according to Zosimus, rejected by Honorius in 410. In the resulting *Rescript of Honorius* of 411, Honorius told the British *civitates* to look to their own defence as his regime was still fighting usurpers in the south of Gaul and trying to deal with the Visigoths who were in southern Italy: 'Honorius, however, wrote letters to the cities in Britain urging them to be on their guard [or: to defend themselves]' (Zosimus 6, 10). At the time the *Rescript* was sent, Honorius was cut off in Ravenna by the Visigoths and was unable to do anything about their sacking of Rome. In addition, by 411, it was all up for Constantine III. His son was killed along with those key supporters who had not turned against him, and he himself was murdered.

So what else had been happening in the wider empire to provoke the *Rescript of Honorius* and necessitate the end of the Roman occupation of Britannia? The withdrawal of the Romans is one of the major episodes in the history of Britain; we should try to put it into some context. It is simply not enough just to record that it happened.

Britannia, though initially well garrisoned and held in some regard in the earlier days, was nevertheless a peripheral province, both geographically and to some extent politically. There were 50,000 or so troops here in AD 150; this fell to 33,500 by the fourth century and possibly as low as 15,000 by then. As a percentage of the total Roman Imperial Army this was a stark decline from twelve-and-a-half per cent to five-and-a-half per cent. The writing was clearly on the wall. Moreover, as time went on the calibre of the troops declined as well, with a preponderance of *limitanei*, second-rate soldiers as opposed to crack *comitatenses*.

Things had gone from very bad to much worse for Flavius Honorius Augustus when the Visigoths invaded Italy in 402 under the command of their formidable king, Alaric. Alaric I was the Christian King of the Visigoths from 395 until his death in 410. He burst onto the world stage as leader of a motley band of Goths who invaded Roman Thrace in 391, but was stopped in his tracks by the half-Vandal Roman general Flavius Stilicho. Alaric then signed up to the Roman army, serving under the Gothic general Gainas. In 394, he led a 20,000-strong Gothic army which helped Theodosius subdue the usurper Flavius Eugenius at the Battle of Frigidus. Alaric's was something of a Pyrrhic victory: he lost a quarter of his own troops.

To add insult to injury, Theodosius was distinctly unimpressed with Alaric's contribution to his war effort, so Alaric deserted the army and was elected *reiks* (tribal leader or king) of the Visigoths in 395. That same year Theodosius died of heart failure and the empire was divided between his two sons, Flavius Arcadius in the east and young Flavius Honorius in the west. Arcadius showed no interest in empire building, while Honorius was still a minor – Theodosius had appointed Stilicho *magister equitum* and guardian of Honorius. Honorius cemented the bond by marrying Stilicho's daughter, Maria. A disappointed and angry Alaric was passed over in his hoped-for permanent command of a Roman army.

Hoping to win such a command, Alaric marched on Constantinople with an army which snowballed in size as he progressed. But Constantinople was then considered too daunting a challenge. He crossed over to Greece, where he sacked the more vulnerable Piraeus and devastated Corinth, Megara, Argos, and Sparta. Athens capitulated and was spared devastation. To prevent further death and destruction Arcadius appointed Alaric *magister militum* in Illyricum. Alaric had finally got the command he craved.

Alaric invaded Italy in 401 and laid siege to Milan, but he was later defeated by Stilicho, first at Pollentia (modern Pollenza) and then, accused of violating the treaty signed after Pollentia, at the Battle of Verona the following year. Amongst Stilicho's prisoners were Alaric's wife and children, and ten years' worth of pillaged booty. Honorius moved the western capital from Rome to Ravenna via Milan, believing it to be more secure against attacks from the Goths.

Now there was trouble in Gaul with Constantine III, who had crossed the Channel from Britannia, and with the Vandals, Sueves and Alans who had crossed the Rhine and invaded.

In 408 Arcadius died after a short illness; Stilicho and Honorius squabbled over who should travel east to settle the succession of the Eastern Empire. But Honorius had had enough and reacted. Stilicho took refuge in a church in Ravenna but, faithful to Honorius to the end, was arrested and executed; his son was also slain. Honorius inflamed the Roman people to massacre tens of thousands of the wives and children of Goths serving in the Roman army . Unsurprisingly, this atrocity led to around 30,000 Gothic soldiers defecting to Alaric, joining him on his march on Rome over the Julian Alps to avenge their slaughtered families. *En route* Alaric sacked Aquileia and Cremona and laid waste to the lands along the Adriatic. In September 408, Alaric was menacingly encamped outside the walls of Rome whence he began his siege of the city and blockaded the Tiber. The hunt was on for scapegoats: one of the victims was Stilicho's widow, Serena; she was strangled in an act of post-mortem 'justice' and became one of ancient history's most tragic afterthoughts.

As in many a siege before, Alaric's greatest ally was starvation. It was not long before the senate capitulated, agreeing in exchange for food to send an envoy to Honorius in Ravenna to urge peace. Alaric agreed, but not before the senate's failed attempt to unsettle Alaric; their flaccid threats were met with derision and a loud guffaw when the Goth retorted: 'The thicker the hay, the easier it is cut down!' The Romans eventually agreed a huge ransom of 5,000 lbs of gold, 30,000 lbs of silver, 4,000 silken tunics, 3,000 hides dyed scarlet, 3,000 lbs of pepper and 40,000 Gothic slaves. According to Gibbon, 'the Senate presumed to ask, in modest and suppliant tone, "If such, O king! are your demands, what do you intend to leave us?" "Your lives," replied the haughty conqueror.' Prodigious as it may seem, the ransom was probably not beyond the deep pockets of some of Rome's more affluent senators. They made little contribution, however – the bill was paid by the official ransacking of pagan temples.

The senate sent envoys, including Pope Innocent I, to Ravenna to encourage the emperor to make a deal with the Goths. Alaric was much more conciliatory this time and went to Ariminum where he discussed terms with Honorius' diplomats. He demanded, quite reasonably, the provinces of Rhaetia and Noricum as a homeland for the Visigoths – a 200 mile long, 150 mile wide strip of territory between the Danube and the Gulf of Venice, grain, and, prize of them all, the rank of *magisterium utriusque militae* – commander-in-chief of the Imperial Army – just as Stilicho had been. Jovius, leader of the imperial delegation agreed, but predictably Honorius refused to see the wider picture and declined. He did not want another barbarian besmirching the imperial hierarchy, and then tried to infiltrate a unit of Illyrian soldiers into Rome. This was intercepted by Alaric and, infuriated by these insults, reacted by besieging Rome a second time and wasting the Roman granaries at Portus for good measure. Starvation loomed again: the high price of relief now was permission from the senate for Alaric to install a rival emperor, a usurper in effect, to Honorius. This was to be the prefect of the city, *praefectus urbi* – the Greek Priscus Attalus, something of a star in Rome; Alaric took Galla Placidia, Honorius' sister, prisoner. Usurpers were always sure to concentrate the mind of an emperor.

Alaric, as we have seen, insisted Attalus make him *magisterium utriusque militae* and his brother-in-law Ataulf, who had arrived with reinforcements, was given the rank of *comes domesticorum equitum*. They then marched on Ravenna to overthrow Honorius and place Attalus on the imperial throne.

Things took their course and, sensing duplicity on the part of Honorius, an outraged Alaric thundered south with his army and stormed through the Porta Salaria to threaten the very existence of Rome. Some say that Alaric bribed elderly senators inside with the promise of Goth slave boys if they opened the gates to him. In any event, Rome was taken. Jerome lamented: 'My voice sticks in my throat, and, as I dictate, sobs choke me. The City which had taken the whole world has itself been taken.' Alaric, a Christian, was busy desecrating a Christian city with his Christian Goths.

Such were the circumstances which forced Honorius to do everything he could to preserve the empire in the face of repeated attacks by Alaric and Attalus. The withdrawal of garrisons at the further reaches of the empire was one obvious way of strengthening his position and the defence of the Roman Empire. Britannia in general and Eboracum in particular were amongst those garrisons.

Alaric

Alaric I was the Christian King of the Visigoths from 395 until his death in 410.

On 24 August 410, as noted above, the Visigoths entered Rome through the Salarian Gate, according to some opened by treachery, according to others forced through hunger, and embarked on a three-day sacking spree.

Many of the city's great buildings were pillaged, including the mausoleums of Augustus and Hadrian; the ashes of the urns in both tombs were scattered to the winds. Anything that could be moved was pillaged throughout the city. The invaders stole a massive, 2,025 lb silver ciborium (a gift from Constantine) from the Lateran Palace. The Gardens of Sallust were burned and never relaid. The Basilica Aemilia and the Basilica Julia were also torched. Many Romans were taken captive, including Honorius' sister, Galla Placidia. Some were ransomed, others sold into slavery, and others raped and killed. Pelagius, a Roman monk from Britannia, survived the siege and wrote an account (Jones, 1838) of the shocking experience in a letter to a woman called Demetrias:

> This dismal calamity is but just over, and you yourself are a witness to how Rome that commanded the world was astonished at the alarm of the Gothic trumpet, when that barbarous and victorious nation stormed her walls, and made her way through the breach. Where were then the privileges of birth, and the distinctions of quality? Were not all ranks and degrees leveled at that time and promiscuously huddled together? Every house was then a scene of misery, and equally filled with grief and confusion. The slave and the man of quality were in the same circumstances, and every where the terror of death and slaughter was the same, unless we may say the fright made the greatest impression on those who had the greatest interest in living.

Other Romans were tortured into revealing the locations of their valuables. One was 85-year-old Saint Marcella, who had no hidden wealth – she lived in poverty. She was a close friend of St Jerome, and he detailed the incident in a letter to a woman, Principia, who had been with Marcella during the pillaging:

> When the soldiers entered [Marcella's house] she is said to have received them without any look of alarm; and when they asked her for gold she pointed to her coarse dress to show them that she had no buried treasure. However they

would not believe in her self-chosen poverty, but whipped her and beat her with cudgels. She is said to have felt no pain but to have thrown herself at their feet and to have pleaded with tears for you [Principia], that you might not be taken from her, or owing to your youth have to endure what she as an old woman had no occasion to fear. Christ softened their hard hearts and even among bloodstained swords natural affection asserted its rights. The barbarians conveyed both you and her to the basilica of the apostle Paul, that you might find there either a place of safety or, if not that, at least a tomb.

> (St Jerome, 'Letter CXXVII. To Principia' *Nicene and Post-Nicene Fathers: Series II*/Volume VI, The Letters of St Jerome/Letter 127, 13)

Marcella died of her injuries a few days later. The sacking had a profound social effect on other parts of the empire, as reported in Wace:

Refugees from Rome poured into the province of Africa, as well as Egypt and the East. Some refugees were robbed as they sought asylum; St Jerome wrote that Heraclian, the Count of Africa, sold some of the young refugees into Eastern brothels.

Who would believe that Rome, built up by the conquest of the whole world, had collapsed, that the mother of nations had become also their tomb; that the shores of the whole East, of Egypt, of Africa, which once belonged to the imperial city, were filled with the hosts of her men-servants and maid-servants, that we should every day be receiving in this holy Bethlehem men and women who once were noble and abounding in every kind of wealth but are now reduced to poverty? We cannot relieve these sufferers: all we can do is to sympathise with them, and unite our tears with theirs ... . There is not a single hour, nor a single moment, in which we are not relieving crowds of brethren, and the quiet of the monastery has been changed into the bustle of a guest house. And so much is this the case that we must either close our doors, or abandon the study of the Scriptures on which we depend for keeping the doors open ... . Who could boast when the flight of the people of the West, and the holy places, crowded as they are with penniless fugitives, naked and wounded, plainly reveal the ravages of the Barbarians? We cannot see what has occurred, without tears and moans. Who would have believed that mighty Rome, with its careless security of wealth, would be reduced to such extremities as to need shelter, food, and clothing? And yet, some are so hard-hearted and cruel that, instead of showing compassion, they break up the rags and bundles of the captives, and expect to find gold about those who are nothing than prisoners.

To summarise, the situation in Britain was just as chaotic and intractable as it was in Ravenna and Rome. The British provinces were isolated, lacking support from the empire, and the soldiers supported the revolts of Marcus (406–407), Gratian (407), and Constantine III. Constantine invaded Gaul in 407, occupying Arles, and while Constantine was in Gaul, his son Constans ruled over Britain. By 410 Britain, as we know, was effectively told to look after its own affairs and expect no aid from Rome. Legio XX *Valeria Victrix* was recalled from Britannia. The absence of coinage from 402 in Britannia may suggest that the army was already going without pay and was in the process of being withdrawn.

Roman Britain, and Eboracum with it, went into a slow but inexorable decline. The city and many of its buildings lived on but in varying degrees of dilapidation. The construction of York churches for one thing benefitted from having a viable quarry right in its very midst. Sacrilegious as it sounds today, the obvious thing for a builder to do then was to recycle all that Roman stone that was lying around in ruinous old buildings – a useful and pragmatic legacy of York's existence as a thriving Roman *colonia*.

The chapters above tell the stories behind the story of Roman Britain. They provide the background and context of why what happened with the Romans in York actually happened, explicating the linear progression of events from early commercial interest, Julius Caesar, the Claudian invasion and occupation through to *colonia*, and eventual departure of the Roman occupying army in AD 410.

PART 2

Roman York –
What Remains?

This second part of the book covers in detail more of what remains of the Roman settlement here and the various artefacts which have been excavated down the years. As such it provides evidence and bears witness to the history of Roman York covered in Part 1.

The Archaeological Investigation of Eboracum 1587–1970

The renaissance of Eboracum from 1,200 years of decay, dilapidation and neglect began in the seventeenth century when it was rescued from an extensive period of oblivion. The first post-Roman recorded reference to Roman York was by the Tudor geographer and historian William Camden (1551–1623). His *Britannia*, published in 1587, gives us a unique survey of the country's historical sites and monuments. With reference to York, Camden recorded such items as a stone coffin (since lost) of Verecundius Diogenes, a *sevir augustalis* (priest of the cult of the deified emperor) found in 1579. Other early treasures included an altar dedicated to Jupiter found in 1638 in Bishophill Senior on the south-west bank of the Ouse, and the tombstone of the *signifer*, standard bearer Lucius Duccius Rufinus, unearthed in 1688 at Holy Trinity Church in Micklegate.

In the eighteenth century, John Horsley's 1732 *Britannia Romana*, or *The Roman Antiquities of Britain,* included a chapter on Roman York. Martin Lister (c. 1638–1712), the prominent zoologist and polymath, contributed papers on such discoveries as the Bishophill altar to the *Philosophical Transactions of the Royal Society*. Lister was also the first to recognise the Multangular Tower as a Roman structure; his work was a major source for the groundbreaking 800-page *Eboracum*, the first definitive history of the city written and published in 1736 by Francis Drake (1696–1771), a local surgeon. Not one to shy away from 'fanciful speculation and misplaced civic pride', Drake got it wrong when he claimed that the emperor Constantine the Great was actually born in York and that Helena (as in St Helen's Church), his mother, was also British. In 1731, the corporation gave Drake £50 to produce plans and maps of the antiquities. For the completist, the full title of the book is the less than pithy *Eboracum: or, the History and Antiquities of the City of York from its Original to the Present Time Together with the History of the Cathedral Church and the Lives of the Archbishops.*

In 1818, William Hargrove, local newspaper proprietor, published his *History of York* which reviewed previous discoveries and such exciting new material as the Mithraic relief found in 1747 near St Martin-cum-Gregory Church as well as the inscription from a temple of Serapis dug up on Toft Green in 1770. Hargrove waxed lyrical:

> In the earliest records of English History, Ebor, Eboracum or York, is represented as a place of great importance; and, in the zenith of meridian splendour, it was the residence of Imperial Power, and the legislative seat of the Roman Empire. Hence we may readily suppose, especially when the ancient historic accounts of this city are contrasted with those of London, that York far exceeded in dignity and consequence, if not in population and extent, the present capital of the British Empire, at that period.

The Rev Charles Wellbeloved (1769–1858), one of the founders of the Yorkshire Philosophical Society and a curator of the antiquities in the Yorkshire Museum until his death in 1858, expatiated systematically on Roman York in his *Eboracum* or *York Under the Romans* in 1842, including first-hand reports of discoveries during excavations in 1835. He included the exposure of the fortress defences wrecked during the creation of St Leonard's Place and Exhibition Square in 1835. Wellbeloved also got the limits of the legionary fortress spot on, although they were not finally proven correct by excavation until the 1950s. What is more, his *Eboracum* comes with the bonus of detailed descriptions of discoveries in the outlying areas on the south-west bank of the Ouse, in particular the remains of a huge baths complex, parts of which were unearthed during the building of the first railway station (the 'Old Station') in 1839–40. He produced a museum guide – *Descriptive accounts of the antiquities in the grounds and in the museum of the Yorkshire Philosophical Society*; published in 1852, it featured thousands of objects held in the Yorkshire Museum collections.

The station project involved breaching the medieval and Roman defences and was described by Patrick Ottaway as 'perhaps the most devastating single episode of destruction ever suffered by York's archaeology'.

More destruction followed during the later nineteenth and early twentieth centuries when York hastily embraced its new role as a national

173

railway hub, developed at any and at all costs. One of the discoveries during the work was a fragment of a commemorative inscription of the reign of Trajan, found in King's Square in 1854 during work on York's first main sewers. In the 1870s, cleric-antiquary, the Rev James Raine, Chancellor of York Minster and curator of antiquities at the Yorkshire Museum 1873–96, watched the large-scale bulldozing operations undertaken for the present railway station which ploughed up one of the main cemeteries of the Roman *colonia*. In some compensation, excavation work at the suburb on The Mount led to the discovery of more of the funerary furniture which had originally lined the main Roman road to York from the south west.

In the 1920s things started to get scientific and more systematic: the first planned and organised archaeological excavations in Roman York were carried out by Stuart Miller, from Glasgow University, on behalf of the York Excavation Committee – a newly formed body. Between 1925 and 1928, Miller concentrated mainly on the fortress defences and it was at the east corner that he exposed, preserved beneath the medieval rampart, the stretch of fortress wall standing some 5 m (16 ft) high, which is still visible today. Other significant digs revealed part of the fortress baths in St Sampson's Square in 1930–1, and more of the baths previously discovered when the first railway station was built.

During the 1950s and 1960s one of the most prolific excavators was Peter Wenham, head of history at St John's College. His invaluable endeavours are recorded in the chapter on recent excavations. Elizabeth Hartley FSA (1947–2018) was the first Keeper of Archaeology at the Yorkshire Museum from 1971 until her retirement in 2007, in which time she organised a number of major exhibitions and made some crucial acquisitions. The 2006 exhibition 'Constantine the Great: York's Roman Emperor' was described as 'the most important archaeological-historical loan exhibition to have been held in a provincial British museum.' Hartley was 'the driving force' behind the exhibition, which drew in over 58,000 visitors.

Religion in Roman York

Religion, like war, was everywhere in the Roman world; as such its ubiquity is evident from numerous tombstones, altars and inscriptions all of which tell us an enormous amount, not just about Roman religion but many other aspects of Roman life in York. By and large the Romans were accepting and tolerant of the religions they encountered in their territorial expansions radiating out to all points of the compass from the Italian peninsula. For the first 1,000 years of their imperial existence, the Romans carted the Olympian gods and goddesses around with them as part of the baggage train, but they practiced a syncretism which allowed local religions and deities to mix and merge with their own complex, incestuous pantheon. Obvious threats such as the druids of Anglesey were an exception and exterminated accordingly, but these were a special case as the following will demonstrate.

As a symbol of just how important the Olympians were to the Romans in the earlier years of the occupation we need go no further than the vestibule of York's Yorkshire Museum. The striking life-size statue of Mars, god of war, confronts and challenges you as you enter the museum. As already described, he is wearing full armour and carries a shield. He has a sword on his hip and in his other hand he was probably carrying a metal spear. The statue would have been painted in bright colours. Mars was dug up in 1880 along with three altars in the grounds of the Bar Convent next to Micklegate Bar. Did these pieces come from a nearby temple to Mars, hastily buried to safeguard them from barbarians, or Christians?

We have in York the dedication of a temple to Serapis – a Hellenistic-Egyptian god – by the Commander of the VIth Legion, Claudius Hieronymianus. This was uncovered in Toft Green in 1770. Other deities populating the city over time include Mithras, Tethys, Veteris, Venus, Silvanus, Toutatis, Chnoubis and the Imperial Numen. Veteris and Sucel(l)us (*RIB* II, 3/2422.21) were imported from the German and

Gallic provinces. Sucelus is carrying a large mallet (also described as a hammer) and an olla or (beer?) barrel. He is associated with prosperity, agriculture and wine, particularly in the lands of the Aedui.

In terms of religion, Eboracum then was decidedly cosmopolitan. The Romans brought with them their polytheistic religion and their complicated, inbreeding pantheon, as well as other faiths adopted, adapted and syncretised over many years of foreign conquest and civilising. The Roman soldiers, the camp followers and the city that grew up around the military fortress signified, with their various deities and the altars and temples which honoured and housed them, the first recorded religious presence in what was to become York.

Mithraism

Mithraism was a mystery religion centred on the god Mithras as practised in the Roman Empire from the first to the fourth century AD. The religion was inspired by Persian Zoroastrianism worship of the god Mithras. Mithras was eternally at war with the forces of evil. According to legend he captured a bull – symbolic of primeval force and vitality – and slew it in a cave, to release its concentrated power for the good of mankind. Mithraism offered an escape from darkness into light but required in return a lifelong commitment; it offered fraternity and was a clubbish benefit society with inspirational ideals embracing duty, *pietas*, endurance and self-discipline – hence its popularity with the military; soldiers were, of course, predisposed to aspire to similar qualities.

Mithraic temples, caves, were typically small, gloomy, semi-subterranean structures, intended to evoke the legendary cave where Mithras killed the bull. Inside, clandestine ceremonies would be followed by ritual feasts, the devotees reclining on benches (*podia*) running along the side walls.

York is the only place in Europe where you can see original carvings of Mithras and Arimanius – good and evil – both together. The followers of Mithras had access to about 400 secret temples, *mithraea*, across the empire where worship and ceremonial feasts took place. Other evidence of Mithraic temples in Britain are in London and at Hadrian's Wall.

The York stone was found in 1747 near St Martin-cum-Gregory Church in Micklegate; the altar stone dedicated to Mithras shows Mithras wearing his distinctive cap and slaughtering a bull, to represent his power over nature. He is surrounded by a number of other figures, including torchbearers representing day and night and other gods – the sun and the moon.

The bull is being worried by a dog and annoyed by a serpent, beasts traditionally associated with Arimanius. Arimanius is the bringer of death: Arimanius occupied the space between earth and Mithras' kingdom, restricting the access of mortals to heaven; he is usually depicted with the head of a lion. The stone statue is of a winged deity (*RIB* 641): dressed in a fringed skirt holding two keys in his left hand, while a serpent girdles his waist and rests its head above his right knee. Found under the city wall during the building the railway station in 1874, it is now in the Yorkshire Museum. The dedication reads:

> Volusius Irenaeus, paying his vow willingly and deservedly to Arimanes, gave (this) gift.

Eboracum (1962) tells us that the dedication is:

> to Arimanius, the Mithraic god of Evil. The missing head was most probably that of a lion, symbolic of all-devouring Death. The snake girdle represents the tortuous course of the sun though the sky; the wings signify the winds; while the keys are those of the heavens and the sceptre is the sign of dominion.

Roman Britain offers a wide variety of shrines and temples dedicated to a range of deities and cults. Examples from York include an inscription to a temple of Serapis-Osiris and an altar to Mother Goddesses of the household by Gaius Julius Crescens found in Nunnery Lane. This altar is dedicated to the Mother Goddesses of the household (*RIB* 652). The dedication reads:

> Gaius Julius Crescens to the Mother Goddesses (*matribus*) of the household served and willingly fulfilled his vow.

Another Crescens was remembered (*RIB* 671) on a tombstone excavated during extension work at the Mount School in 1911; it is still there. The inscription runs:

> To the spirits of the departed: Lucius Bebius Crescens, of Augusta Vindelicum, soldier of the Sixth Legion Pia Fidelis, aged 43, of 23 years' service; his heir had this set up to his friend (?).

The Mother Goddess occurs in a number of other finds: for Rustius, his limestone altar was found in 1850 under Nos. 15 and 16 Park Place, Huntingdon Road (*CIL* 1342) with the inscription:

> To his own mother goddesses Marcus Rustius, a veteran, paid his vow willingly, joyfully and deservedly.

For Marcus Minucius Mudenus, his altar was found in 1752:

> To the mother goddesses of Africa, Italy and Gaul, Marcus Minucius Mudenus, soldier of the Sixth Legion Victorious, river pilot of the Sixth Legion, paid his vow joyfully, willingly and deservedly.

Serapis

Serapis gained popularity in Rome from the first century BC and was first encountered at Memphis, Egypt, where his cult was celebrated in association with that of the sacred Egyptian bull Apis (who was called Osorapis when deceased). He was thus originally a god of the underworld, but was reintroduced as a new deity with many Hellenic aspects by Ptolemy I Soter (r. 305 BC–284 BC), who centred the worship of the deity at Alexandria. The cult of Serapis was a particular favourite of Severus; as noted, the temple was erected and financed by the legionary commander of the VIth, Claudius Hieronymianus, around AD 200; its dedication stone was uncovered in Toft Green. Hieronymianus may well have served in Egypt which is probably where he will have come into contact with Serapis; he went on to become governor of Cappadocia and is mentioned in Tertullian's *Address to Scapula Tertullus*: angry at his wife's conversion to Christianity, Hieronymianus blamed the Christians and brought 'much ill to the Christians' there. Hieronymianus is also identified with the senator mentioned in Ulpian *Digest* 33, 7, 12, 40. His own pagan leanings are, of course, expressed in the dedication stone in which he is named as the benefactor of the rebuilt Roman temple dedicated to Serapis.

The Serapis dedication slab (*RIB* 658) was found in 1770 and is also in the Yorkshire Museum: YORYM 1998.27. It reads:

> To the holy god Serapis Claudius Hieronymianus, legate of the VIth Legion Victrix, built this temple from the ground up.

The Cult of Cybele and Attis

We find Atys on a tomb monument dug up on the Mount. Cybele was an early, and officially sanctioned, import from Asia Minor. As *Magna Mater*, she was a deity with interest to women and fertility; she was a universal earth mother who looked out for all things maternal and represented rebirth and immortality through the resurrection of Attis. Cybele was brought to Rome in 204 BC after consultation of the *Sibylline Books* revealed that victory over the Carthaginians could be ensured by her presence. However, once the cult was established, the Roman authorities must have wished that they had taken more care over what they had hoped for. The orgiastic, frenzied rites, the eunuchs, the dancing, the self-castration and other acts of self-harm by adherents – the Galli – were all quite alien and objectionable to many Romans: measures were taken to control the cult and to marginalise it as far as possible.

Christianity

Eboracum is, of course, famous as the place where strides were taken to decriminalise the worship of Christ and where Constantine I renounced the pagan Olympian gods and converted to Christianity. There must have been a Christian community in the city because Eborius the bishop represented York at the Council of Arles in 314. Two archaeological finds confirm the existence of the religion here, if confirmation were needed. There is a Christian motto on a bone plaque: 'Farewell sister, may you live long in god'; this adorned a lady's jewellery box and was found in a stone coffin with jewellery grave goods in Sycamore Terrace. The grave goods tell us that pagan practices lived on at this time. Then there is the 'chi-ro' stamped tile found in the Minster excavations.

Funerary Inscriptions, Burial and Cemeteries

The Roman presence in York lasted for over 300 years; thousands of Romans were born here during that time, and thousands died here, and were buried or cremated. What do we know about how and where the inhabitants of Eboracum dealt with and disposed of their dead?

Roman law prohibited burials inside inhabited areas, mostly on the grounds of religion and hygiene, but space was also a factor – Roman towns were intensely crowded and there was simply no room for the luxury of an intramural cemetery. Only the imperial family (in the empire) and the Vestal Virgins were exempt. Cremations on funeral pyres would also have posed a serious urban fire hazard.

The sheer importance of this ruling is underlined by the fact that it was one of the twelve laws enshrined in the august and ancient 'The Law of the Twelve Tables' (*Leges Duodecim Tabularum* or *Duodecim Tabulae*) of about 450 BC – legislation that formed the very foundation of Roman law. Table Ten tells us that a 'dead person shall not be buried or burnt in the City'.

It was, therefore, usual practice for interments to take place alongside the principal roads into and out of a fortress, outside the walls. Over the centuries, as today's York was expanding beyond the medieval city walls, we have uncovered much evidence of Roman burials – occasionally as single burials but usually in extensive cemeteries of single and multiple occupation graves. The discoveries have shown us that burial practices varied greatly over time and according to the social or military status of the deceased. Fashions too changed: in some periods we have mostly cremations, at other times burials dominate: until the late second century, cremation was the preferred exit from this life. Then inhumation became the method of dispatch of choice and co-existed with cremation for some seventy years with cremation discontinued from about 270. As we have noted, the emperor Septimius

180

Severus himself was cremated in York in 211 before his remains were returned to Rome.

Inhumation itself was subject to trends in ritual with crouched burials found in the station area, the Mount and Trentholme Drive. Upright burials have been found too, as are inhumations in which, for the well-to-do, favourite objects from a life well lived were buried as grave goods: for example, horses, dogs and goblets (Royal Commission on Historical Monuments *York* p. 85), all indicative of a life devoted to hunting. Those of lower birth benefitted too from this thoughtful charity with less ostentatious goods. Disorganised as it was, Trentholme Drive gives us an excellent picture of lower-order pagan religious belief and ritual. We have found lachrymatories – unguent-filled flask-shaped glass bottles for catching mourners' tears – and gifts including coins, gaming counters, food and pottery. Cinerary urns were routinely holed to render them redundant and useless to grave robbers.

Trentholme Drive has yielded forty cinerary urns and part of the *ustrina* – the place where the dead were incinerated. Unsurprisingly, the charred debris found here contained human and animal bones, nails (from boots, coffins and biers), pottery sherds, rings, pins and brooches. Local wood and coal from Middleton Main and Middleton Little seams near Leeds have also been discovered.

In York, calcined bones have been unearthed in urns and amphorae; a glass jar with a lead bung in the neck found in 1861 contained the ashes of Corellia Optata, a 13-year-old girl whose movingly inscribed tombstone was set up by her grieving father, Quintus Corellius Fortis. Then there are three lead canisters – one of which bore the sad inscription:

> to Ulpia Felicissima, who lived for 8 years 11 months and
> ? days, Marcus Ulpius Felix and ? Andronica, her parents
> had this made

A number of stone coffins or cists have also been found, mainly on the railway station site with another two in the Multangular Tower. Famously there is also a tiled tomb made from eight *tegulae* or flat tiles each with the stamp of Legio IX *Hispana*.

Cemeteries at Burton Stone Lane and Clifton Fields are half a mile from the fortress with others at Heworth; Dringhouses; the Mount (including Trentholme Drive); Holgate; at the railway station, Nunnery

Lane; Bar Convent; Baile Hill; Clementhorpe; Clifford's Tower; Hawthorne Drive; Heworth Green; Bootham near St Peter's School; near what was Queen Anne's Grammar School in Clifton where St Olave's School is now; and Fishergate. There was a small inhumation cemetery near the junction of Haxby and Wigginton Roads comprising twelve burials; it yielded pottery on its discovery in 1833 – all of these, of course, were outside the fortress walls.

Wooden coffins (subject, of course, as they were to decomposition) were the norm, but York is unusual in the large number of stone (ninety) and lead (twenty-five) coffins found. Women (or at least the wealthier women) were often buried adorned with their jewellery and the finest jet items from around Whitby – bracelets, anklets, rings, hair pins, medallions with figures in relief – have been found in York burials. Burials vary from cremated remains either in ceramic pots or holes in the ground to the more common inhumations, and, again for the wealthy or high-ranking military and civic leaders, inscribed sarcophagi sometimes, but rarely, placed in elaborate purpose-built mausoleums. A vaulted tomb discovered in 1807 still survives in the cellar at 104 The Mount. Made from brick and stone it is 3m x 2m, 2.5m high and contains the bones of a woman aged about 40; her finger bones revealed that she had never been troubled by manual work of any kind. Two lachrymatories – glass phials – were found on either side of her skull.

York, then, is blessed with one of the largest collections of stone coffins in Britain. Weighing between 1.5 and 2 tonnes they are made from millstone grit quarried in the Pennines. Fine examples of sarcophagi are in the Yorkshire Museum together with tombstone grave markers erected in remembrance of Eboracum's more prominent citizens.

Twenty-five lead coffins have been excavated here, some lined with wood, some enclosed in wood and one as the lining to a stone coffin – this was discovered in 1875 under the railway station booking office and contained the skeleton of a teenage girl whose auburn hair tied in a bun with two jet pins is now resplendent in the Yorkshire Museum. A stone cist was found in 1952 in Trentholme Drive with the remains of a 40-year-old man in a wooden coffin: an urn had been deliberately placed under the coffin directly beneath the heart of the deceased.

Between 1951 and 1958, a 240 sqm area around Trentholme Drive was excavated yielding the skeletons of over 300 men, women and children.

Two iron arrow heads and an iron shield boss were found but apart from these military objects the cemetery was civilian. Grave goods indicated the dead had been relatively poor. The burials were haphazard with no placement planning in evidence; indeed the cemetery had been used a number of times with subsequent burials overlying earlier occupants and with bones all over the place.

A. F. Norman's vivid description of this morbid recycling in *Religion in Roman York* is worth quoting:

> [Trentholme Drive shows] a continued re-use of the site, with drastic disturbance of existing burials. Nothing is more indicative of the determined, almost ruthless, piety of the family to secure a decent funeral for their own dead, than the mangled remains which have survived from the earlier burials following the intrusion of later funerals. Skeletons are dug through and skulls detached, and the bits and pieces of disarticulated bones hurriedly jumbled together in the filling of these later graves.

Most of the graves were accompanied by a pot, or pots containing food and drink to facilitate the deceased's journey through the underworld into the afterlife. A total of 150 complete or near-complete pots were found in all positions in relation to the bodies. Organised laying out of bodies was absent with every imaginable position represented: five were buried on their faces, some (usually children) were crouched, others on their sides, two were back to back and foot to foot, two teenagers were embracing each other, two were folded up in a sack and had been dumped in a hole. Most, of course, were on their backs, arms at their side or folded across their chests, legs crossed or straight. Some 2,500 nails indicated the presence of coffins. Animal and bird bones suggest they were buried with the dead – another source of post-mortem food; animals included sheep, goats, oxen, horse, cats, pigs and deer. The embracing youths referred to above were found with the complete skeleton of a hen on the uppermost's back. Three of the pots had coins in them, four contained hen's eggshells. Seven skulls contained the obligatory coin to pay surly infernal ferryman Charon the fare required for the perilous crossing of the River Styx.

Charon – Who Pays the Ferryman?

Charon, the unkempt and grumpy ferryman has a long, not very illustrious history. One of our best sources is Book VI of Virgil's *Aeneid*. You met him as you clamoured with hordes of other recently dead, anxious to get over the murky underworld river Styx. Conditions were not good: there were frantic crowds pressing in on you; the ferryman was churlish and repellent, and his gloomy boat leaked. Moreover, some say you even had to help with the rowing, and everyone had to have the right change ready. No obol, no ride. No ride, no afterlife.

Charon's credentials for the job were excellent. He was the son of brother and sister Nyx (night) and Erebus (darkness); he was the brother of Thanatos (death) and Hypnos (sleep). Nyx was born of Chaos and gave birth to Moros (doom), Ker (fate, destruction, death), as well as other morbid characters who included Thanatos, Hypnos, the Oneiroi (dreams), Momus (blame), Oizys (woe, pain, distress), the Moirai (fates), Nemesis; Apate (deceit), Philotes; Geras (old age), and Eris (strife). Not much hope there.

His name comes from χαρωπός (charopós), 'he of the keen gaze', and reflects his piercing, laser-like eyes; Charon is forever a euphemism for doom and death.

Roman Health and Disease

The excavations here did much to advance our knowledge of Roman health and disease: over seventy-five of the people died before 40 – only sixty-five out of 342 reached beyond 45. The tallest man was 6ft 4ins, the average 5ft 5ins; women averaged 5ft 2ins – slightly taller than today's average. Rheumatism and arthritis were present in everyone over 30 – a consequence of the damp and cold. Pott's Disease – tuberculous (TB) spondylitis – extrapulmonary TB affecting the spine – has been found in skeletons in York as well as at Poundbury and Cirencester.

Skeletal evidence shows many of the inhabitants to have lived a life of conflict – not especially surprising given the Romans' endless warring and the lengthy military careers of its soldiery. Twenty-one healed upper and lower-limb fractures have been found, including fractured thigh bones; several more thigh bones displayed depressions consistent with sword cuts. Squatting facets the remodelling of the bones at the front of the *talus*, or ankle joint – in women's bones found at Trentholme

Drive indicate that they spent a lot of time squatting: cooking and tending the fires. Another interesting female skeleton found there gave us a poorly healed right femur which induced a variation in her lumber vertebrae and, no doubt, a pronounced limp: speculation is that she was a professional acrobat. Collarbone injuries and osteoarthritis, mainly in the spine, were common. Two bone tumours were found. There was no sign of tuberculosis, or rickets which suggested a decent enough diet. Dental health was generally good although there were signs of extractions, abscesses and decay; largely free from caries, less than five per cent of the 5,000 teeth examined showed signs of decay although there were signs of impacted wisdom teeth. Grit-lined mortaria, stone querns, as well as plenty of roughage in the diet, no doubt contributed to the well-worn condition of the teeth.

Generally speaking, opticians were to be found throughout the province in both military and civil settings: opticians' stamps impacted on all four sides of small square stone slabs have been found in York; Galen (12 –210), the noted Greek physician, tells us about a Briton call Stolus who prescribed an eye salve or *coryllia*.

Female skulls showed the women to be almost all of Celtic origin but the men were a more diverse group: five came from the eastern Mediterranean, seven were Scandinavian while one was a negro; there were a number of Germans.

To modern sensitivities, the discovery of dead infants, however ancient, is naturally abhorrent. However, the Romans seem to have become relatively inured to infant mortality, probably because it was so prevalent. The skeleton of a baby found in the remains of a barrack block beneath Blake Street was unusual because it was discovered in a military setting. Babies were often buried in houses because they were not considered complete humans until after forty days and so did not qualify for a formal burial in a cemetery. To find a child's skeleton in a barracks is surprising indeed and may suggest that it was a votive offering. An infant's body was found under the ramparts at Winchester – one of a number up and down the country. Babies have been found in stone-lined cists in buildings and under eaves at Catsgore near Taunton with some ceremony, presumably to assist them on their way into the next world. An infant cemetery has been unearthed at Barton Court Farm villa near Abingdon while at York the Trentholme Drive cemetery reveals no neonatals, suggesting they too had their own burial space as yet undiscovered.

Equally disturbing is the report of the skeleton unearthed from a shallow pit at the Vindolanda Roman fort in 2010. Dr Trudi Buck, a biological anthropologist at Durham University, was unable to determine whether it was a boy or girl but it is believed that the child, aged about 10 and who was tied up, died from a blow to the head and that the body was surreptitiously concealed. The pit has been dated to the mid-third century, when the Fourth Cohort of Gauls were the garrison. Tests on the child's tooth enamel showed that he or she grew up in the Mediterranean. 'Until the child was at least 7 or 8, he or she must have been in southern Europe or even North Africa,' Dr Buck told the BBC. Speaking to *The Guardian*, Patricia Birley, director of the Vindolanda Trust, added: 'This definitely looks like a case of foul play. It has been very sad to find a child in this shallow grave under the barrack floor.'

The exposure of infants, particularly female and deformed babies, was rife. It was not until 374 that child exposure was outlawed when infanticide became the legal equivalent of murder. In an earlier bid to restrict the practice, Constantine had offered free food and clothing to new parents and legalised the sale of babies, mainly into slavery, in 329. However, it was still going on some years later: the skeletons of 100 or so infants were excavated from the bottom of a drain in Ashkelon dating from the sixth century AD.

Parasitic Disease in York

What with all those public baths, latrines with washing facilities, sewer systems, fountains and clean drinking water from aqueducts you would think that the Romans (at least the comfortably off ones) would have enjoyed a reasonable level of personal hygiene and were largely free from chronic stomach upsets and intestinal disease generally. Not a bit of it; research led by Piers Mitchell from the Department of Archaeology and Anthropology at the University of Cambridge, and published in the journal *Parasitology*, found that baths and the like did nothing to protect the Romans from those annoying, embarrassing parasites.

Mitchell and his team rolled up their sleeves and used archaeological evidence from cesspits, sewer drains, rubbish pits, burials and other sites to assess the impact of parasites across Roman Europe, the Middle East and North Africa.

Unfortunately for the Romans, analysis of all of the above plus ancient latrines, human burials and coprolites (fossilised faeces) clearly demonstrated that, instead of decreasing as expected, the number of intestinal parasites actually increased compared with the preceding Iron Age. 'The impressive sanitation technologies introduced by the Romans did not seem to have delivered the health benefits that we would expect,' Mitchell said. He found that the most widely spread intestinal parasites in the Roman Empire were whipworm (*Trichuris trichiura*) and roundworm (*Ascaris lumbricoides*), which are transmitted by the contamination of food with faeces. 'It could have been spread by the use of unwashed hands to prepare food or by the use of human faeces as crop fertilizer,' Mitchell concluded. Also prolific was *Entamoeba histolytica*, a protozoan that causes dysentery, with bloody diarrhoea, abdominal pain and fevers. It is contracted by drinking water contaminated by human faeces.

Ectoparasites such as lice and fleas were as common among Romans as in later Viking and medieval populations, where bathing was not so widely practised. Despite all their regular bathing and flushing of latrines, the Romans systematically undid all that good Public Health Britannia work by using as a substitute for toilet paper and for solo hand washing . . . a communal sponge on a stick. These, of course, were breeding grounds for dysentery, diarrhoea and parasites.

Attempts to sweeten things up came with a multitude of perfumes which could be freely splashed over man and woman alike. These were contained in glass flasks called *unguentaria* in various shapes and sizes. From York we have a squat vessel with a tulip-shaped neck, its base stamped with 'Patrimoni', designating the manufacturer of the unguent. There is also a ring-shaped bottle, jet bracelet and a bronze-mounted casket found in a grave here.

The food chain was another culprit, contributing to the gastrointestinal problems. 'Human and animal faeces were often used to fertilize crops, thus leading to reinfection of the population with intestinal parasites when they ate this food,' Mitchell said. The study also found fish tapeworm eggs surprisingly widespread in the Roman Empire, in contrast to the evidence from the Bronze and Iron Ages. The ever-popular fermented fish sauce (*garum*) may not have helped: *garum* was made from pieces of fish, herbs, salt and flavourings but the sauce was not cooked, instead it was allowed to ferment in the sun. 'Fish tapeworm eggs could have been transported large distances across the empire in the *garum* sauce and then consumed,' Mitchell explained.

As noted, two pandemics ravaged the Roman world during the time Eburacum was occupied. The first was the Antonine Plague, AD 165–180 and the second was the Plague of Cyprian in AD 250–271. We have no records of the latter's spread to and within Britannia but there is relatively recent evidence of the Antonine Plague on Hadrian's Wall and in other places. Both the Antonine and Cyprian plagues drained the Roman armies of manpower, skills and experience and wrecked the Roman economy; these would have had a negative effect on the province and would have been keenly felt in major places such as York.

As we have described, the Antonine Plague, or the Plague of Galen, which was probably smallpox, may have claimed the life of Emperor Lucius Verus, who died in 169 and was the co-emperor with Marcus Aurelius. In 168, as Verus and Marcus Aurelius returned to Rome from the field, Verus fell ill with symptoms misdiagnosed with those consistent with food poisoning, dying after a few days. However, scholars now believe that Verus may have succumbed to smallpox. Some also believe that Marcus Aurelius himself died from this plague some eleven years later. We have already seen how this pestilence was probably a contributory factor in the abandonment of the Antonine Wall – so depleted was the army around the empire that troops from Scotland were sent south to consolidate Hadrian's Wall. The depletion in manpower could have been caused either by high mortality amongst the troops or else by having to plug the gaps left by soldiers who had been redeployed elsewhere.

The causative agent of the Plague of Cyprian is highly speculative: suspects have included smallpox, pandemic influenza and viral haemorrhagic fever (filoviruses), such as the Ebola virus. The plague greatly hampered the Roman Empire's ability to ward off barbarian invasions, not helped by additional problems such as depopulation and famine, with many farms abandoned and unproductive as farmers sought refuge in the cities. The absence of consistent leadership and the further dilution of the military during all the political instability, and the ineptitude of a long succession of short-lived emperors all incapable of stemming the contagion – two of them died from the plague, Hostilian in 251 and Claudius II Gothicus in 270 – just added to the empire's parlous state. The relentless march of the disease through every corner of the empire with Christians (who were blamed for it) ennobling it by comparing the suffering it caused with the excruciating pain endured by martyrs. Others grappled with anxiety and panic, believing the contagion to be spread through 'corrupted air' that pervaded the empire, or that the disease was transmitted through the clothes, or simply by being looked at by an infected person. See Appendix 13.

Gypsum Burials

The cemetery beneath the railway station was particularly fruitful after excavations in 1839–41, 1845, and 1870–7. A number of sarcophagi were unearthed including those of Flavius Bellator and Julia Fortunata. Inhumation burial in sarcophagi sometimes entailed pouring gypsum (hydrous calcium chlorate) in as a liquid in order to encase the body in a lead coffin. The gypsum casts, when found undisturbed, often retain an impression of the deceased and their clothing, usually a textile shroud – the numerous sarcophagi from Eboracum have provided a large number of these casts, in some cases with cloth stuck to the gypsum. York is notable for this method; the raw material was quarried at Hillam, near Monk Fryston some fifteen miles from York.

The tombstone of Flavia and Saenius Augusta depicts a set square and mason's hammer. Below a double canopy stands the veteran with his wife on his right. He wears a tunic and long cloak and carries a scroll in the left hand (his will?). His wife wears a tunic and shawl, and holds a bird in her right hand. In front stand a boy and girl, dressed and posed like their parents. It was found at the Mount and used as a lid for Aelia Severa's gypsum coffin. She was wife or daughter to Caecilius Rufus, decurion. Rufus' freedman and heir, Caecilius Musicus, organised Aelia's burial with the tombstone of Flavia Augustina recycled as a lid. A decurion (*decurio*) in this context was a cavalry officer in command of a squadron (*turma*) of cavalrymen.

Julia Victorina's occupancy of her coffin, found in Castle Yard, was short lived as the centurion's wife and her 4-year-old son, Constantius, were evicted to make way for a male gypsum burial (*RIB* 683, 685). The centurion was a former soldier in the Praetorian Guard, Septimius Lupianus presumably attached to the VIth legion. The invading corpse was deliberately positioned so as to obscure Julia's inscription, as was that of Aurelius Super, centurion of the VIth legion (*RIB* 670) also found in 1835 in York Castle Yard:

> To the spirits of the departed (and) to Aurelius Super, centurion of the Sixth Legion, who lived 38 years, 4 months, 13 days; his wife, Aurelia Censorina, set up this memorial.

Two gypsum burials at York have revealed evidence of frankincense and another for *pistacia* (a genus of flowering plants in the cashew family) resin used in funerary rites. This is the northernmost confirmed use of aromatic resins in mortuary contexts during the Roman period.

Gypsum encasing the body of the deceased was no doubt an attempt to embalm and preserve; unfortunately gypsum acts in the opposite way – as an accelerant to decomposition of bones and tissue. Nevertheless, as we have said, the chemical does leave a trace of the body outline and winding sheet – the most interesting example is the outline of a woman with that of a newborn positioned between her legs; casualties no doubt of childbirth mortality. The burial is described in *Eboracum* (1962) as:

> Large coffin, of stone, found in July 1851, at a depth of 3ft under a house at the corner of Price's Lane and Bishopgate Street, containing the skeleton of a woman with the skeleton of a child between her legs. The bodies had been covered in gypsum, forming a cast ... with fragments of cloth still adhering to it. No grave goods are preserved from this coffin, but a hole above the left shoulder of the woman's skeleton shows whence some were removed.

Not surprisingly, ingesting gypsum is not good for you, as Caius Proculeius, a good friend of Augustus found to his cost. A nonchalant-sounding Pliny the Elder (*Natural History* 36, 59) tells us how, 'suffering from violent pains in the stomach, [he] swallowed gypsum, and so put an end to his existence.'

We have seen how funeral feasts are depicted on the tombstones of Julia Velva.

RIB describes it as follows:

> The deceased, Julia Velva, reclines on a couch, though appearing to stand behind it, with a cup in her hand. At the head, in front of a second table, stands her heir Mercurialis, who is bearded and wears tunic, cloak, and boots and holds in his right hand the scroll of the will. On the left of a second three-legged table (in front of Julia's couch) sits a lady in a wicker chair with a bird in her hands. On the right of the table stands a second figure with a jug, presumably

an attendant. The formula suis, 'family', suggests that the figure in the chair is a relative of Mercurialis.

Epigraphical Evidence in York

Many of the funerary inscriptions described above give us much important detail about the Roman army, army careers and troop locations. Civilian epigraphs reveal valuable information about adult and child mortality, morbidity, family life, social status, epigraphy protocol, religious beliefs and ritual, and reactions to death.

The Romans had gods and goddesses for every conceivable stage and facet of life, and death – from conception to life in the afterlife. Deities and *numen*, spirits, attended the Romans' every act and were worshipped accordingly. Excavations in York have revealed the altars and dedication stones devoted to thirty or so different divinities set up at one time or another, including Venus; Mars; Mercury; Bellona (goddess of war); Neptune; Hercules; Castor and Pollux; Jupiter; Tethys; Hospitality and the Home (*Jupiter, Hospitalis et Penates*); Britannia; Veteris; Silvanus; Toutatis; Chnoubis and Fortune; the Divinity of the Emperor (*numen Augusti*) as well as references to the spiritual representation (*genius Eboraci*) of Eboracum, the genius of the Place (*Genius Loci*) and dedications to the Mother Goddess and various local and regional deities. Celtic deities include Boudiga, Arciaco, and Sucelus – the latter two unique to Eboracum in Britannia. The surviving remains of the Temple of Hercules gives us two of the names of the men who rebuilt it: Titus Perpetuus and Aeternus – citizens of York both.

We have already discussed Bellona, the goddess of war, in the context of Severus' victories in Caledonia and his death in York soon after visiting Bellona's temple. As everywhere, the cult of the emperor was alive and well in Eboracum under the aegis of the *seviri augustales* (six men of the emperor). The two we know of from Eboracum are Marcus Aurelius Lunaris and Marcus Vercundus Diogenes. The coffin on which Diogenes' name appeared (found near Scarborough Bridge) is now lost, although his wife's does survive: Sardinian Julia Fortunata (*RIB* 687). It was unearthed during the building of the railway station – but it contained the skeleton of a man. This is a good example of the recycling of sarcophagi which, if anything, would have been cheaper when second hand – sold as having had one careful owner? Or free even, if it was grave-robbed. Verecundus Diogenes was a *sevir augustalis*; these magistrates looked after the cult of the emperor's divinity – a symbol of loyalty – ceremony and entertainment. Diogenes hailed from Bourges, southern France. He was also a *sevir* of the Morini (a Belgic coastal tribe, living around present-day Boulogne-sur-Mer) and trader (*moritix*) who settled at York. Another example of thrifty reuse comes with the demise of Flavius Bellator – a decurion who died age 29; he, or his skeleton, was wearing his official gold ring, set with a ruby (*RIB* 674). His coffin was discovered on the south-west side of the Scarborough Railway Bridge but it contained the remains of someone much younger. The inscription is also notable for its reference to Eboracum:

> D(is) M(anibus)
> Fl[a]vi Bellatoris dec(urionis) col(oniae) Eboracens(is)
> vixit annis XXVIIII mensib[us . . .

Celerinius Vitalis set up an altar to the god of the woods, Silvanus (*RIB* 659). Perhaps he was desperate to get out of his office and into the forests around York. It was found at the Mount with *RIB* 664 in 1884:

> To the holy god Silvanus, Lucius Celerinius Vitalis, cornicularius of the Ninth Legion Hispana, with this offering gladly, willingly, and deservedly fulfilled his vow. Let the gift, this very gift, form part: I must beware of touching.

A *corniculārius* or cornicular was an officer who served as the adjutant to a centurion, so named for wearing a cornicule (*corniculum*), a small, horn-shaped badge.

Marcus Aurelius Lunaris is described as '*sevir Augustalis* of the colonies of Eburacum and Lindum in the province of Lower Britain'. He dedicates to 'Protecting Goddess Boudig' and to Salus on surviving the voyage to Bordeaux in 237. Boudig is a British deity, the Celtic equivalent of Rome's Victoria – the combination of the two reinforces the gradual and discreet Romanisation programme that people such as Lunaris were undergoing.

> To the memory of Julia Fortunata from Sardinia; (she was) a loyal wife to her husband, Verecundius Diogenes.

Sadly for Julia (who was not as lucky as her name might promise) we have all been much more interested in her husband and generally miss the significance of Julia herself. What little we learn from these brief lines is that she was Sardinian and that she was a loyal wife, a true *matrona*. The epigraphs celebrating deceased women found in York are untypical of women's epigraphs empire wide and surprisingly personal, perhaps. Certainly, much of the epigraphical evidence from elsewhere suggests a high degree of subservience, compliance and unobtrusiveness amongst the women honoured and so reflects the general situation in Roman society. More significantly, though, most of what we have is formulaic, trotting out as it does standard qualities and typical domestic virtues; its value as evidence of a woman's actual life and real lifestyle may be diluted as a result.

Fairly typical is 'Here lies Amymone, wife of Marcus, the best and most beautiful, wool spinner, dutiful, modest, careful with money, chaste, stay-at-home' (*CIL* 6, 11602). It ticks all the boxes for the stock eulogy, Amymone's virtues reflect the ideal Roman wife, the compliant *matrona*. Many of the qualifying epithets are here: *optima, pulcherrima, lanifica, pia, pudica, frugi, casta, domiseda*. Claudia was much the same: beautiful, loving, mother of two children (one dead, one living), a bit of a wit (*sermone lepida*), good bearing (*incessu commoda*), looked after the home, and worked the wool (*lanam fecit*) (*CIL* 1, 1007). The six most frequent 'adjectives', as assessed by Werner Riess (*In Rari Exempla Femina* p. 493), are *dulcissima* (sweetest), *pia* (dutiful), *bene merens* (well-deserving), *carissima* (dearest), *optima* (best) and *sanctissima* (most chaste). We could add to the list: (she) valued a traditional lifestyle (*antiqua vita*), friendly and amusing (*comis*), modestly turned out (*ornata non conspiciendi*); a one-man woman (*univira*) and religious, but not with all that superstition stuff (*religiosa sine superstitione*). These epithets crop up with extraordinary regularity. Our Julia Velva is *pientissime*, most dutiful.

At the very least, then, tombstone inscriptions help us because they describe an ideal, if not the absolute reality, of wifely, feminine virtue; they tell us what men expected from a wife or a mother. They probably reflect the normal, everyday, tolerably happy marriage in which husband and wife rub along together, and miss the other when one of them dies. Some wives would have been all the things the standard epigraphs tell us; others less so. Moreover, in a society where the woman's world was usually defined by the confines – physical and social – of the *familia* and the house, the *domus*, the tombstone eulogy – hackneyed as it often seems to us – may be the best a woman could wish for, or even desired: a fitting tribute to a dedicated wife or mother from a loving husband or son for a life well lived. In the wider context, then, our Julia was fortunate to be described as *Verec(undio) Diogeni fida coniuncta marito*: a loyal wife to her husband, Verecundius Diogenes.

RIB 684 is, as we have seen, a plaintive funerary inscription in hexameters for 13-year-old Corellia Optata found at the Mount in 1861. It reads:

> To the spirits of the departed: Corellia Optata, aged 13. You mysterious spirits who dwell in Pluto's Acherusian realms, and whom the meagre ashes and the shade, empty semblance of the body, seek, following the brief light of life; father of an innocent daughter, I, a pitiable victim of unfair hope, bewail her final end. Quintus Corellius Fortis, her father, had this set up.

A large glass vessel inside the coffin, sealed with lead, contained Corellia's ashes. The reference to Dis – god of the underworld – and Acheron – one of the rivers of the underworld – make this epitaph particularly vivid and pathetic. It also adumbrates an aspect of Roman eschatology with its reference to the shade which the body has now become: *simulacrum corpo(r)is umbra*.

Another find is an altar dedicated to Veteris found in the garden of the Bar Convent, in 1880 (*RIB* 660). Veteris was a Celtic god; during the third century AD, the cult was particularly popular in the Roman army.

CIL VI 9143: an inscribed tablet dedicated to Calpurnia found at the site of the old railway station; date about 1840 (*RIB* 662) is more interesting to us for what is on the back: a bronze plate which was originally silvered. *RIB* 663 is one of two bronze votive tablets with its Greek inscription in punched dots...; this one is stuck to the back; it reads:

> To the gods of the legate's residence (*praetorium*) Scribonius Demetrius (set this up).

Demetrius is presumably Scribonius Demetrius of Tarsus, the *grammaticus* (teacher), who took part in Plutarch's dialogue *De Defectu Oraculorum* (410A, 434C) – *On the Dilapidation of the Oracles* – just before the Pythian festival in AD 83–84. Demetrius had recently returned to Tarsus from his visit to Britain where he had accompanied a voyage to the Western Islands of Scotland on imperial orders – 'an Imperial expedition of enquiry and survey'. His report lends credence and strength to the mysterious and frightening reputation enjoyed by our islands: some are named after Celtic spirits and heroes as corroborated by the twenty-seven islands named in the *Ravenna Cosmography*, while the inhabitants of one are 'holy and inviolate'. Demetrius' landing was accompanied by a severe storm with lightning, thunder and waterspouts; only the extinguishing of the Greater Spirits brought storms and disease. Demetrius adds that a slumbering Cronus was imprisoned there, guarded by Briareus.

RIB 662-663 is the second of the two:

To Ocean and Tethys Demetrius (set this up).

This short dedication has considerable significance as it echoes the words used by Alexander the Great on the altars he set up at the mouth of the River Indus in 325 BC (Diodorus 17,104), the furthest east he reached. Demetrius is drawing a direct connection between Alexander's achievement and Rome's parallel achievement in reaching the furthest point west of their empire, their *ultima Thule*. A. F. Norman describes it as 'his individual conception of her as the [Tethys] heir and successor to the greatest conqueror and civiliser of the ancient world.' At the same time it is perhaps evidence of the educational programme established by Agricola at York (Ogilvie p. 33) in order to help Romanise the sons of the tribal aristocracies and replace fear and loathing with an acceptance of the Roman way of doing things (Tacitus, *Agricola* 21). Some of the boys were students, others were hostages who stayed in the governor's house for this.

A dedication to the Divinities of the Emperor and to the goddess Joug (*RIB* 656) found in 1839 on the site of the bank at the junction of Nessgate and Ousegate (with *RIB* 648 and 698) gives us:

To the Divinities of the Emperor and to the goddess Joug[. . .
. . .]sius . . . half of the shrine . . ..

RIB suggests the name of the goddess is formed from Celtic *iougon*, a yoke. It is now in the Yorkshire Museum. Joug was a local York deity and this, along with another local god, Arciacon, are both linked with the divinity of the emperor(s) (*RIB* 640). Another example of religion and loyalty to the emperor conjoined. It was found beneath a pillar in the church of St Denys, Walmgate, in 1839 and is now also in the Yorkshire Museum. The dedication reads:

> To the god Arciaco and to the Divinity of the Emperor, Mat(. . .) Vitalis, centurion, willingly and deservedly fulfilled his vow.

Then there is the dedication (*RIB* 666) slab to Trajan found in 1879 at the north end of the Fine Art Exhibition Building, now the City Art Gallery, north west of Bootham Bar, the site of one of the Roman gates. And the one dedicated to Marcus Aurelius (*RIB* 667) excavated during digging the foundations for the Mechanics' Institute in Clifford Street.

RIB 653 is an altar dedicated to the African, Italian, and Gallic Mother Goddesses found in Micklegate, opposite Holy Trinity Church in 1752. Likewise, the stone altar *RIB* 654 found in 1850, in Park Place, Monkgate, on the line of the road leading north east to Malton.

The altar dedicated to Mars (*RIB* 650) was found in the Bar Convent, in 1880. Described in *Eboracum* (1962) as:

> Altar, of gritstone, 7ins by 1ft by 7ins, found in 1880 in a dump of Roman stones . . . with burials below them, at St Mary's Convent, close to the main Roman road, just outside the built up area of the Roman town. The stones had been gathered together after the Roman period.

It reads:

> To the god Mars, Agrius Auspex pays his vow willingly and deservedly.

The altar dedicated to Jupiter Optimus Maximus (*RIB* 649); on the right side is a weathered figure holding a staff in its left hand. On the left side is a sacrificial scene with a male figure in a knee-length tunic and possibly a hairband, holding an animal; there is a wreath above this animal. It is now believed that the figure is a military figure in profile facing right wearing a crested helmet and possibly armour, with a band sculpted around his neck. The *RIB* archive tentatively describes the right-side relief as possibly Jupiter ('figure with shaft in left hand, weathered away below waist'), and the left-side relief as Hercules ('figure with ? headdress faces sin. And seems to wrestle with an animal (? lion), corona above ? Hercules'). Only the first two lines are preserved; it was found in 1638 while digging the foundation of a house on the site at Castlegate where Fairfax House was later built in 1762. Now among the Chandler Marbles, Ashmolean Museum, Oxford. The dedication reads:

> To Jupiter Best and Greatest, to the gods and goddesses
> of hospitality and to the Penates, for having kept safe the
> welfare of himself and of his household, Publius Aelius
> Marcianus, prefect of the cohort, had this altar set up . . .

The stone altar (*RIB* 646): the capital and part of the base are lost; found at the north end of the current railway station in 1875. It lay at the head of a skeleton with a glass vessel nearby. The dedication is:

> to the god, the Genius of the place, willingly and deservedly
> pays his vow.

The statue base (*RIB* 643) found in 1740 inside Micklegate Bar is now lost but we know the inscription:

> To holy Britannia. Nikomedes, freedman of our Emperors,
> set (this) up.

At the corner of High Ousegate and Nessgate, the foundation stone on the wall of a bank (*RIB* 648) is a copy of an important inscribed stone found (with *RIB* 656 and 698) when the building was being built in 1839. It describes the restoration of a temple dedicated to Hercules and includes something quite special. References to the Roman name for York, Eboracum, found in York are very rare (see Appendix 8), and this is one of only two to have been found. It translates as 'To Hercules . . . Titus Perpetuius (?) Aetern[us . . . of the colony of York . . . restored . . .'. The size of the stone would suggest that at least half is missing.

Other funerary epitaphs include:

> An altar erected by the wife of Antonius Isauricus, Sosia Iuncina, dedicated to Fortuna in the bath house in the *colonia*. Isauricus was *Imperial Legate*, the most senior officer in Eboracum at the time.

The tombstone of Titus Flavius Flavinus, centurion of the VIth *Victrix*, was erected by his heir, Classicius Aprilis; Flavinus was clearly a cautious and prudent man: he must have ordered this before his death (*RIB* 675). It was found at the end of Rawcliffe Lane in 1927.

This is the inscription found at the Mount in 1852 (*RIB* 680). Novaria (modern Novara) lies west of Milan, and belonged to *Claudia tribus*. As the VIth Legion replaced the IXth *Hispana* at York about 120, the deceased must have died by that time, or, if in retirement, within a few years of that date.

> To Gaius . . ., son of Gaius, of the Claudian voting-tribe [*Cl(audia)] (tribu),* from Novaria, . . . of the Ninth Legion Hispana, his heirs and freedmen set this up to their own well-deserving patron.

A *tribus*, or tribe, was a division of the Roman people, making up the voting units of a legislative assembly of the Roman Republic. The word may be derived from *tribuere*, to divide or distribute. Tradition has it that the first three Roman tribes were established by Romulus; each was divided into ten *curiae*, or wards, which were the voting units of the *comitia curiata*. The Claudian voting tribe was quite prestigious and worth reminding people that you were part of it, even if it was on your tombstone. When the Sabine Appius Claudius removed to Rome together with his *clientes*, in 504 BC, he was admitted to the patriciate, and assigned lands in the region around the mouth of the Anio. These settlers became the basis of the *tribus* Claudia, which was admitted in 495 BC, during Claudius' consulship, and subsequently enlarged to become the *tribus Crustumina* or *Clustumina*.

Two of the significant excavations exposing the Roman period are:

Hungate 2006–2012

This major archaeological excavation was the largest developer-funded project to take place in York up to 2006, and the biggest urban excavation in the city for twenty-five years, covering a 26,900 sq ft area. York Archaeological Trust (YAT) spent five years on the dig before handing the site back to developers. Hungate has been under continuous occupation for most of the past 2,000 years. Part of the site contains the remains of an early Roman cemetery.

Project director Peter Connelly told the BBC: 'It is the largest Roman cemetery excavated in York for a century. We've discovered amazing pieces of Roman jewellery.' These jewels include a Roman necklace consisting of 299 small glass beads and rare jet jewellery dating from the third or fourth centuries.

Newington Hotel 2017–18 Cemetery Adjacent to the Trentholme Drive Site

The redevelopment of the former Newington Hotel gave YAT a chance to explore and study an important aspect of York's Roman past.

The site is on Mount Vale, only about 200 yards from where YAT uncovered the headless Roman skeletons of Driffield Terrace; it is part of a Roman cemetery that was first excavated by Peter Wenham on the neighbouring Trentholme Drive site in the 1950s – one of the first Romano-British burial grounds to be fully published in the UK.

In April 2018, seventy-five Roman skeletons were discovered on the site; they were unearthed under the swimming pool, in an extension to the Roman burial ground further up Mount Vale. YAT describes it as follows:

> Included among exciting finds have been grave goods in the form of pottery, dishes, jars, flagons and beakers and also traces of the coffins in which the dead were laid to rest. These burials are currently thought to date to a period spanning the 2nd to 4th centuries AD and, as the finds suggest, to have been of people of a relatively lowly social status.

The seventy-five graves were mostly very shallow indicating that many of them had been plough damaged throughout the medieval period and nineteenth-century construction.

YAT adds:

> At first glance, the image is decidedly chaotic: rather than lying in regimented rows the graves crowd together, oriented towards all points of the compass and frequently intercutting. As for who was buried there, this was a demographically diverse cemetery, populated by both men and women, and individuals of all ages from infants to elderly adults – although they seem to have been broadly of the same social class.
>
> Nor was there anything immediately spectacular about the objects that accompanied these everyday individuals to the grave – only two contained any items of personal adornment. One grave yielded a jet pin, while another individual had been interred wearing some kind of copper alloy head ornament whose flaky, corroded remains had left a green stain on their forehead. Otherwise, grave goods were limited to pots, which were found interred with young and old alike.

The Wold Newton Hoard – 'A Once in a Lifetime Find'

One day in 2014, metal detectorist David Blakey was out detecting near the village of Wold Newton, East Yorkshire when he came across this hugely important hoard in a ceramic pot.

The quick-witted David Blakey filmed its discovery and immediately reported it to the Portable Antiquities Scheme (PAS) rather than just emptying it out. This has allowed archaeologists the rare opportunity to excavate it in different layers to see how different coins were added to the vessel.

As the museum website tells us:

> insect remains attached to some of the coins also offer another way of analysing the contents. All this means there is huge potential for getting a greater understanding of the

period and why it was buried. The hoard can be dated quite precisely, with the latest coins in the hoard suggesting it was hidden in 307. This is shortly after the death of the emperor Constantius in York, and the rise to power of his son, Constantine the Great. The hoard provides a link to events which would reshape the empire and the history of Europe.

The Wold Newton hoard is the largest of that period found in northern Britain. It contains 1,857 copper coins which were concealed within a ceramic pot. This is a large store of wealth, roughly equivalent to a legionary's annual salary, three year's salary for a carpenter or six years for a farm labourer. It could buy 700 chickens, 2,000 of the finest fish or 11,000 pints of beer!

On being declared treasure, the hoard was valued at just over £44,200. The Yorkshire Museum ran a fundraising campaign (launched on 25 July 2016 to raise the money, which included donations from hundreds of people from around the world, £10,000 from the Arts Council/Victoria and Albert Museum Purchase Grant Fund and a donation of £9,981 from the American Friends of the Arts Fund). The hoard went on public display on 1 June 2017 in the Yorkshire Museum as part of the York Roman Festival.

The Women and Children of Roman York

The previous chapter gives us much of our knowledge about the women and children of Eboracum. In addition to these we also know about Empress Helena, wife to Constantius and mother to Constantine. The other empress York can boast is, of course, Julia Domna, empress to Septimius Severus. Julia Domna is famous for the encounter reported by Dio between Julia and the wife of a Caledonian chieftain in Britannia. Julia remarked primly on how the tribal women are somewhat free with their sexual favours; the barbarian woman replied tartly, 'We satisfy our desires in a better way than you Roman women do. We have sex openly with the best men while you are seduced in secret by the worst.' That was probably the end of that particular edge of empire tête-à-tête diplomacy.

Julia was renowned for her impressive learning, her extraordinary political influence, and for her expertise in, and patronage of, philosophy. Julia had her fair share of political enemies, who accused her of treason and adultery, neither of which were proven. She and Severus were very close; he insisting she accompany him in the campaign in Britannia from 208. Julia was awarded the title of *Mater Castrorum* (Mother of the Camps) in 195.

A reference by the epigrammist Martial (AD 41–102) is interesting (11, 53): he describes a Claudia Rufina; she is of British stock, a barbarian, but nevertheless is a Latin at heart and would pass any time for a Roman or a Greek. Like all good *matronae* she is fertile, *fecunda*, *univira* and looking forward to her childrens' marriages. We obviously have no way of knowing where in Britannia Claudia came from – it could have been York but probably was not – it nevertheless shows that by Martial's time, foreign women were being appreciated for their matronly qualities just like any Roman woman. Coming from a poet not noted for his liberal views on gender equality and for his xenophobia this is praise indeed: the women of Roman Britain, and this would include Roman

York, were, it seems, becoming more and more Roman under the spread of Romanisation by the end of the first century.

The Grave of a Rich Lady

In 1901, a stone coffin was discovered near Sycamore Terrace, Bootham. The treasure trove of unusual grave goods found in the coffin is dated to the second half of the fourth century and tells us much about the middle-class Roman preoccupation with personal appearance and ostentatious display. The goods include jet, elephant ivory and blue glass bead bracelets, earrings, pendants, and beads. Also in there was a blue glass jug 123 mm tall, likely to have contained perfumes, as well as a glass mirror.

The deceased was a truly wealthy lady as indicated by the exotic (and therefore expensive) provenances of many of the grave goods. Ivory was a rare material in Roman Britain, although it has been found in the nearby cemetery discovered during the construction of the railway station in the 1870s. Jet, as we have noted, became very popular in the third and fourth centuries, and may have had associations with the cult of Bacchus and with Christianity.

But the rich lady is of more interest to us than for being just the owner of fine and exotic jewellery, or for her religion. The 'Ivory Bangle Lady', as she has been christened, assumed a secret when she was lowered into the ground; it was not just her grave goods which had an interesting provenance. She was one of a number of multiracial people of African origin to be exhumed in York and who hailed from the southern borders of the Roman Empire; as such she and the others are indicative of the diverse, highly mobile, cosmopolitan nature of the Romans, a variegated demographic which was highly mobile, extensively travelled and multinational.

How do we know that 'the Ivory Bangle Lady' was African? Radioisotope analysis and other major advances in osteoarchaeology provide the answer. Radioisotope analysis is the process by which oxygen and strontium isotopes are deployed to reveal chemical signatures in bones and teeth which in turn tells us where long dead skeletons came from and where they passed their childhood. This allows us to differentiate people who lived thousands of years ago in warm climates from those emanating from cooler climes, and to differentiate locals from immigrants. In York, skeletons from two different cemeteries – one for the comfortably off, the other for the poor – showed, through cranial anatomy and radioisotope analysis, a significant number (about twelve per cent) were of North African origin; the diversity in York was not just of ethnic origin but it was also evident in all levels of society. In particular the radioisotope and cranial-skeletal anatomy analyses performed on our 'Ivory Bangle Lady' and the traces revealed by the food and drink she consumed in childhood reveal her origins, and probably those of her parents and grandparents. The lady died age 23; she was probably the wife of a high-ranking Roman soldier posted to York.

Significantly, as David Olusoga concludes in his *Black and British: a Forgotten History*, she and the others provide good evidence that Eburacum in the later empire was considerably more ethnically and racially diverse than York is today.

Carvings etched into a stone in a Cumbrian village tell us that a group of soldiers called the Aurelian Moors were garrisoned in the nearby fortress of Aballava. Moors indicates North African origin while Aurelian dates them in the reign of Marcus Aurelius. Confirmation of their presence here is found in a Roman official's travel list. But the auxiliaries probably did not stay in Aballava: studies of over 200 skulls in York revealed that over one in ten exhibited features very similar to the North African auxiliaries.

The women who have become known to us from their tombstones are:

Julia Velva – shown feasting for the next life, as described above.

Aelia Severa – a member by marriage of the *honestiores* – the upper echelon of citizens in positions of high standing in local government – as opposed to the second class *humiliores;* Aelia's family were wealthy enough to have given one of their slaves, Musicus, his freedom and he himself became a member of the local nouveau riche.

Julia Brica – *RIB* 686. The draped figure of Julia Brica stands in the niche holding a cup in her hands. To her right is the draped figure of her daughter, holding in her right hand an object which may be a pet. Found with *RIB* 693 on the site of the Mount Hotel in 1892.

Candida Barita – died with her two daughters Mantia and Tetrica.

Emilia Theodora – *RIB* 677 shows the most distressing of functions some mothers had to perform: organising the burial of her son, namely Valerius Theodorianus, of Nomentum, who lived for thirty-five years and six months. The *York Museum Handbook* (1891) described the skull as 'of noble proportions'. He had his tomb set up by Emilia, his mother and heir. His coffin was found in the early 1800s in a garden at the Mount.

Aelia Aeliana – *RIB* 682 is the funerary inscription for Aelia Aeliana, found during the building of the current railway station in 1872. Her tombstone depicts a three-legged table with claw-feet, laden with food.

As noted, Aelia is one of three women (Julia Velva and Mantinia Maercia are the other two) where dining scenes can be seen on their tombstones to cater for their needs in the afterlife; they are shown reclining on a couch and being served food and wine.

RIB 134. This tomb, found on the Mount, shows a triple tragedy commemorated by a retired soldier, Gaius Aeresius Saenus, and the tombstone he erected for his wife, Flavia Augustina, and his two infant 2-year-old children. Perhaps this is how Aeresius liked to think how things might have turned out.

Generally speaking, as mentioned, the Roman soldier took up a posting unaccompanied by his wife or partner; relationships were nevertheless, quite naturally, fostered with local women and seem not to have been discouraged or punished. The ruling came in the form of the Augustan *Lex Julia de Maritandis Ordinibus* prohibiting marriage between senators, and their near relatives and freedwomen; marriage to convicted adulteresses or those in a dubious profession (actors, dancers, prostitutes); and serving soldiers below a certain rank until the reign of Septimius Severus when the ban was relaxed in 197; provincial officials were prohibited from marrying women from the province; guardians could not marry their wards.

Legionary commanders, the *legatus legionis* or legate, second-in-command to the governor were, like the governor, exempt from this order and enjoyed the privilege of having their wives with them on their postings. We know that between AD 86 and AD 213, 127 legates served in Britannia but we can only identify twenty or so; rarer still are the legates' wives – but York throws up a rare example in Sosia Juncina by way of her appearance on the altar dedicated to Fortuna by herself and her husband Quintus Antonius Isauricus, legate of the VIth. Stoically following the drum was the order if the day – either in the fortress *praetoria* or, less comfortably and potentially more dangerously, on campaign.

Despite the long absences from home, wife and children, some soldiers welcomed the regulation. We have the opinions of a veteran commander and seasoned politician, Aulus Caecina Severus, who adopts what is possibly an extreme view, exaggerated in his unsuccessful speech in the senate of AD 21, as recorded by Tacitus (*Annals* 3, 32-35); but it contains within it the arguments which no doubt moulded the regulations relating to accompanied postings. Severus gets on with his wife and they have had six children together – however, he has left her at home for the forty years he has been away in the provinces. Why? Because women encourage extravagance in peace time and weakness during war; they are feeble and tire easily; left unrestrained they get angry, they scheme and boss the commanders about; he cites instances of women running patrols and exercises, how they attract spivs and embrace extortion.

Centurians too were, amongst other privileges, allowed to be accompanied by their wives. Claudia Marcia Capitolina came to York with her husband, the super veteran Petronius Fortunatus, with the VIth *Victrix* and after time with the XXXth *Ulpia Victix* on the Lower Rhine and before his posting to Arabia with the *III Cyrenaica* but not before they had had a son in York when Claudia was 30 and he 45. Petronius could point to fifty years' service to his name and time with thirteen legions. How do we know this? Because of the monument the 80-year-old Fortunatus erected to himself and to Claudia, and his son, Marcus Petronius Fortunatus, proudly and painstakingly listing his military career – an army service record etched in stone.

Salvenia Meteliana came to Housesteads with her centurion husband. He was born in Cologne and died at Lambaesis in Egypt. These wives, like many army wives today, were highly organised, unflinching and adaptable to any situation. Papyri found in Egypt show the women to take moving the family from posting to posting in their stride while husband goes on ahead to his new legion.

Other wealthy women who may well have lived in York at some time with military or administrative connections through a husband include:

Candiedinia Fortunata, whose tombstone (*RIB* 632 now lost) was found before 1702 at Adel Mill, just south of the Roman site at Adel, Leeds. Candiedinia was described as having lived fifteen years as a devoted (*pia*) wife.

Titia Pinta (38 years old), whose coffin (*RIB* 720) was found about 1615 at Eastness near Hovingham, inscribed:

(To) Titia Pinta (who) lived 38 years and to Valerius Adjutor (who) lived 20 years and to Varialus (who) lived 15 years Valerius Vindicianus had (this) set up to his wife and sons

And Cosconia Mammiola (*RIB* 3209) whose damaged coffin is now in store in the Yorkshire Museum. It was found during ploughing at Hood Grange farm near Sutton-under-Whitestonecliffe. It contained human bones which included pieces of four male femora, indicating that it had been re-used. Cosconia's epitaph describes her as *piissim(ae)*, extremely devoted.

Children include:

Sepronia Martina, Julia Brica's daughter who died aged 6. This sad epitaph for mother and daughter (*RIB* 686) set up by husband and father was found in 1892 on the site of the Mount Hotel, beside the Roman road leading south west to Tadcaster. The epitaph reads:

> To the spirits of the departed (and) of Julia Brica, aged 31, and of Sepronia Martina, aged 6, Sepronius Martinus had this set up.

Mantia and *Tetrica Barita* who died with their mother.

Corellia Optata, who died aged 13.

Felix. In 1872 a tombstone was excavated from under the road opposite the current railway station (*RIB* 672) reading:

> To the memory of . . . Bassaeus Julius and of his very sweet son Felix.

Simplicia Florentia. Another desperately sad inscription (*RIB* 690) comes with the epitaph for 10-month-old Simplicia Florentia found in a coffin on the south side of the bridge over the railway in Holgate Road in 1838; the coffin contained a skeleton set in gypsum:

> To the spirits of the departed (and) of Simplicia Florentina, a most innocent soul (*anime inocentissimae*), who lived ten months; her father, Felicius Simplex, made this: centurion of the Sixth Legion Victrix.

207

It has been suggested that this was in fact a Christian burial.

Crescens (*RIB* 695) is another child death – this time of 3-year-old Crescens buried with his 30-year-old mother, Eglecta. The right-hand side of the tombstone was found built into the south wall of All Saints' Church, North Street about 1682 while the left was discovered while the church was being underpinned in 1931.

> To the spirits of the departed (and) to Eglecta, aged 30, here buried beside their son Crescens, aged 3; Antonius Stephanus had this set up to his wife.

RIB 696:

> to her child, (who) lived 13 years, the mother, Vitellia Procula, as heir in part, (set this up).

This had been reused in a medieval building and spotted in 1865 in a heap of rubble near Ebor Street, Clementhorpe, on the west bank of the River Ouse and south east of the Roman *colonia*. The text reveals something about the Roman laws of inheritance: Vitellia Procula had part of the family estate coming to her anyway, a legacy possibly split with 'her child', which could have been a girl or a boy as Roman girls achieved adulthood at 12, two years before boys. The ancient but revered *XII Tables* permitted women to inherit and to be named in wills – one of the few areas of equality in Roman jurisprudence and society – likewise Emilia Theodora (*RIB* 677) was due to inherit after burying husband Valerius Theodorianus. Aurelius Mercurialis describes himself as Julia Velva's heir in the tomb he erected for her so she may have inherited from parents perhaps at some point during their marriage.

Finally there is the sad coffin, complete with cupids, in which Septimius Lucianus laid his wife, Julia Victorina, to rest, and his infant son, Constantius.

Perinatal, Neonatal and Child Mortality

Infant mortality in Britannia and Roman York may have been as high as thirty deaths in every 100 pregnancies, compared with 9.1 per 1,000 in western Caucasian populations today. It is worth noting that improvements on those shocking Roman statistics only came about relatively recently: the London Bills of Mortality for 1762–1771 show that fifty per cent of infants died before age 2. Susan Treggiari has usefully compiled some revealing statistics extrapolated from an assumption that female life expectancy at birth was 25. A woman, of course, would not expect to die at that age, rather it means that thirty per cent of all babies died before their first year and fifty per cent by the age of 10; these survivors would then have a fifty per cent chance of reaching 50. Seventeen percent would see 70. This reveals a lot about the demographics of women in Roman society, and the number of women available for marriage, and for remarriage .

Pliny gives some of the (mainly outrageous by our thinking) reasons suggested to explain the very high rate of maternal and infant mortality. Babies born before the seventh month do not survive and only those babies born in the seventh month survive if they are conceived the day before or after a full moon or during a new moon; eighth-month babies are common, despite what Aristotle says, however, they are vulnerable until they are 40 days old. For mothers, the fourth and eighth months are the most critical; abortions at that time are fatal. He goes on to record how, in a normal pregnancy, the ninth day after conception sees the onset of headaches, dizziness, blurred vision, loss of appetite and nausea, indicating that the foetus is forming; male foetuses produce a healthier complexion in the mother and make for an easier delivery; movements in the womb begin on the fortieth day with males, for females after ninety days. Babies are particularly vulnerable when they start to grow hair and during the full moon; if the pregnant mother eats too much salt then the baby will be born without nails; excessive maternal yawning can be fatal during delivery.

It has been estimated that the average early Roman Empire woman had to give birth to five babies if she was to ensure the survival of two and to do her bit to maintain the required birth rate.

In reality the main causes of neonatal mortality, death within the first twenty-nine days of life, were insanitary conditions at the birth, over swaddling and trauma; infant morbidity and deaths were often caused by intestinal disorders, particularly enteritis and dysentery. Celsus recorded that the latter was particularly virulent in children up to the age of 10 and in their pregnant mothers, when the unborn baby would also be lost. Over-zealous swaddling – where the limbs are confined and the heartbeat slowed down dangerously – dirty laundry, and mastication of baby foods by wet nurses who themselves might be carrying an infection, may also have taken their toll. As indeed would goat's and cow's milk, which can contain infectious organisms and would have been used not just by reluctant breastfeeders but by poorer, undernourished women who were unable to feed and could not afford a wet nurse.

Aulus Cornelius Celsus (c. 25 BC–c. AD 50) was a Roman encyclopaedist, known for his *De Medicina* – the only surviving section of a much larger encyclopedia. The *De Medicina* is a primary source on diet, pharmacy, surgery and related fields, and it is one of the best sources concerning medical knowledge in the Roman world.

We have already noted that, due to the high rate of infant mortality, Roman parents inured themselves to the harsh fact that their baby might well die so as to minimise the grief that is normal in such a tragic situation. The employment of wet nurses, and the knowledge that some Romans 'farmed out' their infants for the first two years or so of their lives, may suggest a level of parental indifference. Cicero says as much: 'no one pays any notice if he dies in the cradle.' The tombstone of 12-year-old Julia Pothousa from Arcadia may endorse this: her parents wish was that she had died earlier, before they had grown to love her.

There is inscriptional evidence for maternal mortality, and pain in childbirth, and a *matrona*'s concern for her offspring at the end of the first century BC in Egypt. Dosithea, aged 25, died in childbirth; she died 'in pain, escaping the pangs of childbirth'. Rusticeia Matrona died in childbirth and from 'malignant fate' at the same age in Mauretania; she urges her husband to look after their son. Also 25, Daphne, from Carthage, died giving birth; her epitaph records her aching concern for the baby: 'who will feed him, look after him for the rest of his life?' Socratea died of a haemorrhage in childbirth aged 36. This 15 year old died giving birth, with her baby, in Tusculum in the first century BC: 'the tomb [holds] two deaths in one body, the [urn] of ashes contains twin funerals.' It is highly likely that similar tragedies occurred in York on a regular basis.

The situation, of course, cannot have been helped by the conjecture surrounding, and ignorance about, the length of gestation. Aulus Gellius inclined to the view that babies could be born in the seventh, ninth and tenth months – but never in the eighth. Strenuous work in the fields and poor diet was the lot of many women and this can only have exacerbated the problem.

Roman York in the Yorkshire Museum

The Yorkshire Museum in York is one the best repositories of Roman artefacts in the UK. This chapter offers a tour of the place, highlighting some of the museum's most striking and significant exhibits.

Perhaps the Yorkshire Museum exhibit with the most impact is, as mentioned briefly above, a preserved head of hair, with jet hairpins and cantharus-shaped heads in situ, from a fourth-century inhumation burial found at the railway station booking office site. The hair is fashioned into a loose bun. It is exhibits like this which bring Roman York to life, allowing you to experience day-to-day living and to get inside the lives of the Romans.

On hairstyles generally, the Julia Velva tombstone shows Julia and her daughter both with a middle parting fixed into a roll framing the face, ears covered, and hair drawn back and tied at the nape of the neck, maybe in a bun. A tombstone of about the same date honouring Candida is markedly different: her ears are exposed, the parting is on the left. Empress Julia Domna's visit to York will have started a craze for Syrian hair styles, which meant hair hanging in crimped waves on either side of the face and gathered back into a roll at the back. The mid-third century saw a variation in the arrival of the Syrian 'helmet style' in which, like a crested helmet, the waves were worn clear of the ears but the hair at the back was carried in a single strip or a band of small plaits straight up the back of the head from the nape to the crown. This can be seen on an anonymous woman's head found in Fishergate (*Corpus Signorum Imperii Romani – CSIR* 1.3, #7) and adopted by Aelia Aeliana and her daughter (*RIB* 682).

Empresses, however, did not have a monopoly on hair styles. Celtic fashion prevails with York's Decimina and her wavy hair parted in the middle and fashioned in two long braids loose down her back, partly over her ears. Scpronia Martina's hair is long and loose while her mother, Julia Brica, wears her hair without a parting and tied back at the nape.

The anonymous woman on a Micklegate tombstone has shoulder length hair (*CSIR* 1,3 # 54). York can boast a burial in which auburn ringlets have been found.

Other fascinating exhibits include:

'Millefiori' is Italian for 1,000 flowers. It denotes the fine and beautiful decoration formed by joining and stretching coloured strips of glass which are then cut to reveal a pattern. You can see an example of this on a Roman soldier's belt plate – third-century military 'bling'. This was found at 9 Blake Street.

Julius Alexander's salve for irritations: this domino-sized piece of stone found on the Mount is engraved with the words 'Julius Alexander's salve for irritations'. The words are in reverse, indicating that the stone was used in printing, and is one of only sixty such stamps found worldwide.

A water bucket found on Skeldergate, close to the River Ouse, near a 6 metre wood-lined well.

An unusual roofed coffin using roof tiles.

Two splendid vases; the one celebrating a good harvest, the other Dionysius – god of wine and orgiastic behaviour. Both were found in Apulia, Italy.

The magnificent head of Caracalla who came with his father, Septimius Severus, to Eboracum to learn how to be an emperor.

An example of a bronze diploma awarded to a retiring soldier. This granted citizenship and the right to marry to a soldier in the Fifth Cohort Raetorum under the command of Sextus Cornelius Dexter from Saldae in Mauretania.

A fragment showing two gladiators fighting, in incredible detail.

Another Mars, very different from the one in the doorway. As god of war it was extremely important to keep Mars on side to ensure victory and survival in battle.

Two examples of *Lares* – household gods – which were religiously observed in order to bring good fortune and safety to the household; they were integrated into the roofwork of the house.

The skull of a carnivorous man from a warm country. Osteoarchaeology tells us from his teeth and bones that this man, found in York at Trentholme Drive in 1951, was a meat-eater and lived in a warm climate – perhaps a Berber from Numidia travelling the empire as a mosaic maker from North Africa, the place where some of the finest Roman mosaics survive?

Another star exhibit is the large head of Constantine found in Stonegate.

We also can see a fan or parasol handle with an ivory catch with ivory ribs forming the frame protected by silver sheathing; the fan itself was probably made from leather. There are also lamps, keys, spoons and combs as well as pins and brooches and a lot of ceramics. The bone plaque inscribed 'Lord Victor, good luck and victory' found on the skeleton of a gladiator or charioteer is, of course, pagan.

Roman York and its Connectivity

Communications and connectivity were everything in the Roman world. Much of Rome's enduring success as world leader can be attributed to the Roman obsession with, and expertise in, road building, bridge building and its postal service. The fact that the site of Eboracum was at the confluence of two navigable rivers (leading eventually to the Humber and to the North Sea only some fifty miles to the east) would have been influential factors in the decision the Romans made to site their northern stronghold where they did. As with any occupying army, the Romans had to move men and supplies and they had to trade. The rivers Foss and Ouse were connected to the Humber, Trent and Fosse Dyke, which gave access to the Witham at Lincoln and the Nene at Peterborough and so to the fertile farmlands of East Anglia; they also brought materiel, supplies, food, weapons, soldiers and horses to the fortress quickly and efficiently. They fostered trade and provided a launching place for the deployment of soldiers in times of crisis or of routine defence or to go north to build roads, forts or defensive walls. The Romans, then, put their rivers to good use: shiploads of goods would have come in on the Ouse via the Humber from the North Sea, and on the Foss; two possible wharves on the east bank of the River Foss support this idea. We have already noted the large deposit of incinerated grain, found in a timber structure beneath modern-day Coney Street, on the north bank of the Ouse; it points to storehouses for the movement and storage of goods via the river.

One man who would have been familiar with this mercantile activity was Marcus Minucius Mudinus, *gubernator* (helmsman) of the VIth legion who worked on the cargo boats plying up and down the Ouse. His altar (*RIB* 613) found in Micklegate is dedicated to the 'Mother Goddess of Africa, Italy and Gaul' – adding a nice international flavour to the trade in and through York.

The Romans maintained four legions in Britain, in total about 20,000 soldiers supported by a further 20,000 auxiliaries, so deploying a full legion would on average entail moving around 5,000 men, their carts, mules and horses, equipment and supplies, and the extensive baggage train.

As well as the rivers, an efficient road system and supply chain was therefore required to support all of these needs. No doubt this volume of people and their encumbrances in some areas would clog up and damage trackways, bridges and fords making them difficult to use, often causing the column to be strung out and therefore vulnerable to attack. The ordinary Roman soldier carried all of his kit and weapons with him. This is where the Roman road comes in and, while not all road building was driven by military considerations and stretches of road were built to service farms, villas and other places with no military significance, the Roman army had to be able to move from A to B in the most expeditious way possible. It was not until the German Bundesautobahn network was initiated in the 1930s that anything like a comparable road scheme was completed; however, unlike in the Roman Empire, the military value to the Germans was limited as most major military transports in Nazi Germany were made by train to save fuel.

In almost four centuries of occupation the Romans built about 2,000 miles of roads in Britain with the aim of connecting key locations by the most direct possible route. The roads were all paved and all-season and all-weather, to permit heavy freight wagons to be used the year round.

Before the Romans came, Britain had few, if any, substantial bridges, so all rivers and streams would have been crossed by fords. Even well after the Romans had come and gone, many towns were at fording points, and the point nearest to the sea that a river could be forded was a major consideration in most journeys and military manoeuvres. In York the Ouse was bridged.

The Roman army was multi-skilled, with skilled soldiers who could quickly and efficiently construct bridges, plan and organise the building of defensive forts, signal stations and other structures in wood and stone; they could also build boats. Indeed, their skill sets were not so dissimilar to the mechanical engineering function of the Royal Electrical and Mechanical Engineers in the modern British Army. Ordinary soldiers were expected to build walls, camps and fortresses as required, competent as they were at digging, quarrying, cutting and shifting stone. Apart from military facilities, many villas and towns were built by the soldiery.

The roads we know involving York include:

> Dere Street leading north west from the city north through Clifton towards the site of Cataractonium (modern Catterick).
>
> Cade's Road west towards Petuaria (modern Brough).
>
> Ermine Street south towards Lindum (modern Lincoln).

A road bypassing the south wall of the fortress, between the fortress and the Ouse has not been formally tracked, although its path is thought to run beneath Museum Gardens. Other roads came in to York from Malton and Stamford Bridge; in all eleven roads are known to converge on the city, full details of which can be found at www.british-history.ac.uk/ rchme/york/vol1/

The initial road network was, of course, built by the army to facilitate military communications. The emphasis was on linking up army bases, rather than anything else. To that end, three important cross-routes were established connecting the major legionary bases by AD 80 as the frontier of the Roman-occupied zone advanced:

> Exeter (Isca) – Lincoln (Lindum)
> Gloucester (Glevum) – York (Eboracum)
> Caerleon (Isca) – York via Wroxeter (Viroconium) and Chester (Deva)

The roads leading into and out of Eboracum would have formed an integral part not just of the road network in Britannia but also of the empire-wide *cursus publicus*. Augustus formalised all routes of official communication when he established the *cursus publicus* (literally, the public way), a state-run courier and logistics service. Apart from acting as a means for distributing the general post, the *cursus* gave the legions the tactical opportunity to summon reinforcements and issue status reports before any situation got out of hand; slaves were also sent through the system.

Essentially, it was made up of thousands of posting stations (*mutationes* or *mansiones*) along the major road systems of the empire where horses were watered, shoed, cared for by vets, stabled, and passed over to dispatch riders (initially imperial *tabellarii* but later soldiers as the system became militarised). In 1969, the carved base of what was probably a milestone was found in the forecourt of the Eboracum *principia*.

Roman Streets In and Out of York

Today, three of York's main streets, Chapter House Street, Stonegate and Petergate, more or less trace the line of the two principal streets in the fortress, the *via praetoria* and the *via principalis* so we can see how the layout of the fortress has determined the layout of the modern city. The *via praetoria* led to the south-west gate (*porta praetoria*) where St Helen's Square now is, revealing that the fortress faced south west towards the River Ouse. The *via principalis* linked the gates on the north west and south-east sides – the *portae principales* – on the sites of Bootham Bar and King's Square. *The porta decumana* – a rear gate central on the north-east sides remains hidden under the medieval rampart. Bootham and Clifton follow the track of a road which issued from the north-west gate (*porta principalis dextra*) all the way to Cataractonium (Catterick). From the north-east gate (*porta decumana*), the road to Malton came via the Groves and Heworth golf course along the Malton Road to Malton (*Derventio*).

In March 2020, it was reported that archaeologists had discovered a previously unknown 'road' under the Guildhall which was being restored and redeveloped at the time. 'A silver coin and an abundance of Roman pottery' have been unearthed by YAT who tell us that: 'the excavation of new foundation trenches recently revealed an area of cobbled surface . . . buried over 1.5 m below modern street level.' The archaeologists conclude that the area may have been a yard or lane rather than a main road 'but its location was significant, as it was close to the projected location of the Roman crossing over the river' – in other words 'part of an important crossroad that once connected the fortress to the main approach from the south'.

Roman Life and
Culture in Roman York

If anything characterises Roman culture and interior design, it is the wall painting and the quintessentially Roman mosaic. In York, the big houses, villas and *mansiones*, continued to be built into the late third to early fourth century, evidenced by the remains of town houses decorated with mosaic pavements. Where there are mosaics there is, or was, money. We have evidence of town houses with mosaic floors at St Mary, Castlegate and in Aldwark, Bar Lane, Toft Green and Clementhorpe. Particularly impressive is the extensive, high-end town house in Bishophill built in the late third century; it can boast at least two ranges of rooms around a central courtyard.

The Mosaic With a Woman's Head

This impressive section of flooring, probably the floor of a corridor, boasts complex patterns and a woman's face staring straight back at you. The pupils of her eyes are made from single pieces of rounded black jet and her right cheekbone and the side of her nose are highlighted in white. It was found beneath a medieval church floor in Aldwark; her gaze into the future is probably one of the most memorable vestiges of Roman York.

The Ophiotaurus

A fabulous creation: a fantastic sea creature from a mosaic found in Toft Green. According to its sole classical reference in Ovid's *Fasti* (3.793 ff), the Ophiotaurus (Οφιόταυρος Serpent Bull) was powerful enough to enable whoever slew it and then burnt its entrails to bring down the gods no less. The monster was killed by an ally of the Titans during the Titanomachy, but the entrails were retrieved by an eagle sent by Zeus before they could be burned. The creature had emerged from Chaos with Gaia and Ouranos. If anything was going to impress your visitors and dinner guests then this piece of fabulous decoration was it – a guaranteed conversation starter and certain to provoke dining room envy.

The Four Seasons Mosaic

Another conversation piece. The magnificent 'Four Seasons Mosaic' was uncovered in 1853 in the course of drainage work at Tanner Row. Three other mosaics were also found in the same house, obviously suggesting someone very wealthy lived there. A coin of the emperor Claudius Gothicus was discovered underneath it, thereby telling us that the mosaic must have been laid down during or after his reign (268–270).

The mosaic depicts the head and shoulders of Medusa who is surrounded by the four seasons. Medusa was a popular image in Roman homes: her petrifying ability to turn people to stone was thought to ward off evil. The four seasons are each shown with emblems associated with their particular season. Spring is depicted with a bird, summer with a bunch of grapes, autumn with a rake and winter with a bare branch. The grapes, though, have caused some controversy. It is now believed that the original summer depiction was of 'fruit and foliage' – the grapes being the work of nineteenth-century conservationists rather than Roman mosaic makers. Unfortunately, the well-intentioned conservationists sacrificed summer fruits with something more closely associated with the characteristic 'mellow fruitfulness' of autumn.

A section of wall painting can be seen in the crypt under York Minster.

In Search of a Palace and an Amphitheatre

Did York have an imperial palace? Did it have an amphitheatre for gladiatorial games and the ritual slaughter of criminals, prisoners and nonconformists, especially Christians? The answer is probably yes – in both cases.

The palace?

So where was the tantalising imperial palace built to keep emperors Severus, Constantius and Constantine in the manner to which they were accustomed? Aelius Spartianus, in the admittedly unreliable *Scriptores Historiae Augustae*, describes Severus when at York living in a *palatium* (palace) and in a *domus palatine* (*Severus* 22,7). Do we believe him or was he just making an assumption or, worse, making it up? Severus certainly had to have somewhere roomy enough to accommodate that huge retinue, and in which to woo the local hangers-on who would have swarmed round.

The Search for the Missing Amphitheatre, King's Manor, 2017

It may not just be Richard III who suffered the indignity of being buried under what became a city car park. York's undiscovered and hitherto elusive amphitheatre may also be languishing under a similarly mundane public amenity. Two other British legionary fortresses, Chester and Caerleon, each boast an amphitheatre, and a cemetery on the Mount appears to have been the burial ground for scores of gladiators. However, as yet, conclusive archaeological evidence for an amphitheatre in Eboracum remains elusive. It may, though, be under the car park at King's Manor. Stewart Ainsworth, Chester University archaeologist and part of Channel 4's *Time Team* fame asserts: '[York is] a massive legionary presence. It should have an amphitheatre – it will have one, it just hasn't been found in my opinion.'

Tim Sutherland, a specialist on battlefields and archaeology at the University of York, also became convinced that the King's Manor site could have been where the amphitheatre lies when he noticed that the surrounding buildings had, over the years, tilted in the direction of a depression. 'We need to know what the hollow is,' he said. 'We are hoping to start something that could become very big news indeed.' The team used ground-penetrating radar to look underneath King's Manor for evidence of an amphitheatre.

A fragment from about AD 160 from a samian mortarium shows two gladiators fighting, in incredible detail. It is now in the Yorkshire Museum and although it is not proof of the existence of an amphitheatre, the piece shows just how universal gladiatorial combat scenes were in the Roman world.

That discovery of decapitated male skeletons in the cemetery in Driffield Terrace has lent weight and credence to the belief that an amphitheatre flourished nearby. Evidence is pointing to the conclusion that these were gladiators who had been decapitated. Here is a summary of that evidence, most of which relies heavily on a report by the York Archaeological Trust (YAT 2015). The burials took place during the second and third centuries AD, perhaps into the fourth.

Things got interesting in 2004–5, when eighty-two inhumations and fourteen cremated burials were excavated at 3 and 6 Driffield Terrace; all were young male adults on whom cuts to the neck bones of forty individuals (around forty-eight per cent) suggested they had been decapitated, although the number of decapitations could have been higher. The severed heads of a number of individuals had been placed in the graves in unusual positions, such as near the feet.

Twenty-five of the decapitations exhibited a single cut to the neck. Multiple cut marks on some of the skeletons suggested that the victim was relatively still at the time of assault and the majority of blows were delivered from behind, soon after death. As well as the decapitations, there were three cases of unhealed blade injuries, two to the backs of the hands and one to the femur. Three individuals had cuts to the neck. There was also evidence of large carnivore bite marks on one individual, maybe from a bear, lion or tiger? Kurt Hunter-Mann adds in his *Driffield Terrace: An Insight Report* (2015) that the decapitations were 'remarkable' because

> In the rest of Roman Britain, the prevalence of decapitations is about 5% (mostly in rural contexts), usually from the front and probably some time after death. In many cases the decapitations were achieved with a single blow, but more than one cut was involved in a number of cases, 11 in one instance. However, the complete removal of the head was not always the primary aim, as in some instances the cut was not complete and the head apparently remained attached to the body.

Hunter-Mann reveals that most of the deceased seem to have taken a savage beating or have been tortured before death:

> Nearly a third of the adults had one or more fractured teeth, mostly upper front teeth and molars (back teeth). The majority of the upper tooth fractures were on the left side, indicating a blow from a right-handed opponent wielding a blunt object. The back tooth fractures were more evenly distributed and can be attributed to blows delivered to the chin or to teeth clenching. Thirteen individuals had healed cranial trauma, and there were a couple of cases of possible peri-mortem blunt force injuries to the cranium. Trauma to the rest of the body included a fractured scapula blade; several fractures of vertebral processes; a healed blade cut to the left thigh; two fibula fractures; and five metacarpal fractures, all in the right hand. There was also a high prevalence of broken ribs. Fractured clavicles, wrists, ulnas and a vertebra suggest injuries due to falls, whereas fractures and soft tissue injuries evident in the feet and ankles indicate twisted ankles. Stress injuries indicative of an active, athletic even, lifestyle were also common.

YAT reveals that finds include an unusual pair of iron rings around the ankles of one young male between 26 and 35 which cannot be fetters; other material was found including a set of miniature silver smiths' tongs which may have been offerings. His bones revealed a life punctuated by injury as well as one that might have caused considerable chronic pain due to a growth in his right scapula. His injuries included skull fractures, soft tissue damage to his right hand, and a broken left leg. At the time of his death he had an active chest infection.

Were the skeletons those of gladiators, soldiers, criminals or slaves? YAT concludes:

> The high proportion of younger adult males and frequency of violent trauma could indicate they were gladiators. The demographic profile at Driffield Terrace most closely resembles a burial ground of the 2nd and 3rd century AD at Ephesus, in ancient Greece. Excavated in 1993, this has been interpreted as a burial ground for gladiators.

They were probably not slaves as the skeletons were found in a cemetery for the relatively well off. Soldiers they could well have been as the deceased all complied with the minimum height in force for recruitment.

Few of the burials included grave goods. Some had complete pottery vessels, pairs of hobnailed shoes; a bone hairpin, a miniature silver tong and some glass sherds, a bridle cheek-piece, a copper alloy pelta mount, an iron pen nib or goad and a fragment of pipeclay figurine. The odd single animal bone indicated a joint of meat, to keep the occupant going on his journey to the afterlife; the masses of horse bone deposited in two graves were also grave goods.

Timeline: Rome – Britannia – York

As stated in the Introduction, nothing in Roman York, or in Britannia for that matter, happened in historical isolation. Much, if not all, that occurred in Roman York was a direct consequence of an event, political decision or aspect of foreign policy which happened or was formulated in Rome and thence disseminated to the various provinces of the empire for local implementation. This timeline will show the interrelationship between Rome, Britannia and York.

55–54 BC: Julius Caesar invades Britain.

37–41 AD: Caligula emperor; Cunobelinus was ruling most of south-east England.

41–54: Emperor Claudius.

43–49: Invasion of Britain by Claudius and Aulus Plautius. Conquest of Southern Britain. Brigantes become a client kingdom allied to Rome.

43 (August): The Romans capture the capital of the Catuvellauni tribe, Colchester.

44 (June): The Romans take the hills forts of Dorset, including Maiden Castle.

47: The Romans force their allies, the Iceni tribe of East Anglia, to surrender their weapons. The Iceni resist but their revolt is short lived.

48: The Romans have now conquered all territory between the Humber estuary and the Severn estuary. Parts that remain under British control include Dumnonii (Cornwell and Devon), Wales and North West England.

49: The Romans found a *colonia* at Colchester for retired soldiers – the first civilian centre of Roman Britain and, for a time, the capital.

51: The leader of the exiled Catuvellauni tribe, Caratacus, is captured. He had led a long guerrilla war against the Roman forces for years, but was eventually defeated by the Roman governor Publius Ostorius Scapula. Caratacus spent the remainder of his days in in Italy.

54–68: Emperor Nero.

60: The Romans attack the druid stronghold of Anglesey. The campaign to occupy Wales was cut short by the Iceni revolt in south-east England.

61: After attempting to fully annexe East Anglia, Boudica leads a rebellion against the Romans. After razing Colchester, London and St Albans, Boudica was eventually defeated at the Battle of Watling Street.

68–69: The Brigantes break with Rome.

69–79: Vespasian emperor.

71–72: IX Legion installed at York: Eboracum wooden fortress built.

71–74: Petillius Cerialis defeats the Brigantes.

75: The palace at Fishbourne built.

78–85: Agricola governor.

80: London now houses a forum, *basilica*, governor's palace and probably even an amphitheatre.

79–83: Agricola's campaigns in northern Britain and Caledonia.

c. 80: Eboracum fortress strengthened.

84: The Romans do battle with the Caledonians at Mons Graupius, somewhere in modern-day Aberdeenshire.

90–96: Foundation of *colonia* at Lindum; Inchtuthil abandoned; Gleva fortress built.

98–117: Emperor Trajan; he orders a complete withdrawal from Scotland and the construction of a new frontier between Newcastle-on-Tyne and Carlisle.

100: Many of the 8,000 miles of Roman roads in Britain are completed, allowing troops and goods to travel easily across the country.

107–8: Eboracum fortress rebuilt in stone.

117–138: Emperor Hadrian.

c. 117: Roman defeat, heavy casualties.

122: Hadrian in Britain.

122–128: To strengthen the border between Roman-occupied Britain and Scotland, Hadrian orders the famous wall to be built. Significantly, many of the early forts along Hadrian's Wall face south into the intractable Brigantes' territory, showing the ongoing threat they posed.

c. 122: VIth Legion replaces IXth Legion.

125–130: Major fire in London.

139–140: The Antonine Wall built, dramatically shifting Rome's northern border. It is built of earth and timber, strengthened by a series of forts.

155: St Albans, one of the largest towns in Roman Britain, is destroyed by fire.

155–158: The Antonine Wall is abandoned and Roman troops withdraw back to Hadrian's Wall. Perhaps an uprising by the Brigantes was the cause, or the Antonine smallpox plague?

165–180: Antonine smallpox plague ravages the Roman army and civilian population empire-wide.

182: The Brigantes, along with tribes of southern Scotland and northern England, rise again against the Romans. Fighting continued for years along Hadrian's Wall, with towns further south building precautionary preventative defences.

193–211: Emperor Septimius Severus.

193–7: Albinus, governor of Britain, attempts to become emperor, taking the army of Britain to the continent; Hadrian's Wall overrun.

197: Destruction of York's fortress by the Maeatae: subsequent rebuilding; Hadrian's Wall fortified.

197: Severus defeats Albinus near Lyons.

208–11: Severus in Britain: political and military administration reorganised. Caledonia invaded.

211: Severus dies in York; area between the two walls now a protectorate – Britain is divided up into two separate provinces; the south called 'Britannia Superior' ('superior' indicating that it was closer to Rome), with the north called 'Britannia Inferior'. London the new capital of the south, with York the capital of the north. The adjacent civil town becomes a *colonia*.

211–217: Emperor Marcus Antoninus.

250–271: Plague of Cyprian assails the Roman Empire.

250 onwards: New threats to Britannia emerge from the Picts from Scotland, as well as the Angles, Saxon and Jutes from Germany and Scandinavia.

259: Britain, Gaul and Spain secede from the Roman Empire, creating the so-called 'Gallic Empire'.

274: The Gallic Empire is re-absorbed into the main Roman Empire.

284: Diocletian introduces the system of two *Augusti* and two *Caesars*.

287: The admiral of the Roman Channel fleet, Carausius, declares himself Emperor of Britain and Northern Gaul, and starts minting his own coins.

293: Carausius is assassinated by his treasurer, Allectus, who starts to build his palace in London to strengthen his claim to authority. He also builds the famous 'Saxon Shore Forts' along the coasts of Britain, both to strengthen defences against the Germanic tribes to the east but also to prevent Rome from sending a fleet to reclaim Britain for the empire.

296: The Roman Empire retakes Britannia and Allectus is killed in battle near Silchester. Britain is then divided into four provinces; Maxima Caesariensis (northern England up to Hadrian's Wall), Britannia Prima (the south of England), Flavia Caesariensis (the Midlands and East Anglia) and Britannia Secunda (Wales).

293: Constantius I (Chlorus) *Caesar* of the West.

296: Constantius Caesar defeats Allectus and retakes Britain. Northern tribes overrun northern half of Roman Britain. York and Chester destroyed: subsequently rebuilt.

300: Hadrian's Wall increasingly dilapidated. Repaired and rebuilt. New military command – *Dux Britanniarum* – in charge of the field army. HQ in York.

306: Constantius I defeats the Picts and invades Caledonia. Death of Constantius I at York. Constantine proclaimed emperor.

313: Edict of Milan grants tolerance to Christian Church.

314: Christianity now legal in the Roman Empire, thanks to Constantine amongst others; Bishop of York at Council of Arles.

343: Emperor Constans visits Britain.

364–369: Major raids by Picts, Scots, Attacotti and Saxon pirates. Hadrian's Wall rebuilt.

367–383: Emperor Gratian.

367–369: Combined raids by Saxons, Picts and Scots. Hadrian's Wall outflanked. Fullofaudes, Duke of Britain, routed. Count Theodosius in Britain – repairs wall.

383–388: Usurpation by Magnus Maximus, commander in Britain, who conquers Gaul and Spain.

388: Magnus Maximus defeated by Theodosia at Aquileia.

395–423: Emperor Honorius; Sertorius reorganises Britain; troops being withdrawn.

396: Massive barbarian attacks on Britain resume. Large naval engagements are ordered against the invaders, with reinforcements arriving from other parts of the empire.

399: Peace is fully restored throughout Britannia.

401: Many troops are withdrawn from Britain to assist with the war against the Goths led by Alaric I, who is intent on sacking Rome.

407: The remaining Roman garrisons in Britain proclaim one of their generals, Constantine III, Emperor of the Western Roman Empire. Constantine quickly levies an army and crosses the English Channel to invade Gaul and Spain, leaving Britain with only a skeleton force to defend itself.

410: With more and more incursions from the Saxons, Scots, Picts and Angles, Britannia turns to the Roman emperor Honorius for help. He responds, telling them to 'look to their own defences' and refuses to send any aid. This effectively marked the end of Roman Britain.

Appendixes

1. Select List of Roman Emperors
2. Governors of Britannia: AD 43–97
3. Roman Units Serving in Britannia
4. The Roman Britain Sat Navs
5. Ermine Street and York
6. York's Medieval Churches Built Using Roman Masonry
7. The York Historic Pageant: the Roman Bits
8. References to Ebo(u)racum in *RIB*
9. Typical *cursus honorum* in the First Century AD
10. Roman Assemblies
11. The Etymology of Eburacum
12. The Antonine Plague
13. The Plague of Cyprian
14. Roman York – More Interesting Facts

Appendix 1

Select List of Roman Emperors

Emperors from Augustus to Constantine

Emperor	Reign
Augustus (Imp. Caesar Augustus)	27 BC–AD 14
Tiberius (Ti. Caesar Augustus)	AD 14–37
Gaius / Caligula (C. Caesar Augustus Germanicus)	37–41
Claudius (Ti. Claudius Caesar Augustus Germanicus)	41–54
Nero (Imp. Nero Claudius Caesar Augustus Germanicus)	54–68
Galba (Ser. Sulpicius Galba Imp. Caesar Augustus)	68–69
Otho (Imp. M. Otho Caesar Augustus)	69
Vitellius (A. Vitellius Augustus Germanicus Imp.)	69
Vespasian (Imp. Caesar Vespasianus Augustus)	69–79
Titus (Imp. Titus Caesar Vespasianus Augustus)	79–81
Domitian (Imp. Caesar Domitianus Augustus)	81–96
Nerva (Imp. Caesar Nerva Augustus)	96–98
Trajan (Imp. Caesar Nerva Traianus Augustus)	98–117
Hadrian (Imp. Caesar Traianus Hadrianus Augustus)	117–138
Antoninus Pius (Imp. Caesar T. Aelius Hadrianus Antoninus Augustus Pius)	138–161
Marcus Aurelius (Imp. Caesar M. Aurelius Antoninus Augustus)	161–180
Lucius Verus (Imp. Caesar L. Aurelius Verus Augustus)	161–169
Commodus (Imp. Caesar M. Aurelius Commodus Antoninus Augustus)	176–192
Pertinax (Imp. Caesar P. Helvius Pertinax Augustus)	193

Emperor	Reign
Didius Julianus (Imp. Caesar M. Didius Severus Julianus Augustus)	193
Septimius Severus (Imp. Caesar L. Septimius Severus Pertinax Augustus)	193–211
Clodius Albinus (Imp. Caesar D. Clodius Septimius Albinus Augustus)	193–197
Pescennius Niger (Imp. Caesar C. Pescennius Niger Justus Augustus)	193–194
Caracalla (Imp. Caesar M. Aurelius Antoninus Augustus)	198–217
Geta (Imp. Caesar P. Septimius Geta Augustus)	209–211
Macrinus (Imp. Caesar M. Opellius Macrinus Augustus)	217–218
Diadumenianus (Imp. Caesar M. Opellius Antoninus Diadumenianus Augustus)	218
Elagabal (Imp. Caesar M. Aurelius Antoninus Augustus)	218–222
Severus Alexander (Imp. Caesar M. Aurelius Severus Alexander Augustus)	222–235
Maximinus (Imp. Caesar C. Julius Verus Maximinus Augustus)	235–238
Gordian I (Imp. Caesar M. Antonius Gordianus Sempronianus Romanus Africanus Senior Augustus)	238
Gordian II (Imp. Caesar M. Antonius Gordianus Sempronianus Africanus Iunior Augustus)	238
Balbinus (Imp. Caesar D. Caelius Calvinus Balbinus Augustus)	238
Pupienus (Imp. Caesar M. Clodius Pupienus Augustus)	238
Gordian III (Imp. Caesar M. Antonius Gordianus Augustus)	238–244
Philip (Imp. Caesar M. Julius Philippus Augustus)	244–249

Emperor	Reign
Decius (Imp. Caesar C. Messius Quintus Traianus Decius Augustus)	249–251
Trebonianus Gallus (Imp. Caesar C. Vibius Trebonianus Gallus Augustus)	251–253
Volusianus (Imp. Caesar C. Vibius Afinius Gallus Veldumianus Volusianus Augustus)	251–253
Aemilianus (Imp. Caesar M. Aemilius Aemilianus Augustus)	253
Valerian (Imp. Caesar P. Licinius Valerianus Augustus)	253–260
Gallienus (Imp. Caesar P. Licinius Egnatius Gallienus Augustus)	253–268
Claudius II (Imp. Caesar M. Aurelius Claudius Augustus)	268–270
Quintillus (Imp. Caesar M. Aurelius Claudius Quintillus Augustus)	270
Aurelian (Imp. Caesar Domitius Aurelianus Augustus)	270–275
Tacitus (Imp. Caesar M. Claudius Tacitus Augustus)	275–276
Florianus (Imp. Caesar M. Annius Florianus Augustus)	276
Probus (Imp. Caesar M. Aurelius Probus Augustus)	276–282
Carus (Imp. Caesar M. Aurelius Carus Augustus)	282–283
Carinus (Imp. Caesar M. Aurelius Carinus Augustus)	283–285
Numerianus (Imp. Caesar M. Aurelius Numerius Numerianus Augustus)	283–284
Diocletian (Imp. Caesar C. Aurelius Valerius Diocletianus Augustus)	284–305
Maximian (Imp. Caesar M. Aurelius Valerius Maximianus Augustus)	286–305
Constantius (Imp. Caesar Flavius Valerius Constantius Augustus)	305–306

Emperor	Reign
Galerius (Imp. Caesar C. Galerius Valerius Maximianus Augustus)	305–311
Severus (Flavius Valerius Severus Augustus)	306–307
Maxentius (M. Aurelius Valerius Maxentius Augustus)	306–312
Constantine (Imp. Caesar Flavius Valerius Constantinus Augustus)	307–337
Licinius (Imp. Caesar Valerius Licinianus Licinius Augustus)	308–324
Maximin (C. Valerius Galerius Maximinus Augustus)	308/9–313

Emperors from Diocletian to Romulus

Emperor West	Reign	Emperor East	Reign
Maximian	C. 285–286, A. 286-305, 307–310	Diocletian	A. 284–305
Constantius I	C. 293–305, A. 305–306	Galerius	C. 293–305, A. 305–311
Constantine	C. 306–308, A. 308–337	Maximian	C. 305–308, A. 308–313
Severus	A. 306–307		
Maxentius	A. 307–312	Licinius	A. 308–324
		Licinianus	C. 317–323
Crispus	C. 317–325	Martinianus	C. 324
		Constantine	A. 324–337
Constantine II	C. 317–337, A. 337–340	Constantius II	C. 324–337, A. 337–361
Constans	C. 333–337, A. 337–350		
Dalmatius	C. 335–337	Gallus	C. 350–354
Constantius II	A. 351–361		
Julian	C. 355–360, A. 360–363	Julian	A. 361–363

Emperor West	Reign	Emperor East	Reign
Jovian	A. 363–364	Jovian	A. 363–364
Valentinian I	A. 364–375	Valens	A. 364–378
Gratian	A. 375–383		
Maximus	A. 383–387	Theodosius I	A. 379–395
Valentinian II	A. 383–392		
Theodosius I	A. 394–395		
Honorius	A. 395–423	Arcadius	A. 395–408
Constantius III	A. 421	Theodosius II	A. 408–450
Valentinian III	A. 425–455	Marcian	A. 450–457
Petronius Maximus	A. 455		
Avitus	A. 455–456		
Majorian	A. 457–461	Leo I	A. 457–474
Libius Severus	A. 461–465		
Anthemius	A. 467–472		
Olybrius	A. 472		
Glycerius	A. 473		
Julius Nepos	A. 473–480	Leo II	A. 474
Romulus	A. 475–476	Zeno	A. 474–491
		Anastasius	A. 491–518
		Justin I	A. 518–527
		Justinian	A. 527–565
		Justin II	A. 565–578
		Tiberius Constantine	C. 574–578, A. 578–582
		Maurice	A. 582–602

Appendix 2

Governors of Britannia: AD 43–97

Britannia was a consular province, so its governors had first to serve as a consul in Rome before they could be governor.

Claudian governors

Aulus Plautius (43–47)
Publius Ostorius Scapula (47–52)
Aulus Didius Gallus (52–57)
Quintus Veranius (57)
Gaius Suetonius Paulinus (58–62)
Publius Petronius Turpilianus (62–63)
Marcus Trebellius Maximus (63–69)

Flavian governors

Marcus Vettius Bolanus (69–71)
Quintus Petillius Cerialis (71–74)
Sextus Julius Frontinus (74–78), also a military writer
Gnaeus Julius Agricola (78–84), conqueror of Caledonia
Sallustius Lucullus (c. 84–c. 89)
Aulus Vicirius Proculus (fl. 93)
Publius Metilius Nepos (c. 96–c. 97)

Appendix 3

Roman Units Serving in Britannia

The Roman Legions of Britain

Legio II *Augusta* – The Second Augustan Legion

Legio II *Adiutrix Pia Fidelis* – The Second Legion, the Rescuer, Loyal and Faithful

Legio VI *Victrix* – The Sixth Victorious Legion

Legio VII *Gemina* – The Seventh Twin Legion

Legio VIII *Augusta* – The Eighth Augustan Legion

Legio IX *Hispana* – The Ninth Spanish Legion

Legio XIV *Gemina* – The Fourteenth Twin Legion

Legio XX *Valeria* – The Twentieth Legion, Valiant and Victorious

Legio XXII *Deiotariana* – The Twenty-Second Deiotarian Legion

Legio XXII *Primigenia* – The Twenty-Second Firstborn Legion

Selected Auxiliary Cavalry Wings (*alae*) of Britain

This gives a good picture of the diverse provenance of the *alae*:

Ala I Hispanorum Asturum – The first Spanish Wing of Astures

Ala Gallorum Indiana – Indus' Wing of Gauls

Ala I Herculaea – The first Herculean Wing

Ala I Thracum – The first Wing of Thracians

Ala I Tungrorum – The First Tungrian Wing

Ala Hispanorum Vettonum – The Spanish Wing of Vettones

Ala Augusta Vocontiorum – The August Wing of Vocontii

Formations, Mounted Units, Companies and Detachments – and Source

Cuneus Frisiavonum Vercovicensium – The Formation of Frisians from Vercovicium

Equites Catafractariorum – The Heavily Armoured Horsemen

Equites Crispianorum – The Crispian Horsemen

Equites Dalmatarum Branodunensium – The Dalmatian Horsemen of Branodunum

Equites stablesianorum Gariannonensium – The Horsemen from the Stables at Gariannum

Milites Tungrecanorum – The Soldiers of the Tungrecani

Numerus Defensorum – The Company of Guards

Numerus Directorum – The Company of Upright Men

Numerus Equitum Sarmatarum – The Company of Sarmatian Horsemen

Numerus Exploratorum Bremenio – The Company of Scouts from Bremenium

Numerus Exploratorum Habitanco – The Company of Scouts from Habitancum

Numerus Fortensium – The Company of Brave Men

Numerus Hnaudifridi – The Company of Hnaudifridius

Numerus Longovicanorum – The Company from Longovicium

Numerus Maurorum Aurelianorum – The Company of Aurelian's own Mauri

Numerus Superventientium Petueriensium – The Company of Newcomers from Petuaria

Numerus Syrorum Saggitariorum – The Company of Syrian Archers

Numerus Barcariorum Tigrisiensium – The Company of Tigris Bargemen

Numerus Vigilum – The Company of Watchmen

Venatores Bannienses – The Hunters from Banna

Vexillatio Germanorum Voredis – The Detachment of Germans from Voreda

Vexillatio Equitata Provincae Germaniae – The part-mounted Detachment from the German Provinces

Vexillatio Raetorum et Noricorum – The Detachment from Raetia and Noricum

Vexillatio Sueborum Longovicanorum – The Detachment of Suebi from Longovicium

The information above owes everything to M. G. Jarrett 'Non-legionary troops in Roman Britain: Part One, The Units' *Britannia* Volume XXV. The definitive list of British auxiliary units.

Appendix 4

The Roman Britain Sat Navs

The following maps and road maps help us to understand the relative geographical position of Britannia and the impressive road system on the islands. York's crucial position in this is made all the clearer.

The Peutinger Map

Tabula Peutingeriana – The Peutinger Map is an illustrated *itinerarium* (ancient Roman road map) showing the layout of the *cursus publicus*, the road network of the Roman Empire.

The map is a thirteenth-century parchment copy of a possible Roman original. It covers Europe (without the Iberian Peninsula and the British Isles), North Africa, and parts of Asia, including the Middle East, Persia, and India. The *Tabula* originates from the map prepared by Marcus Vipsanius Agrippa, the Roman general, architect, and friend of Emperor Augustus. After Agrippa's death in 12 BC, that map was engraved in marble and put on display in the Porticus Vipsania in the Campus Agrippae area in Rome, near the Ara Pacis building.

The Antonine Itinerary

The Antonine Itinerary (*Itinerarium Antonini Augusti*, 'The Itinerary of the Emperor Antoninus') is a register of the 225 stations and distances along various roads based on official documents; it describes the roads of the Roman Empire. Owing to the scarcity of other extant records of this type, it is an invaluable historical record.

The title has led this to be ascribed to Antoninus Pius (r. 138–161), but this cannot be so. The British section, crucially, is titled *Iter Britanniarum*; Britanniarum is plural, indicating that the collection was put together after Britain was divided into two provinces by Septimius Severus c. 197 (Rivet and Smith, 1979, p. 154). Almost nothing is known of its date or author, although it is likely that the original edition was compiled over nearly two centuries. The oldest extant copy has been assigned to the time of Diocletian and the most likely imperial patron – if the work had one – would have been Caracalla.

The British section, the *Iter Britanniarum*, is *the* 'road map' of Roman Britain (although it includes less than twenty-five per cent of all the roads in Roman Britain), one of fifteen such itineraries applying to different geographic areas around the empire. The itinerary measures distances in Roman miles.

What was its purpose? Some say it shows routes of the *cursus publicus* (the imperial postal service); others assert that they are routes of journeys planned for emperors or their armies. Nicholas Reed has given the most plausible explanation; he argues that the itineraries are a collection of routes to be used for the collection of *annona militaris*, a tax of food and supplies originally imposed by Septimius Severus to provide for the Roman army. Casado sums this up:

> This would explain the arbitrary way in which the routes contained in the document were selected, and would also account for the strange 'detour-type' layouts chosen, on some occasions, to link two cities relatively close to each other, when the second city is reached after passing through other places that would have made the route much longer than was really necessary.

Here are the four sections of the *Iter* which involve Eboracum:

Iter I Breenium (High Rochester) to Brough via Corbridge, Aldborough, York intersecting with Itera II, V

Iter II Bratobulgium (Barrens) to Rutupiae (Richborough) via Carlisle, Aldborough, York, Chester, Wroxeter, St Albans, London, Canterbury intersecting with Itera I, III, IV, V

Iter V Londinium to Luguvalium (Carlisle) via London, Colchester, Caistor, Lincoln, York, Aldborough, Carlisle intersecting with Itera I, II, IX

Iter VIII Eboracum to Londinium via York, Lincoln, Leicester, St Albans, London

The Ravenna Cosmography

Ravennatis Anonymi Cosmographia, 'The Cosmography of the Unknown Ravennese', is a list of place names covering the known world from India to Ireland, compiled by an anonymous cleric in Ravenna around AD 700.

The naming of places in Roman Britain has traditionally depended on Ptolemy's *Geography*, the *Antonine Itinerary* and the *Peutinger Table*, as the *Cosmography* was notoriously corrupt and unreliable – the lists of place names being haphazard to say the least. However, the *Cosmography* is more comprehensive than the other documents. When archaeological investigations began to uncover sites that had evidence of occupation in the Roman period, the *Antonine Itinerary* and Richard of Cirencester's *De Situ Britanniae* were increasingly used to corroborate entries, until, that is, Richard's work was found to be an eighteenth-century hoax. The *Cosmography* remained relatively impenetrable until the mid-twentieth century.

In 1949, Sir Ian Richmond and O. G. S. Crawford published a paper originally submitted to *Archaeologia*, which suggested that the sources for the document had included maps or road books, and that many place names described geographical features. The book was seen as a significant advance in the study both of the document and of Romano-British place names; A. L. F. Rivet and Colin Smith published their landmark *The Place-Names of Roman Britain* in 1979.

Ptolemy's World Map – Britain

Ptolemy's *Prima Europe Tabula*. The Ptolemy world map is a map of the world as known to Hellenistic society in c. 150 BC and is one of the earliest surviving copies of Ptolemy's second-century map of the British Isles. Originally published in Ptolemy's *Geographia*, this is the second issue of the 1482 map, printed at Ulm, which was the first woodcut map of the British Isles and the first to be printed outside Italy. It is dated 1486 and in the National Library of Wales.

Based on an inscription in several of the earliest surviving manuscripts, it is traditionally credited to Agathodaemon of Alexandria and so is not really by Ptolemy.

Appendix 5

Ermine Street and York

The following is from *Roman Roads in Britain* by Thomas Codrington, published by the Society for Promoting Christian Knowledge, London, 1903; it covers those reaches of Ermine Street which impinge on Eboracum. Starting in London, the road heads into Lincoln via Godmanchester and Caistor, then over the Humber estuary up to York via Tadcaster.

(8) Tadcaster to York

Tadcaster is no doubt the site of the Roman Calcaria, which must have been at Castle Hill on the south-west of the river Wharfe. The river was probably crossed to the north of the church in the line of an old street on the east of the river. About half-a-mile from Tadcaster the Roman road appears a quarter of a mile north of the modern York road as a wide grass-grown farm road, at one part with a hedge on one side only, and so continues in a straight line for a mile and a half with a parish boundary along it. It was formerly called 'The Old Street'. At Street Houses the present road takes the line, but soon leaves it, the parish boundary continuing . . . on across fields without any other trace of the old road for a mile, and then a lane with a parish boundary along it continues the line to Queen's Arms Inn. There the present road rejoins the old road, which kept on the ridge of high ground crossed by the Great Northern Railway about two miles from York. Parish boundaries follow the road for two miles from Queen's Arms, making seven miles of parish boundaries along the nine miles of road from Tadcaster to York. Blossom Street and Micklegate Bar are probably on the line of the Roman road, pointing one to Stonegate, the street which passes through the Roman city Eboracum on the east side of the river Ouse. The original rectangle seems to have been about 550 yards from south-west to north-east, and if Stonegate represents the middle street, about 470 yards from north-west to south-east. The breadth in this direction is, however, sometimes stated to be 650 yards, the position of the Roman wall on the south -east being uncertain.

(9) York to Stamford Bridge and Malton: Wade's Causeway

From the south-east gate of York a Roman road followed the course of the present road along a ridge of ground rising above the moors and curving round to Stamford Bridge . . . at the beginning of the last century it was visible in Cawthorne village, and was very distinct on approaching Cawthorne camps – a remarkable group of camps situated on a high ridge (650') overlooking a deep valley on the north. There are four camps; the most westerly is rectangular, with a double ditch, and measures 133 yards by 120 yards from crest to crest of the rampart ... . The course of the Roman road northwards from these camps is much plainer. It is called Wade's Causeway, the story being that a giant of that name made it for his wife's convenience in going to the moors to milk her cows. The general course of the road for two and three-quarters miles appears to have been laid out in a straight line from the west of the Roman camps (650') to a point (825') on Pickering Moor, a quarter of a mile to the north of Stape.

(11) York to the North-east and North

A Roman road probably left York in a line with Stonegate, following the course of the present Malton road, along which there are some lengths of parish boundary. It must have joined a Roman road shown on Warburton's map from the north of Stamford Bridge, through Sutton-le-Forest, Easingwold, Thirsk, and Northallerton, and joining Erming Street on the north of Catterick. It is marked by Warburton on his map as visible through Thormanby and by Thirsk to Northallerton, and he mentions it in a letter to Gale as more entire from Easingwold to Thirsk. It was faintly distinguishable at the beginning of last century between Thirsk and Northallerton, and there seem to have been some remains between the latter town and Catterick. The only trace now appears to be the road called 'The Street', passing through Old Thirsk in the direction of Easingwold.

Another road left York by what is now Bootham Bar, outside which many Roman interments have been found. Boundaries run along the road for about a mile from York, and in places further on along the road and across country in the direction of Easingwold, where it probably joined the road last mentioned. Drake continued the road by Newburgh to the Hambleton Hills and Teesmouth. Another Roman road seems to have branches northwards from the Thirsk and Catterick road near Thornton-le-Street. At about two and a half miles north of the latter place a parish boundary begins to follow a lane, first for two miles, and then on in the same line for half-a-mile, then nearly the same line is taken up by a lane and a parish boundary to Bullamoor, and after a break of one and a quarter miles, boundaries continue in a straight line from Hallikeld for five miles to the Wiske river, lanes following the same line for most of the way. After a gap of a quarter of a mile the line is taken up by a lane, joined in five-eighths of a mile by parish boundaries which follow it for two and a half miles almost to the river Tees. For 123 miles the indications of a Roman road are thus evident, and on the north side of the Tees a line of highways continues on nearly due north for about eight miles, by Fighting Cocks, with boundaries along it for two miles, and on by Street House and Stanton-le-Street. This would give a road to the north on the east of the rivers Ouse and the Swale, in the direction of Chester-le-Street.

Appendix 6

York's Medieval Churches Built Using Roman Masonry

All Saints, North Street	1166	*Active*
St Andrew, Fishergate	Pre conquest	*Demolished 14th c*
St Andrew, St Andrewgate	1194	*Converted use*
St Cuthbert, Peasholme Green	Pre conquest	*Converted use*
St Helen on the Walls, Aldwark	Late 9th c	*Demolished 16th c*
St Mary Bishophill Jnr	Pre conquest	*Active*

York Churches with a Roman Connection

St Cuthbert, Peaseholme Green
York's oldest church after the Minster, close to Layerthorpe Postern on York city walls near Layerthorpe; the east wall of the chancel is built from Roman masonry and is situated at the north-east corner of the fortress where excavations have shown large gaps in the fortress' perimeter wall. A tile bearing the stamped inscription LEG IX HISP has been found.

St Denys, Walmgate
There is evidence of previous Roman and Viking and Anglo-Saxon buildings on the site: a third-century Roman altar unearthed in 1846 from underneath a church pillar was dedicated to the Roman God Arciaco, erected by the Roman centurion Maternius Vitalis; it is now in the Yorkshire Museum. The inscription reads: 'To the god Arciaco and to the Divinity of the Emperor, Mat(. . .) Vitalis, centurion, willingly and deservedly fulfilled his vow.'

St Helen, Stonegate
This church is dedicated to St Helen, mother of Constantine the Great. St Helen appears in the stained glass.

St Helen-on-the-Walls, Aldwark

This church was on or near the east corner of York's Roman walls; it was a small rectangular building, with stone walls that included re-used Roman stones and built in the late ninth or early tenth century. Camden would have us believe that the emperor Constantius I was buried here in 306; so far so good . . . Camden then adds that in the sixteenth century excavations revealed a vault in which a candle from 306 was still burning!

St Martin-cum-Gregory, Micklegate

The 1844 tower plinth is made from stone pillaged from the Roman temple of Mithras.

St Mary, Bishophill Junior

One of the tiles used as the base of a culvert discovered under St Mary Bishophill Junior by Peter Wenham bore the imprint of an animal's paw over the impression of a child's sandal which, in turn, showed the stitching on the sole.

St Mary, Bishophill Senior

St Mary has the unenviable distinction of being the last medieval church in York to be demolished. There were Roman walls underneath the church; pieces of Roman tilework can be seen in the tower. Excavations in the vicinity in the 1960s revealed a ninth-century Anglian antler comb together with numerous oyster shells.

The remains of nearly 2,000 fish were collected in a compacted mass making it reasonable to conclude that something in the region of 40,000 fish were present within the excavated area, with many more unexcavated. The fish were small herrings (*Clupea herengus*) and sprats (*Clupea sprattus*) imported into York in the late Roman period. All were 4–6 inches long. They were dried and not smoked or salted, possibly rejected as being too small to bother with.

St Mary, Castlegate

The church is eleventh century, but most of what can be seen is fifteenth century; it boasts a dedication stone denoting the church a minster, and records that it was founded by [Ef]rard, Grim and Æse. A recycled Roman column capital and fragments of three column drums have been revealed under the chancel arch.

St Michael, Spurrriergate

St Michael was thought to be more than a match for the devil, so it is no surprise that many churches from the earliest times were dedicated to him on pagan sites. This church of St Michael stands on what was the site of the Roman temple of Hercules.

St Sampson, Church Street

St Sampson is the only church in the country dedicated to St Sampson. According to Geoffrey of Monmouth's *History of the Kings of Britain*, he was installed by King Arthur's uncle, Ambrosius Aurelianus, as Archbishop of York after repelling a force of Saxon invaders in AD 466. This Sampson, of course, has nothing to do with the Samson in the Bible – he of the long hair and Delilah. The church was built into the wall of the old Roman fortress.

York Minster

In the excavations under the central tower the remains of the earlier Norman church show it to be built of Roman ashlars, including a centurial stone.

Appendix 7

The York Historic Pageant – the Roman Bits

The 1909 *Pageant* was a dramatisation of York's history in seven episodes from 800 BC to AD 1644. With a cast of 2,500, the truly epic production involved 800 costume designs by forty different artists. Some 2,000 tracings were made and coloured – all based on information supplied by such authorities as the British Museum, Magdalen College, Oxford and Ampleforth College; the chorus comprised 220 singers; numerous horses also took to the stage. Total receipts over the seven performances were £14,439 18s 9d; profit was £762 9s 7d, which went to charities.

In their early days, the world-famous Mystery Plays had been bowdlerised (with scenes involving the Virgin Mary cut) and then completely suppressed in 1569; it was not until 1909 when this pageant, a spectacular revival of sorts, Mystery Plays-lite, took place, performed in and around the Museum Gardens. It included chapters from the history of York, including, of course, the Roman period, and a parade of the banners of the York Guilds through the streets, accompanying a wagon representing the Nativity. Later that year, a selection of six plays was performed as a fundraising venture for St Olave's Church. The *Pageant* was never intended as a religious ceremony although it inevitably included religious episodes: these are inextricably wound up in any 'dramatic representation of the evolution of the old northern capital of Britain.' The conversion of Constantine is naturally in there.

The author was Louis Napoleon Parker, the father of modern historical pageantry; he had decided to bring the curtain down on his career as a pageant master in 1909 with his swansong as a director of this large-scale pageant at York.

Parker was at pains to show that York had an illustrious history reaching back into the mists of time; a city contemporary with Jerusalem no less and more ancient even than ancient Rome. Accordingly, his Episode I begins not with imperial Roman York but with a legend that a band of wandering

Trojans had in fact founded York after their own city, Troy, had been comprehensively sacked by Agamemnon's perfidious Greeks. Parker was thus able to trace the English bloodline back beyond the Romans. He had little time for the Romans though: 'the Romans by his way of thinking had attempted to displace a culture that was assertively British and proud of it.' The Romans inevitably make their appearance, but Parker ends the episode not with anything remotely like the grandeur that was Rome but with the nascent rise of Christianity in the shape of the emperor Constantine.

Here is a summary of Episode II which covers the Roman period; it is abridged, with permission, from www.historicalpageants.ac.uk/pageants/1354/

Episode II: Altera Roma

Scene I. AD 53
The scene 'deals with the treachery of Queen Cartismandua [Cartimandua], the betrayal of Caradoc [Caratacus], and the compact between Cartismandua and the Roman – Ostorius Scapula.' It begins with Cartismandua seated on the throne; she receives homage from several princes but Venusius refuses to bow to her. The queen attempts to persuade the attendant crowds that they must throw in their lot with Rome, but Venusius calls for war and the crowds support him. Boduoc takes the queen's side; a fight takes place between him and Venusius in which the latter triumphs, thus strengthening his cause. Caradoc then arrives exhausted from battle with the Romans; he is greeted cordially by the queen ... . The Romans then appear led by Scapula. The queen allows Caradoc to be taken prisoner by the Romans; Caradoc wakes to find himself in shackles. A druid priest – Abaris – challenges the queen but she does not yield. Venusius threatens to overthrow her and declare himself overlord; but Cartismandua counters this by stating she will take his sisters (Aska and Ailaedia) as hostages. Abaris detains Venusius stating that he must stay his wrath meantime.

Scene II. AD 78–89
The Britons discuss the imminent arrival of Agricola and the IXth Legion; they flee to their altar as the Romans appear. The Romans are weary from battle and decide to set camp at the village; Agricola orders his officer Amicus to barter with the natives for food. Amicus returns and states

the natives are friendly. Agricola asks to speak with their representative. Bran comes forward and Agricola asks the name of their village: Bran states that it has no name. Agricola insists on knowing ... . Agricola takes advice and determines the place will henceforth be called Eboracum. The natives accept this reluctantly.

Scene III. AD 117–120

Members of the IXth Legion bemoan being stationed in Britain; they are homesick for Rome. The VIth Legion arrives. The leaders of the VIth are surprised by the primitive camp which has no baths. A trumpet sounds and Adrianus [Hadrian] enters accompanied by soldiers, nobles and ladies. The 'natives' stare on the scene with awe. Adrianus orders the building of forts, great walls and towers – including 'A tower facing many ways, that whencever the barbarians come, you may hurl arrows at them' [the Multangular Tower]. He calls for priests and orders that altars are built to the Roman gods, but also to Egyptian and Persian deities. He enquires about local gods and is told there are many; further altars are ordered. Adrianus goes on to dictate that comforts such as baths and a theatre must be provided. Adrianus and his men depart leaving the court behind. One member of the IXth orders the Britons to begin building and refers to them as slaves. The Britons are angry and the Roman ladies become afraid. The ladies are then persuaded to perform a Roman dance; this closes the scene.

Scene IV. AD 206

The emperor Septimius Severus arrives leaning on Papinianus; his sons Geta and Caracalla follow. Septimius states he wishes to make progress with the history of his life that he has been writing, but ill health impedes this. He comments on his sons stating, 'Geta is gentle ... . But Caracalla is a wolf!' Septimius begins to write as Papinianus retires. Geta then leaves to watch some games in which the soldiers are engaged, and is greeted heartily by all. Caracalla remains with his father and is resentful that the soldiers hold Geta in such affection; he is eager to be emperor. Caracalla steals up behind his father and makes to strike him with his sword, but Septimius is alert to this move and grabs his wrist. Caracalla tries to make light of his actions but his father calls for Papinianus and tells him that his son has tried to kill him. Septimius, distressed, takes out a phial of poison but is prevented from swallowing its contents by Papinianus. He then announces that he will travel on to the north and leave government in the hands of his sons. The soldiers show favouritism towards Geta and Caracalla's jealousy is given full vent when he attempts to destroy a statue of his brother. Septimius returns and it is announced that he is dying; Geta runs to be with his father who bids him perform the last rites (to close his eyes and place a coin in his mouth) before he dies. Geta does this and prepares for his father's funeral, but Caracalla and his allies leave immediately for Rome. The scene ends with the funeral procession.

Scene V. AD 294

Women are chatting excitedly at the riverside; they are first to see the arrival of Carausius by ship. They call out 'Woe! Woe! The Pirate!' Britons and Romans respond and rush to arms but are easily overpowered by Carausius and his men, including his associate Alectus. Carausius declares that 'Rome grows weak. She is tottering to her fall. Wherefore here and now, I seize the sovereignty.' Carausius is hailed as emperor. Alectus demands his reward and is dismissed contemptuously by Carausius. Alectus responds by stabbing Carausius and declaring himself emperor. A messenger enters stating that Constantius Chlorus is on his way. Alectus and the soldiers depart. The Britons discuss the situation; it is of no interest to them who rules from Rome. A messenger returns from the battle stating that both Alectus and Constantius Chlorus are dead. The new ruler is Constantius' son – Constantinus – whose mother [Helena] was a Briton. The Britons are surprised and happy that they will now be ruled by one of their own kind. The scene ends with the arrival of Constantinus.

Scene VI. AD 306

Constantinus enters in pomp, accompanied by a large company of attendants including senators and magistrates, nobles, ladies, dancers, and also some captives in chains. The procession approaches an altar where priests wait. Constantinus calls for thanks to be given for the recent victory; a 'Hymn to Apollo' is sung. Then a 'lowly and humble' procession approaches; in this are the bishop Eborius and two attendants—they chant the 23rd Psalm. A Roman priest calls for the Christians to be slain but Constantinus forbids this and asks to hear more about the 'God of Love' from Eborius. All then exit. A chorus is sung which rejoices in the arrival of Christianity to Britain.

Appendix 8

References to Ebo(u)racum in *RIB*

Most of the many inscriptions featured in the book come from *Roman Inscriptions of Britain* (*RIB*), the authoritative and indispensable catalogue of Roman inscriptions found in Britain. According to www.romaninscriptionsofbritain.org/:

> *RIB* online . . . hosts Volume One of *The Roman Inscriptions of Britain*, R. G. Collingwood's and R. P. Wright's magisterial edition of 2,401 monumental inscriptions from Britain found prior to 1955. It also incorporates all Addenda and Corrigenda published in the 1995 reprint of *RIB* (edited by R. S. O. Tomlin) and the annual survey of inscriptions published in Britannia . . . *RIB* Online endeavours to faithfully reproduce the printed edition and the relevant addenda and corrigenda published in *Journal of Roman Studies* and *Britannia*.

EBORACVM or EBVRACVM, fortress of Legio VI *Victrix* on the left bank of the R. Ouse, and COLONIA EBORACENSIS on the right bank.

Mentions of Eboracum
Col(onia) Ebor(acensis)

RIB 674, 678; Collingwood, *JRS* 11 (1921) 102
Col(oniae) Ebor[acensis]

RIB 3203
Ebur[. . .

RIB 648
Eb(oraco)

RIB 2274
Eb[or(aci)

253

RIB 657
Εβόρακον
Ptol. *Geogr.* ii 3, 16; Ptol. *Geogr.* viii 3, 7

Eboraci
Codex Iustinianus 3, 32, 1 (a.d. 210). Eburacum It. Ant. 466, 1; It. Ant. 468, 4; It. Ant. 475, 7; It. Ant. 478, 6

Eboraci
SHA (Spartian) Severus 19, 1

Civitate Eboracensi
Haddan and Stubbs, *Councils and Ecclesiastical Documents* (1869) i, 7 (a.d. 314, Council of Arles)

Eboraci
Eutropius 8, 10

Eburacum
Rav. 137 (Rav. 33)

Eburaci
Vindolanda Inv. No. 87.575

Eburac[ ]
Tab. Vindol. III, 850

[Ebura(?)]co
Tab. Vindol. III, app. 154

Ebora[ci]
AE 1986, 628

RIB 640
Altar dedicated to Arciaco and to the Divinity of the Emperor (third century)

RIB 641
Statue dedicated to Arimanius (AD 43–410)

RIB 642
Dedication to Bonus Eventus and Fortuna (AD 43–410)

RIB 643
Dedication to Holy Britannia (AD 43–410)

RIB 644
Altar dedicated to Fortune (mid–AD 130s)

RIB 645
Dedication to Fortune (AD 43–410)

RIB 646
Altar dedicated to the Genius Loci (AD 43–410)

RIB 647
Dedication to the Genius Loci (AD 43–410)

RIB 648
Fragmentary dedication to Hercules (AD 43–410)

RIB 649
Altar dedicated to Jupiter Optimus Maximus, to the gods and goddesses of hospitality and to the Penates (AD 43–410)

RIB 650
Altar dedicated to Mars (AD 43–410)

RIB 651
Altar dedicated to Mars (AD 43–410)

RIB 652
Altar dedicated to the Mother Goddesses of the household (AD 43–410)

RIB 653
Altar dedicated to the African, Italian, and Gallic Mother Goddesses (AD 43–410)

RIB 654
Altar dedicated to the Mother Goddesses (AD 43–410)

RIB 655
Relief and Altar dedicated to Mercury (AD 43–410)

RIB 656
Dedication to the Divinities of the Emperor and to the goddess Joug . . . (AD 43–410)

RIB 657
Dedication to Divinity of the Emperor and the Genius of Eboracum (AD 43–410)

RIB 658
Dedication to Serapis (AD 190–212)

RIB 659
Altar dedicated to Silvanus (before about AD 120)

RIB 660
Altar dedicated to Veteris (AD 43–410)

RIB 662
Dedication to the gods of the praetorium (AD 43–410)

RIB 663
Dedication to Ocean and Tethys (AD 43–410)

RIB 665
Building inscription of Trajan (AD 107–108)

RIB 668
Building inscription of the Tenth Cohort (AD 43–410)

RIB 670
Funerary inscription for Aurelius Super (AD 43–410)

RIB 671
Funerary inscription for Lucius Bebius Crescens (AD 43–410)

RIB 672
Funerary inscription for Bassaeus Julius and Felix (AD 43–410)

RIB 673
Funerary inscription for Lucius Duccius Rufinus (AD 43–410)

RIB 674
Funerary inscription for Flavius Bellator (AD 43–410)

RIB 675
Funerary inscription for Titus Flavius Flavinus (AD 43–410)

RIB 677
Funerary inscription for Valerius Theodorianus (AD 43–410)

RIB 678
Funerary inscription for Marcus Verecundius Diogenes (AD 43–410)

RIB 679
Funerary inscription for Gaius (AD 43–410)

RIB 681
Funerary inscription for Hyllus (AD 43–410)

RIB 682
Funerary inscription for Aelia Aeliana (AD 43–410)

RIB 683
Funerary inscription for Aelia Severa (AD 43–410)

RIB 684
Funerary inscription for Corellia Optata (AD 43–410)

RIB 685
Funerary inscription for Flavia and Saenius Augustina (AD 43–410)

RIB 686
Funerary inscription for Julia Brica and Sepronia Martina (AD 43–410)

RIB 687
Funerary inscription for Julia Fortunata (AD 43–410)

RIB 688
Funerary inscription for Julia Velva (AD 43–410)

RIB 689
Funerary inscription for Mantinia Maerica and Candida Barita (AD 43–410)

RIB 690
Funerary inscription for Simplicia Florentina (AD 200–300)

RIB 691
Funerary inscription for Ulpia Felicissima (AD 43–410)

RIB 692
Funerary inscription for Decimina (AD 43–410)

RIB 694
Funerary inscription for Minna (AD 43–410)

RIB 695
Funerary inscription for Eglecta (AD 43–410)

RIB 705
Fragmentary funerary inscription (AD 43–410)

RIB 706
Magical inscription (AD 43–410)

RIB 3193
Dedication to the Genius of the Collegium (AD 43–410)

RIB 3194
Altar to the Genius Loci (AD 43–410)

RIB 3198
Building stone of the Ninth cohort (AD 43–410)

RIB 3199
Centurial stone of Iullinus (AD 43–410)

RIB 3201
Coffin for Antonius Gargilianus (early third century AD and seventh–ninth century AD)

RIB 3202
Coffin for Julia Victorina and Constantius (AD 43–410)

RIB 3206
Fragmentary tombstone (?) (mid-second century AD or earlier)

www.romaninscriptionsofbritain.org/sites/york

The texts of RIB and the TEI XML from which they are derived are published under a Creative Commons Attribution 4.0 International License.

Appendix 9

Typical *cursus honorum* in the First Century AD

Ten years military service in cavalry or on the political staff of a relative or friend.

Minimum Age

30 *quaestor* (8–12 in number): financial admin in Rome, or in a province, as second-in-command to the governor.

'*tribune of the plebs*'(10): preside over the *concilium plebis*.

36 *aedile* (4, 2 curule and 2 plebeian): admin role in Rome; responsible for the corn supply, festivals *etc.*; optional.

39 *praetor* (6): judicial role in Rome; in charge of provinces not allocated to consuls; commanded one legion and allies.

40 *consul* (2): governed larger provinces and held major commands in all wars; led two legions and two allied *alae*. Other roles: to preside over the senate and assemblies.

censor: magistracy held by most distinguished ex-consuls. Two in office for five years; function: to carry out the census.

Appendix 10

Roman Assemblies

Senate

Three hundred members regulated by the censors. Members were from the eighteen senior centuries, i.e. they had property worth more than 400,000 HS. Role was to advise magistrates, especially the consuls.

Concilium Plebis

Made up of plebeians; divided into thirty-five tribes; membership based on ancestry; role was to elect the tribune and the *aedile*; passed laws.

Comitia Tributa

Made up of citizens, including patricians; role as above, but elected *curule aediles* and *quaestors*.

Comitia Centuriata

Comprised citizens divided into 193 voting centuries; originally formed from citizen militia, with membership based on possession of military equipment. Presided over by a consul or praetor. Function: election of consuls, praetors, and censors; declarations of war and ratification of peace treaties.

Appendix 11

The Etymology of Eburacum

Eburacum is mentioned by all the main ancient sources, including Ptolemy 2, 3, 17 Εβορακον, RC Eburacum, AI Eburacum and Eburaco, plus various inscriptions and early writers, some with vowel U, some with O.

Name origin: Latin *ebur* (whose genitive *eboris* contains an O) 'ivory', referring to boars' tusks, offers a perfect fit to the observed name. The -acum part was a common adjectival ending seen in early place names, especially in Gaul. York's later strong association with boars has been dismissed as a reinterpretation based upon Germanic words such as OE *eofor* 'wild boar', but, long before Romans lost control of York, a traveller from there set up a stone altar in Bordeaux with a detailed image of a boar on one side, securely dated to AD 237. How ebur may have evolved linguistically is discussed at length here.

Legio IX *Hispana*, which built the Roman fortress at York around AD 71, was originally recruited in the part of Iberia where ancient personal names based on Ebur were most prevalent and where Verraco 'boar' monuments are common. Presumably boars had a symbolic/religious significance there much like that in India for Varaha 'boar'. The implication is that the name Eburacum had nothing directly to do with boar hunting or the ivory trade, and the widely promoted idea of an association with Celtic words for 'yew' is a big red herring.

Source: www.romaneranames.uk

Appendix 12

The Antonine Plague, AD 165–AD 180

The Antonine Plague was the first of three devastating pandemics which ravaged the Roman Empire and the early Byzantine Empire, the others being the Plague of Cyprian (AD 249–AD 262) and the Justinian Plague (AD 541–AD 542).

As we have observed, it was never only the booty which victorious troops returning from war brought back to the homeland and their families and friends. Sexually transmitted infections and other diseases were sometimes incubating in the soldiers themselves and infecting their baggage trains, only too ready to spread into new populations. The Antonine Plague, or the Plague of Galen, which was probably smallpox, took hold during the reign of Marcus Aurelius (r. AD 161–AD 180); it devastated the Roman army and may have killed over five million people in the Roman Empire after the army came home from the war in Parthia (161–166). It has even been suggested that a quarter to a third of the entire population of the empire perished, estimated at 60-70 million.

The plague may have claimed the life of emperor Lucius Verus, who died in 169 and was the co-emperor with Marcus Aurelius. In 168, as Verus and Marcus Aurelius returned to Rome from the field, Verus fell ill with symptoms consistent with food poisoning, dying after a few days. However, scholars now believe that he may have succumbed to smallpox. Some also believe that Marcus Aurelius himself died from this plague some eleven years later.

A blend of legend and historical fact give two different explanations as to how the plague developed to infect the human population. In one, Lucius Verus is said to have opened a closed tomb in Seleucia during the sacking of the city and in so doing released, Pandora-like, the disease. This suggests that the epidemic was a supernatural punishment because the Romans violated an oath to the gods not to pillage the city. In the second story, a Roman soldier opened a golden casket in the temple of Apollo in Babylon allowing the plague to escape. Two different fourth-century sources, *Res Gestae* by Ammianus Marcellinus (c. AD 330–AD 400) and the biographies of Lucius Verus and Marcus Aurelius in the *Historia Augusta,* ascribe the outbreak to a sacrilege by the Romans when violating the sanctuary of a god. Other Romans preferred to blame Christians for angering the pagan gods by refusing to worship them, believing that angry gods sent the plague as a punishment.

Marcus Aurelius accordingly embarked on a programme of persecutions against Christians but these backfired when the tenets of Christianity started to exert themselves: Christians of course felt an obligation to help others in time of need, including those suffering from a lethal illness, and to 'love thy neighbour'. Therefore, they made themselves available to provide the most basic needs, food and water, for those too ill to fend for themselves. This not only helped the needy but it inculcated good feelings between Christians and their pagan counterparts. Christians stayed to help while pagans fled. At an eschatological and existential level, Christianity offered meaning to life and death in times of crisis and an assurance of life after death. Those who survived gained solace in knowing that loved ones, who died as Christians, could receive their reward in heaven. This promise of salvation in the afterlife triggered a spike in recruitment to the faith which, in the longer term, facilitated the acceptance of Christianity as the sole, official religion of the empire in the reign of Constantine I.

It seems that the Antonine Plague first emerged as a Roman public health problem during the siege of Seleucia in Mesopotamia (a major city on the Tigris River) as prosecuted by the Romans in the winter of 165–166. All sources agree that Verus' troops brought disease back west with them on their victorious return. Rome and the provinces were all affected, and the army was particularly badly hit; a concern with compromised Roman manpower is noted in many sources, for example Ammianus Marcellinus and Orosius and Eutropius who reports that the plague was so severe that 'in Rome and throughout Italy and the provinces most people, and almost all soldiers in the army, were afflicted by weakness.' This was especially problematic since the empire was now under threat along its north-eastern frontiers, and had some difficulty mobilising sufficient forces for the Marcommanic Wars at the end of the AD 160s. Ammianus Marcellinus records that the plague rampaged through the western empire to Gaul and to the legions stationed along the Rhine.

The spread of the contagion through the armed forces would have been accelerated by soldiers and sailors who had been on leave returning to active duty and infecting other legionaries and crews. Twenty-eight legions totalling approximately 150,000 highly and expensively trained men were exposed to the virus: many succumbed. As a result, Marcus Aurelius was desperate to recruit any able-bodied man who could fight: freed slaves, prisoners of war, criminals and gladiators were all signed up. Fewer gladiators meant fewer games in Rome and around the empire, which antagonised the Roman people who demanded more, not less, entertainment during a time of intense national stress. The resulting poorly trained and ill-disciplined army failed badly: in AD 167, Germanic tribes crossed the Rhine for the first time in more than 200 years. Such enemy successes served to expedite the decline of the Roman military, which, along with economic crises, were early steps in the decline and fall of the empire.

Eutropius stated that a large population died throughout the empire. According to Cassius Dio, the disease broke out again nine years later in AD 189 and led to up to 2,000 deaths a day in Rome, one quarter of those who were infected. The total death count has been estimated at 5 million, and the disease killed as much as one third of the population in some areas and again devastated the ranks of the Roman army.

This prodigious death toll severely reduced the number of people paying tax and contributing to the state's coffers, so government revenues plummeted. It diminished recruits for the army, candidates for public office, businessmen and farmers. Production on the farms fell as fewer farmers meant that so much more land was uncultivated with a further adverse effect on tax revenues. Crop shortages led to inflation and steep price increases along with decreasing food supplies. Fewer craftsmen and artisans also meant a downturn in productivity, which impacted local economies. Workforce shortages led to higher wages for those who survived the epidemic, and fewer businessmen, merchants, traders and financiers caused profound interruptions in domestic and international trade.

So, a long term effect of the Antonine Plague was to set off a gradual progression to the decline of the Roman Empire in the west: Hanna, in *The Route to Crisis* would have it that 'Roman culture, urbanism, and the interdependence between cities and provinces' helped the spread of infectious disease thus creating the basis for the collapse of the empire. Overcrowded cities, poor diet and malnutrition, and a lack of sanitary measures made Roman cities reservoirs for disease transmission. The contagions spread unchecked along the land and sea trade routes which connected the cities to the outlying provinces, surely including Britannia and Roman York.

Harper (*The Fate of Rome*) suggests that 'the paradoxes of social development and the inherent unpredictability of nature, worked in concert to bring about Rome's demise.'

The earliest outbreak of this plague recorded in Jerome's *Chronicle*, the universal chronology he compiled in the late fourth century, is listed for AD 168, when, 'A plague (*lues*) took hold of many provinces, and affected Rome.' Four years later things were even worse: 'There was such a great plague throughout the whole world that the Roman army was reduced almost to extinction.' Dio alleges that death by disease was augmented by mass-scale poisoning, performed by paid criminals equipped with sharp needles and a deadly compound in what to him was the worst plague he had ever come across and that 'two thousand often died in a single day' in Rome.

Herodian confirms that there was a severe plague outbreak in Rome around AD 190. All Italy was affected and infected, 'great destruction of both men and livestock resulted'. Doctors advised Commodus, the emperor at the time, to flee Rome to a safer place, and recommended those who remained in the city to make good use of incense and other aromatics. This would either keep the corrupt air out of their bodies, or overcome any that did manage to enter. The remedy failed for both humans and the animals they shared their living space with.

A second wave struck during the reigns of Decius (AD 249–251) and Gallus (AD 251–253) This plague broke out in Egypt in 251, and from there infected the whole of the Roman Empire. Its mortality rate severely depleted the ranks of the army, and caused massive labour shortages. According to Zosimus, the plague was still raging in 270, when it claimed the emperor Claudius Gothicus (r. 268–270).

Based on demographic studies, the average mortality rate during the Antonine plague was probably seven to ten per cent and possibly thirteen to fifteen per cent in cities and armies. In 1807, evidence emerged which confirmed the existence of the plague at Housesteads on Hadrian's Wall. (*RIB* 1579) It comes in the form of a funerary slab with the inscription: 'To the gods and goddesses according to the interpretation of the oracle of Clarian Apollo the First Cohort of Tungrians (set this up)'. While this is formulaic (we know of at least ten others) and would have been trotted out by all units, it seems likely that it was a reaction to a general order from Marcus Aurelius to invoke Apollo in a bid to safeguard their forts and cities from rampant smallpox. An identical inscription has been found at Ravenglass.

In 2011, Roger Tomlin provided more evidence for the plague's spread to Britannia when he published research on an amulet found in 1989 at Vintry in the City of London: it gives us thirty lines of Greek, and was written for a man with the Greek name Demetri(o)s. It translates as:

> send away the noisy clatter of raging plague, air-borne ...
> penetrating pain, heavy-spiriting, flesh-wasting, melting,
> from the hollows of the veins. Great Iao, great Sabaoth,
> protect the bearer. Phoebus [Apollo] of the unshorn hair,
> archer, drive away the cloud of plague....! Lord God, watch
> over Demetrios.

Appendix 13

The Plague of Cyprian:
AD 250–AD 271

In AD 250, the Roman Empire was losing its way, badly. The Imperial Crisis exploded when the Roman Empire was destabilised by a seemingly endless series of barbarian invasions, rebellions and imperial pretenders queuing up to wrestle power from the man in charge.

We have seen how the Antonine Plague in the previous century drained the Roman armies of manpower, skills and experience and wrecked the Roman economy. From AD 250 to AD 271, the Plague of Cyprian also laid waste the Roman Empire to such an extent that some cities, such as Alexandria, experienced a sixty-two per cent decline in population from something like 500,000 to 190,000, although not all of these people may have died of plague: some may have fled in panic.

The plague greatly hampered the Roman Empire's ability to ward off barbarian invasions, not helped by additional problems such as famine, with many farms abandoned and unproductive as farmers sought refuge in the cities. The absence of consistent leadership and the further dilution of the army during all the political instability, plus the ineptitude of a long succession of short-lived emperors all incapable of stemming the contagion just added to the parlous state the empire was in. Two of these emperors died of the plague: Hostilian in 251 and Claudius II Gothicus in 270.

Named after St Cyprian, a bishop of Carthage who saw the epidemic as signalling the end of the world, the Plague of Cyprian was estimated to be killing 5,000 people a day in Rome alone. What disease caused the pandemic? It may well have been smallpox, pandemic influenza or viral hemorrhagic fever, the Ebola virus.

Whatever it was, the Cyprian Plague destroyed whole populations throughout the empire causing widespread shortages in manpower, food production and army recruitment – just as the Antonine Plague had done in the previous century. Its effect was to severely weaken further the empire during the Crisis of the Third Century.

Cyprian, ever moralising and desperate to reassure his flock who were no more immune for being Christian than anyone else the pestilence encountered, gives graphic descriptions of the horrible physical symptoms in his *De Mortalitate*:

> The pain in the eyes, the febrile attacks, and the aching in all the limbs are the same among us and among the others, so long as we share the common flesh of this age … . These are proof of faith: that, as the strength of the body dissolves, the bowels dissipate in a flow; that a fire that begins in the inmost depths burns up into wounds in the throat; that the intestines are shaken with continuous vomiting; that the eyes are set on fire from the force of the blood; that the infection of the deadly putrefaction amputates the feet or other extremities of some; and that as weakness prevails through the failings and losses of the bodies, you go lame, deaf or blind.
>
> Cyprian, *De Mortalitate*. Adapted
> from Harper, *The Fate of Rome*.

All the while the Crisis of the Third Century rumbled on and the barrack emperors persisted with their corrupting policies, bribing armies to ensure their support in the civil wars, debasing the coinage, igniting rampant inflation and generally wrecking the economy. The people resorted to a black market economy, thus depriving the treasury of essential taxes; taxes were paid in kind in food or goods.

The various armies were so distracted by their own differences and battling that they ignored the incursions on their borders by the Carpians, Goths, Vandals and Alamanni on the Rhine and Danube with raids by the Sassanids in the east. Climate change in what are now the Low Countries caused sea levels to rise, forcing the displacement of inhabitants there in search of new land to settle.

The crisis, aided and abetted by the plague, forced wholesale changes in the military – the Romans, if anything, were going to learn from this perfect storm, chaos and mayhem to try and prevent it from recurring. Under Gallienus (r. 253–268), senators were barred from serving in the army: this had the dual benefit of reducing the likelihood of senatorial insurrection against Gallienus and eliminating the old hoary aristocratic hierarchy in the military. Officers would now have to work their way up through the ranks, no longer reliant on their privileged status. The result was a much more experienced and rigorous officer corps. To win his victories over the Gallic and Palmyrene secessionists, Aurelian deployed fleet cavalry rather than the usual infantry. Diocletian increased even further the cavalry element to ensure speedy and flexible deployment wherever armies were required. Diocletian reigned from the regions as well as Rome so that his fast reaction forces were nearer to potential trouble spots.

These appendixes are adapted from chapters in my book, *The History of the World in 100 Pandemics, Plagues and Epidemics* (2021).

Appendix 14

Roman York – More Interesting Facts

Here are just some of the visible remains of Roman York which can be easily seen today.

1. Outside the south door of York Minster at the **statue of emperor Constantine the Great** sitting regally, surveying his fortress. There is a descriptive plaque next to the statue which reads:

   > CONSTANTINE THE GREAT 274–337. Near this place Constantine was proclaimed Roman Emperor in 303. His recognition of the civil liberties of his Christian subjects, and his own conversion to the faith, established the religious foundations of Western Christendom.

   The sculptor, Philip Jackson, was fastidious in his research on the clothing, seating and armour of the period. The result is a 'fascinating medley of fact and conjecture'. The emperor gazes down at his broken sword, which forms the shape of a cross, a moving emblem of Constantine's world-changing act of making Christianity a legal and (largely) tolerated religion of the hitherto predominantly pagan Roman Empire.

2. **The Undercroft Museum** is accessible from inside the minster. It features structural remains of the Roman fortress headquarters (*principium*) and parts of the First Cohort centurions' quarters, along with one of the sewers serving the fortress. Entrance to the Undercroft Museum is through the west end of the minster. Remains of the Roman *basilica* building, at the north side of the *principia,* are visible in the undercroft.

3. While you are in the minster, take time to see **St Stephen's Chapel** at the north-east corner beyond the choir; its terracotta panel is called

The First Hour of the Crucifixion and was created by the ceramic artist George Tinworth. The relief shows early afternoon on Good Friday when the other two of the three crosses are just being erected. Roman soldiers are casting lots as to who should get Christ's robes after his crucifixion and the same soldiers are shown dividing up his clothes. Note the Victorian moustaches sported by the soldiers and the little boy on the right who seems to be enjoying the Eucharist wine.

4. Once outside again head towards the 25ft **column** which formed part of the *principia*, and was discovered when the minster's central tower was underpinned in the 1960s.

5. Bootham Bar overlies another gateway in the fortress – the *porta principalis dextra* – part of which is preserved in the floor of the modern building (currently a café) adjoining the bar. In the coffee house (Bean & Gone), you can see the lower courses of the **fortress wall** immediately next to the *porta principalis dextra* (i.e. the main gate on the right side) through a glass panel in the floor. This is a fragment of the foundations of the western curtain wall. The remains were first revealed and recorded in 1910 during building works on the site, but the wall was then concealed in a shallow basement for more than 100 years. Opposite, on the grassed area between the pavement and the car park, you can see another small section of the fortress wall. A plaque records that it was built under the emperor Constantius Chlorus in about AD 300.

   Back over the road, under the stage in the Theatre Royal, there are the remains of a **Roman well**. Unfortunately, but for obvious reasons, you can only see this on one of the organised tours of the theatre.

6. One of the stones of the **Multangular Tower** in Museum Gardens is 21ft by 11ft wide and bears the legible inscription '*Genio loci feliciter*': 'good luck to the guardian spirit of this place' (*RIB* 647). It was uncovered in 1702 when digging a cellar below the Black Swan Inn in Coney Street outside the south angle of the fortress and is now in the Yorkshire Museum (YORYM: 2007.6197).

7. Exit the Gardens and head down to the end of Lendal along Davygate and go into St Helen's Square. Here, a **slave market** is said to have

existed during the Roman occupation. Later, Bede tells us that Pope Gregory I (d. 604) admired English slaves, punning *'non Angli sed angeli'*: 'they're not Angles, but angels'.

The following may also be of interest:

Treasurer's House

Behind the Chapter House at the minster. A Roman street, the via decumana, was excavated here under the cellar of the house in the 1960s, lending credence to stories about ghostly legionaries marching through.

Stonegate

Stonegate refers to the road leading to and from the Roman *Porta Praetoria*, a gate into the Roman garrison. The old Roman stone paving – which gives us the modern name – survives under the cobbles complete with the central gulley for the chariots' skid wheels.

Streets (*viae*) and gates (*portae*) in Eboracum

Via principalis, main street – Petergate
Via praetoria, Stonegate
Via decumana, Chapter House Street
Porta pricipalis dextra – under Bootham Bar
Porta principalis sinistra – under King's Square
Porta praetoria – under St Helen's Square
Porta decumana – in the garden at Gray's Court

Plaques celebrating Roman York are at Bootham Bar; Praetorian Gate, St Helen's Square; the Roman Column; Stonegate; Petergate; Constantine the Great statue; Roman Wall in St Leonard's Place, the Anglian Tower in Library Gardens.

Further Reading

Addyman, P. V. 1975, Excavations in York, 1972-1973, first interim report, *Antiquaries Journal*, Vol 54, pp. 200-31

Addyman, P. V. 2015, *York: British Historic Towns Atlas*, Vol 5

Aldhouse-Green, M., 2005, *Exploring the World of the Druids*, London

Aldhouse-Green, M., 2018 *Sacred Britannia: The Gods and Rituals of Roman Britain*, London

Allason-Jones, L., 1989, *Women in Roman Britain*, London

Allason-Jones, L., 1996, *Roman Jet in the Yorkshire Museum*, York

Allason-Jones, L., 2012, *Women in Roman Britain*, pp. 467-477

Allen, D.; Bryan, M., 2020, *Roman Britain and Where to Find It*, Stroud

Anderson, A. S., 1984, *Roman Military Tombstones*, Aylesbury

Arnheim, M. T. W., 1972, *The Senatorial Aristocracy in the Later Roman Empire*, Oxford

Barclay, C.; Allason-Jones, L., 2006, *Shiptonthorpe, East Yorkshire: Archaeological Studies of a Romano-British Roadside Settlement*. Yorkshire Archaeological Society

Barnes, T. D., 1981, *Constantine and Eusebius*, Cambridge MA

Barnes, T. D., 1982, *The New Empire of Diocletian and Constantine*, Cambridge MA

Barnes, T. D., 1993, *Athanasius and Constantius: Theology and Politics in the Constantinian Empire*, Cambridge MA

Barnes, T. D., 1996, 'Emperors, panegyrics, prefects, provinces and palaces (284–317)', *Journal of Roman Archaeology* Vol 9, pp. 532-552

Barrett, A., 2005, 'Aulus Caecina Severus and the Military Woman', *Historia: Zeitschrift Für Alte Geschichte*, 54 (3), pp. 301-314

Bartie, A. 'The York Pageant', *The Redress of the Past*, www.historicalpageants.ac.uk/pageants/1354/

Bartie, A., 2016, 'The Redress of the Past: Historical Pageants in Twentieth-Century England', *International Journal of Research on History Didactics, History Education and History Culture* – Yearbook, Vol 37, Issue 1, pp. 9-35

Bartie, A., 2018, 'Pageants and the Medieval Past in Twentieth-Century England', *English Historical Review*, Vol 133, pp. 866-902

Bartie, A., 2020, *Restaging the Past: Historical Pageants, Culture and Society in Modern Britain*, London

Bennett, J., 2001, *Towns in Roman Britain*, Oxford

Bidwell, P., 'Constantius and Constantine in York', in Hartley, E., 2006, *Constantine the Great: York's Roman Emperor*, York

Bidwell, P., 2009, *The Roman Army in Northern England*, Newcastle

Bietenholz, Peter G., 1994, *Historia and Fabula: Myths and Legends in Historical Thought from Antiquity to the Modern Age*, Leiden

Birley, A. R., 1992, The People of Roman Britain, Berkeley

Birley, A. R., 1996, 'Iulius Agricola, Cn.', in Hornblower, Simon (Ed), *Oxford Classical Dictionary*, Oxford

Birley, A. R., 2005, *The Roman Government of Britain*, Oxford

Birley, E. B., 1966, 'The Roman inscriptions of York', *Yorkshire Archaeological Journal*, Vol 41, pp. 726-34

Birley, E. B., 1971, *The Fate of the Ninth Legion*, in Butler R. M. (Ed), 1971, *Soldier and Civilian in Roman Yorkshire*, Leicester, pp. 71-80

Birley, E. B., 1974. 'Cohors I Tungrorum and the Oracle of the Clarian Apollo', *Chiron*, 4, pp. 511-513.

Bishop, M. C., 2013 *Handbook to Roman Legionary Fortresses*, Barnsley

Bishop, M. C, 2014, *The Secret History of the Roman Roads of Britain*, Barnsley

Bodel, J., 2001, *Epigraphic Evidence: Ancient History from Inscriptions*, London

Boin, D., 2020, *Alaric the Goth: an Outsider's History of the Fall of Rome*, New York

Boutwood, Y., 1996, 'Roman Fort and Vicus, Newton Kyme, North Yorkshire', *Britannia,* Vol 27, pp. 340-344

Bowman, A. K., 1994, *Life and Letters on the Roman Frontier: Vindolandia and its People*, London

Bragg, M., Podcast, 5 Oct 2017: BBC Radio 4, *In Our Time*, 'Constantine the Great', www.bbc.co.uk/programmes/b096gjw0

Branigan, K., 1980, *Roman Britain: Life in an Imperial Province*, London

Branigan, K., 1980, *Rome and the Brigantes: the Impact of Rome on Northern England*, Sheffield

Brauer, G. C., 1975, *The Age of the Soldier Emperors: Imperial Rome, AD 244–284*, New Jersey

Breeze, D. J., 1985, 'Roman Military Deployment in North England', *Britannia*, Vol 16, pp. 1-19

Breeze, D. J., 2002, *Roman Forts in Britain*, Oxford

Breeze, D. J., 2011, *The Frontiers of Imperial Rome*, Barnsley

Brendel, O., 1979, *Prolegomena to the Study of Roman Art*, New Haven

Brinklow, D. 1987: 'Fortress wall in bus lay-by', *Interim: the Archaeology of York*, Vol 12, pp. 16-18

Brittany, T., 2016, 'Imperial Statues and Public Spaces in Late Antiquity: Conceptualising 'Constantine' at York as an Ancient Public Commission' In Mandichs, (Ed), Proceedings of the Twenty-Fifth Annual Theoretical Roman Archaeology Conference, pp. 177-187

Broadhead, W., 2007, 'Colonization, Land Distribution, and Veteran Settlement' in *A Companion to the Roman Army*, Erdkamp, P., (Ed), Oxford, pp. 148-163

Brown, P., 1989, *The World of Late Antiquity: AD 150–750*, New York

Brown, P., 2003, *The Rise of Western Christendom: Triumph and Diversity AD 200–1000*, Oxford

Buckland, P. C., 1976: 'The Environmental Evidence from the Church Street Roman Sewer System', *The Archaeology of York*, Vol 14 Fasc 1, York

Buckland, P. C., 1984, 'The "Anglian Tower" and the use of Jurassic limestone in York' in Addyman, P., (Ed), *Archaeological papers from York presented to M. W. Barley*, York, pp. 51- 57

Burckhardt, Jacob, 1949, *The Age of Constantine the Great*, Moses Hadas, trans., New York

Burn, A. R., 1953, *Agricola and Roman Britain*, London

Burn, A. R., 1969, *The Romans in Britain – An Anthology of Inscriptions*, Oxford

Burnham, B. C., 1990, *The Small Towns of Roman Britain*, London

Bury, J. B., 1889, *A History of the Later Roman Empire from Arcadius to Irene*, Vol I, London

Butler, R. M., (Ed), 1971, *Soldier and Civilian in Roman Yorkshire*, Leicester

Butler, R. M., 1971, 'The Defences of the Fourth Century Fortress at York', in Butler, *Soldier and Civilian*, pp. 97-106

Cameron, A., 1993, *The later Roman Empire: AD 284–430,* Cambridge, MA

Cameron A., 1999, *Eusebius: Life of Constantine*, Oxford

Campbell, D. B., 1986, 'The consulship of Agricola', *Zeitschrift für Papyrologie und Epigraphik*, Vol 63, pp. 197-200

Campbell, D. B., 2009, *Roman Auxiliary Forts 27 BC-AD 378*, Oxford

Campbell, D. B., 2010, *Mons Graupius AD 83: Rome's Battle at the Edge of the World*, Oxford

Campbell, D. B., 2010, 'Women in Roman forts: Residents, visitors or barred from entry?', *Ancient Warfare*, IV (6), pp. 48-53

Campbell, D. B., 2018 *Fortifying a Roman Camp: The Liber de munitionibus castrorum of Hyginus*

Campbell, D. B., 2019, 'The Fate of the Ninth: the Curious Disappearance of the VIIII Legio Hispana', *Ancient Warfare*, IV (5)

Casado, C., 2013, 'Roman Roads: The Backbone of Empire', *Fundacion Juanelo Turriano*, pp. 69-86.

Casey, P. J., 1994. *Carausius and Allectus: The British Usurpers*, London

Charlesworth, D., 1971, 'The Defences of Isurium Brigantum', in Butler, *Soldier and Civilian*, pp. 155-164

Christol, M., 2014, *Rome et Son Empire*, Paris

Chrystal. P., 2016, *Roman Military Disasters*, Barnsley

Chrystal, P., 2017, *How to Be a Roman*, Stroud

Chrystal, P., 2017, *When in Rome: A Social History of Rome*, Stroud

Chrystal, P., 2017 and 2020, *Women at War in the Ancient World*, Barnsley

Chrystal, P., 2018, *Roman Records and Communication*, Stroud

Chrystal. P., 2019, *Reportage from Ancient Greece and Rome,* Stroud

Chrystal, P., 2019, *The Romans in the North of England*, Darlington

Chrystal, P., 2020, 'Death' in *Oxford Bibliographies in Classics*. Scodel, R., (Ed), New York

Chrystal, P., 2021, *The History of the World in 100 Pandemics, Epidemics and Plagues from the Plague of Athens to COVID-19*, Barnsley

Collingwood, R. G., 1930, *The Archaeology of Roman Britain*, London

Collingwood, R. G., 1965, *The Roman Inscriptions of Britain*, Oxford

Collins, R., 2014, *Life in the Limes: Studies of the people and objects of the Roman frontiers*, Oxford

Collins, R., 2020, *Living on the Edge of Empire: The Objects and People of Hadrian's Wall*, Barnsley

Combe, W., 1785, *The History and Antiquities of the City of York*

Cool, H. E. M., 1995, 'Finds from the Fortress', *The Archaeology of York*, Vol 17 Fasc 10, York

Cool, H. E. M., 1999. 'Glass-making and the Sixth Legion at York', *Britannia*, Vol 30, pp. 147-62

Cool, H. E. M., 2002. 'Craft and industry in Roman York', in Wilson, P., (Ed), *Aspects of Industry in Roman York and the North*, Oxford, pp. 1-11

Cool, H. E. M., 2014, 'Which "Romans"; what "home"? The myth of the "end" of Roman Britain' in Haarer, F. K., (Ed), AD 410: *The History and Archaeology of Late and Post-Roman Britain*, Society for the Promotion of Roman Studies

Corcoran, S., 1996, *The Empire of the Tetrarchs, Imperial Pronouncements and Government AD 284–324*, Oxford

Corcoran, S., 2006, 'Before Constantine' in *The Cambridge Companion to the Age of Constantine*, Lenski, N., (Ed), pp. 35-58, Cambridge

Crawford, P., 2016, *Constantius II: Usurpers, Eunuchs, and the Antichrist*, Barnsley

Cunliffe, B., 2004, *Iron Age Britain*, London

Cunliffe, B., 2005, *Iron Age Communities in Britain: An Account of England, Scotland and Wales from the Seventh Century BC until the Roman Conquest* (Fourth Edition), London

Dark, K., 2000, *Britain and the End of the Roman Empire*, Stroud

Dayton, L., 1994, 'The Fat, Hairy Women of Pompeii', *New Scientist*

Dean, W. T., 2007, 'Yorkshire jet and its links to Pliny the Elder', *Proceedings of the Yorkshire Geological Society*, Vol 56, pp. 261-265

De la Bedoyere, G., 1989, *The Finds Of Roman Britain*, London

Doyle, C., 2014, *The Endgame of Treason: Suppressing Rebellion and Usurpation in the Late Roman Empire AD 397-411*, National University of Ireland Galway. Unpublished doctoral thesis

Dickinson, B. M., 1971, 'The Evidence of Potters' Stamps on Samian Ware and on Mortarie for the Trading Connections of York' in Butler *Soldier and Civilian*, pp. 127-142

DiMaio, M., 'Constans I (337–350 AD)', in *De Imperatoribus Romanis*, An Online Encyclopedia of Roman Emperors

Dobinson, C., 1995, *Aldborough Roman Town*, London

Downes, A., 2016, *50 Finds from Yorkshire: Objects from the Portable Antiquities Scheme*, Stroud

Drake, F., 1788, *Eboracum: or the History and Antiquities of the City of York, from its Original to the Present Times*

Drake, H. A., 2002, *Constantine and the Bishops, The Politics of Intolerance*, Baltimore

Drijvers, J. W., 1992, *Helena Augusta: The Mother of Constantine the Great and her Finding of the True Cross*, Leiden

Drijvers, J. W., 2000 'Evelyn Waugh, Helena and the True Cross' *Classics Ireland 7*

Dudley, D. R., 1965, *The Roman Conquest of Britain*, London

Dumville, D. N., 1977, 'Sub-Roman Britain: History and Legend' *History*, Vol 62 (205), pp. 173-92

Duncan-Jones, R. P., 1996, 'The impact of the Antonine plague', *Journal of Roman Archaeology*, 9, pp. 108-36

Dunham, S. B., 1995, 'Caesar's perception of Gallic social structures' in Arnold, B., (Ed), *Celtic Chiefdom, Celtic State*, Cambridge

Dunnett, R., 1975, *The Trinovantes*, London

Dyer, J., 1967, 'Excavations and discoveries in a cellar in Messrs. Chas. Hart's premises, Feasgate, York, 1956', *Yorkshire Archaeological Journal*, Vol 39, pp. 419-25

Eaton, J. M., 2020, *Leading the Roman Army*, Barnsley

Elliott, S., 2018, *The Scottish Campaigns of Septimius Severus: The Northern Campaigns of the First Hammer of the Scots*, Barnsley

Elliott, S., 2021, *Roman Britain's Missing Legion*, Barnsley

Elliott, T. G., 1996, *The Christianity of Constantine the Great*, Scranton, PA

Elsner, Ja., 1998, *Imperial Rome and Christian Triumph*, Oxford

Engels, D., 1980, 'The Problem of Female Infanticide in the Greco-Roman World', *Classical Philology*, Vol 75, pp. 112-120

Esmonde-Cleary, A. S., 1989, *The Ending of Roman Britain*, London

Evans, D. T., 1998, 'Excavations at the former Daveygate Centre', *Interim: the Archaeology of York*, Vol 22 (4), pp. 5-9

Evans, D. T., 2000, 'The former Primitive Methodist chapel, 3 Little Stonegate', *Interim: the Archaeology of York,* Vol 23(2), pp. 24-8

Evans, J. K., 1991, *War, Women and Children in Ancient Rome*, London

Faulkner, N., 2000, *The Decline & Fall of Roman Britain*, Stroud

Fenton, T., 1995, 'The Late Roman Infant Cemetery Near Lugnano', *Journal of Paleopathology*, pp. 13-42

Ferraby, R., 2020, *Isurium Brigantum: An Archaeological Survey of Roman Aldborough*, London

Fleming, R., 2011, *Britain After Rome: The Fall and Rise, 400 to 1070: Anglo-Saxon Britain*, London

Forder, S., 2019, *The Romans in Scotland and The Battle of Mons Graupius*, Stroud

Frakes, R. M., 2006, 'The Dynasty of Constantine down to 363' in Lenski, N., (Ed), *The Cambridge Companion to the Age of Constantine*, Cambridge

Frank, R. I., 1975, 'Augustus' Legislation on Marriage and Children', *California Studies in Classical Antiquity*, Vol 8, pp. 41-52

Frere, S., 1978, *Britannia: A History of Roman Britain*, Revised Edition, London

Gerrard, J., 2013, *The Ruin of Roman Britain An Archaeological Perspective*, Cambridge

Gibbon, E., 1888, *The Decline and Fall of the Roman Empire*, Philadelphia

Gillespie, C. C., 2018, *Boudica: Warrior Woman of Roman Britain*, Oxford

Golden, M., 1988, 'Did the Ancients Care When their Children Died?' *Greece and Rome*, Vol 35, pp. 152-163

Goodyear, F. R. D., 1970, *Tacitus*, (Greece and Rome, New Surveys in the Classics 4), Oxford

Grainger, J. D., 2020, *The Roman Imperial Succession*, Barnsley

Grant, M., 1994, *Constantine the Great: the Man and His Times*, New York

Hall, R. A., 1986, 'Roman warehouses and other riverside structures in Coney Street', in Brinklow, D., *Coney Street, Aldwark and Clementhorpe, Minor Sites and Roman Roads*, York

Hall, R. A., 1997, 'Excavations in the Praetentura: 9 Blake Street', *The Archaeology of York,* Vol 3 Fasc 4, York

Hall, R. A., 2004, 'The Topography of Anglo-Scandinavian York', in Hall R. A., et al (Eds), *Aspects of Anglo-Scandinavian York*, York pp. 488-97

Hanson, W. S., 1991, *Agricola and the Conquest of the North*, London

Hanson, W. S., 'Roman campaigns north of the Forth-Clyde isthmus: the evidence of the temporary camps', *Proceedings of the Society of Antiquaries or Scotland*, Vol 109, pp. 14-150

Hargrove, W., 1818, *History and Description of the Ancient City of York; Comprising all the Most Interesting Information, Already Published in Drake's Eboracum*

Harris, W. V., 1982, 'The Theoretical Possibility of Extensive Female Infanticide in the Graeco-Roman World', *The Classical Quarterly*, Vol 32, pp. 114-116

Hartley, B. R., 1971, 'Roman York and the Northern Military Command to the Third Century AD', in Butler*, Soldier and Civilian*, pp. 55-70

Hartley, B. R., 1988, *The Brigantes*, Stroud

Hartley, E., 1985, *Roman Life at the Yorkshire Museum*, York

Hartley, E., (Ed), 2006, *Constantine the Great: York's Roman Emperor*, York

Haselgrove, C., (Ed), 2016, 'Cartimandua's Capital? The late Iron Age royal site at Stanwick, North Yorkshire: Fieldwork and Analysis 1981–2011', *Council for British Archaeology, Research Report* 175

Haverfield, F., 1912, *The Romanization of Roman Britain*, Second Edition, Oxford

Heather, P., 2005, *The Fall of the Roman Empire*, Basingstoke

Hell, J., 2019, *The Conquest of Ruins: The Third Reich and the Fall of Rome*, Chicago

Heyob, S. K., 1975, *The Cult of Isis Amongst Women of the Graeco-Roman World*, Leiden

Higham, N., 1985, *The Carvetii*, Stroud

Higham, N., 1992, *Rome, Britain and the Anglo-Saxons*, London

Higham, N., 1994, *The English Conquest: Gildas and Britain in the Fifth Century*, Manchester

Highways England, 2018, *A1 Leeming to Barton improvement scheme Archaeological Discoveries*, Guildford

Hodgson, N., podcast 21 March 2021: The Antonine Plague: evidence from the collection of the Society of Antiquaries of Newcastle-upon-Tyne

Hoffmann, B., 2019, *The Roman Invasion of Britain: Archaeology versus History*, Barnsley

Holst, M., 19 May 2017, 'The Headless Gladiators of York', *Ancient Mysteries Series*, Channel 5

Hopkins, K., 1965, 'The Age of Roman Girls at Marriage', *Population Studies,* Vol 18, pp. 309-327

Hoyos, D., 2019, *Rome Victorious: The Irresistible Rise of the Roman Empire*, London

Hughes, I., 2020, *A Military Life of Constantine the Great*, Barnsley

Hunt, D., 1998, 'The successors of Constantine' in Cameron, A., (Ed), *The Cambridge Ancient History: The Late Empire, AD 337–425,* Vol 13 (Second Edition), Cambridge, pp. 1-43.

Hunter-Mann, K., 2006, 'Romans lose their heads in York', *York Historian*, Vol 23, pp. 2-7

Ireland, S., 2009, *Roman Britain: A Sourcebook,* (Third Edition), London

Jackson, R., 1988, *Doctors and Diseases in the Roman Empire*, London

Jackson, R., 2020, *The Roman Occupation of Britain and its Legacy*, London

James, S. L., 2012, *A Companion to Women in the Ancient World*, Chichester

Jarrett, M. G., 1994, 'Non-legionary troops in Roman Britain: Part One, The Units', *Britannia,* Vol 25, pp. 35-77

Johnson, P., 1995 *Romano-British Mosaics*, Princes Risborough

Jones, A. H. M., 1948, *Constantine and the Conversion of Europe* Buffalo NY

Jones, A. H. M., 1954, 'The Date and Value of the Verona List', *The Journal of Roman Studies* Vol 44, pp. 21-29

Jones, A. H. M., 1971, *The Prosopography of the Later Roman Empire: Volume I: AD 260–395*, Cambridge

Jones, B.; Mattingly, D., 2007, *An Atlas of Roman Britain*, Oxford

Jones, C., 2012, *York: Archaeological Walking Guides*, Stroud

Jones, C. P., 2005, 'Ten dedications "to the gods and goddesses" and the Antonine plague', *Journal of Roman Archaeology*, 18, pp. 293-301

Jones, M. E., 1996, *The End of Roman Britain*, Ithaca NY

Jones, R. H., 2012, *Roman Camps in Britain*, Stroud

Jones, W., 1838, *Ecclesiastical History, in a Course of Lectures*, Vol. 1, London

Kenny, J., 2013, 'Investigating the Roman Road from Eboracum Towards Aldborough, Near Hessay and Moor Monkton', *York Historian*, Vol 30, pp. 43-45

Kenward, H. K., 1986, 'Environmental Evidence from a Roman Well and Anglian Pits in the Legionary Fortress', *The Archaeology of York*, Vol 14 Fasc 5, York

Keppie, L., 'The Fate of the Ninth Legion: a Problem for the Eastern Provinces?', in *Legions and Veterans: Roman Army Papers 1971–2000*, pp. 247 ff

Kolb, A., 2019, *Roman Roads: New Evidence – New Perspectives*, Amsterdam

Kulikowski, M., 2000, 'Barbarians in Gaul, Usurpers in Britain', *Britannia*, Vol 31, pp. 325-345

Laes, C., 2009, *Children in the Roman Empire: Outsiders Within*, Cambridge

Laing, L., 1975, *The Archaeology of Late Celtic Britain and Ireland, c. 400–1200 AD*, Frome

Laycock, S., 2008, *Britannia – The Failed State: Tribal Conflict and the End of Roman Britain*, Stroud

Leach, S., et al., 2010, 'A Lady of York: Migration, Ethnicity and Identity in Roman Britain', *Antiquity*, Vol 84 Issue 323, pp. 131-145.

Lenski, N., (Ed.), 2005, *The Cambridge Companion to the Age of Constantine*, Cambridge

Lenski, N., 2006, 'The Reign of Constantine' in *The Cambridge Companion to the Age of Constantine*, pp. 59-90

Levick, B., 2007, *Julia Domna: Syrian Empress*, London

Levitt, P. C., 2019, *Yorkshire: A Story of Invasion, Uprising and Conflict*, Stroud

Lewis, M. J. T., 1966, *Temples in Roman Britain*, Cambridge

Lieu, S. N. C., 1996, *From Constantine to Julian: Pagan and Byzantine Views*, New York

Ling, R., 1983, 'The Seasons in Romano-British Mosaic Pavements', *Britannia*, Vol 14, pp. 13-22

Ling, R., 1985, *Romano-British Wall Painting*, Princes Risborough

Ling. R., 1991, 'Brading, Brantingham and York: A New Look at Some Fourth-Century Mosaics', *Britannia*, Vol 22

Lister, M., 1683, 'Some Observations upon the Ruins of a Roman Wall and Multangular-Tower at York', *Philosophical Transactions of the Royal Society*, Vol 13, pp. 238-242

Liversidge, J., (1968) *Britain in the Roman Empire*, London

Liversidge, J., 'Brantingham Roman Villa: Discoveries in 1962', *Britannia* Vol 4

Livingstone, H., 1995, *In the Footsteps of Caesar: Walking Roman Roads*, Shepperton

MacGregor, A., 1976, 'Finds from a Roman Sewer and an Adjacent Building in Church Street', *The Archaeology of York*, Vol 17 Fasc 1, York

MacKendrick, P. L., 1952, 'Roman Colonization', *Phoenix*, Vol 6 Issue 4, pp. 139-146

MacMullen, R.; Lane, E., 1992, *Paganism and Christianity, 100–425 C.E.: A Sourcebook*, Minneapolis

Macnab, N., 2000, 'More on the Roman fortress: a lift-pit excavation behind 3 Little Stonegate', *Interim: the Archaeology of York*, Vol 23(3), pp. 31-46

Mainman, A., 2004, 'Craft and Economy in Anglo-Scandinavian York', in Hall, R. A., et al. (Eds), *Aspects of Anglo-Scandinavian York*, York, pp. 459-87

Mander, J., 2012, *Portraits of Children on Roman Funerary Monuments*, Cambridge

Mango, C., 1994, 'The Empress Helena, Helenopolis, Pylae', *Travaux et Mémoires*, Vol 12, pp. 143-58.

Mann, J. C., 1975, *The Romans in the North*, Durham

Mann, J. C., 1998, 'The Creation of Four Provinces in Britain by Diocletian', *Britannia,* Vol 29, pp. 339-341

Margary, I. D., 1957, *Roman Roads in Britain: Volume II North of the Foss Way – Bristol Channel*, London

Margary I. D., 1973, *Roman Roads in Britain* (Third Edition), London

Marshall, A. J., 1975, 'Roman Women in the Provinces', *Ancient Society*, Vol 6, pp. 109-127

Martin, C., 1995, *British Archaeology*

Mattingly, D. J., 2004, 'Being Roman: Expressing Identity in a Provincial Setting', *Journal of Roman Archaeology*, Vol 17, p. 13

Mattingly, D., 2006, *An Imperial Possession: Britain in the Roman Empire*, London

McCarthy, M., 2012, *The Romano-British Peasant: Towards a Study of People, Landscapes and Work During the Roman Occupation of Britain*, Oxford

Merlat, P., 1947, 'Jupiter Dolichenus, Serapis et Isis', *Revue Archéologique,* Vol 27, pp. 10-31

Merrow, A., 2020, Caesar's *Great Success: Sustaining the Roman Army on Campaign*, Barnsley

Millet, M., 1990, 'Romanization: historical issues and archaeological interpretation', in Blagg, T., & Millett, M., (Eds), *The Early Roman Empire in the West*, Oxford, pp. 35-44

Miller, S., 1925, 'Roman York: excavations of 1925', *Journal of Roman Studies*, Vol 15, pp. 176-94

Miller, S., 1928. 'Roman York: Excavations of 1926–1927', *Journal of Roman Studies*, Vol 18, pp. 61-99.

Millett, M., 1990, *The Romanization of Britain: An Essay in Archaeological Interpretation*, Cambridge

Milsted, I., 2010, 'The Roman Landscape of Blossom Street', *York Historian*, Vol 27

Miranda, F., 2002, 'Castra et Coloniae: The Role of the Roman Army in the Romanization and Urbanization of Spain', *Quaestio: The UCLA Undergraduate History Journal*

Moffat, A., 2005, *Before Scotland: The Story of Scotland Before History*, London

Mohler, S. L., 1932, 'Feminism in the Corpus Inscriptonium Latinarum', *Classical Weekly*, Vol 25 Issue 1, pp. 13-116

Monaghan, J., 1993, 'Roman Pottery from the Fortress: 9 Blake Street', *The Archaeology of York,* Vol 16 Fasc 7, York

Monaghan, J., 1997, 'Roman Pottery From York', *The Archaeology of York*, Vol 16 Fasc 8, York

Moore A., 2009, 'Hearth and Home: The Burial of Infants within Romano-British Domestic Contexts', *Childhood in the Past*, Vol 2 Issue 1, pp. 33-54

Moorhead, S.; Stuttard, D., 2012, *The Romans Who Shaped Britain*, London

Mustakallio, K., 2005, *Hoping for Continuity: Childhood Education and Death in Antiquity*, Helsinki

Myres, J., 1960, 'Pelagius and the End of Roman Rule in Britain', *Journal of Roman Studies*, Vol 50 (1-2), pp. 21-36

Neal, D. S., 2002, *Roman Mosaics of Britain: Volume I: Northern Britain*, London

Norman, A. F. 1960, *The Romans In East Yorkshire* (PDF). East Yorkshire Local History Society, Hull

Norman, A. F., 1971, 'Religion in Roman York', in Butler, *Soldier and Civilian*, pp. 143-154

O'Connor, T., 1988, 'Bones from the General Accident Site', *The Archaeology of York*, Vol 15 Fasc 2

Odahl, C. M., 2004, *Constantine and the Christian Empire*, New York

Ogilvie, R. M.; Richmond, A., (Eds), 1967, *Cornelii Taciti de Vita Agricolae*, Oxford

Olusoga, D., 2016, *Black and British: a Forgotten History*, London

Omissi, A., 2018, *Emperors and Usurpers in the late Roman Empire*, Oxford

Ordnance Survey, 1994 *Roman Britain; Historical Map and Guide*

Orlin, E., (Ed), 2015, *Routledge Encyclopedia of Ancient Mediterranean Religions*, London

Orwell, G., 1962, *Coming Up for Air*, London

Ottaway, P., 1985, '7–9 Aldwark', *Interim: the Archaeology of York*, Vol 10, pp, 13–15

Ottaway, P., 1987, *A Traveller's Guide to Roman Britain*, London

Ottaway, P., 1991, 'The Roman fortress: planning for the future', *Interim: the Archaeology of York*, Vol 16(3), pp. 3-13

Ottaway, P., 1992, *The English Heritage Book of Roman York*, London

Ottaway, P., 1996, 'Excavations and Observations on the Defences and Adjacent Sites, 1971– 90', *The Archaeology of York*, Vol 3 Fasc 3

Ottaway, P., 1997, 'The sewer trenches in Low Lane, Petergate', *Interim: the Archaeology of York* Vol 22(3), pp. 15-23

Ottaway, P, 2004, *Roman York*, Stroud

Ottaway, P., 2013, *Roman Yorkshire: People, Culture and Landscape*, Pickering

Parker, A., 2019, *The Archaeology of Roman York*, Stroud

Pearson, N. F., 1986: 'The Purey Cust Nuffield Hospital', *Interim: the Archaeology of York*, Vol 11, pp. 15-18

Pearson, N. F., 1990: 'Swinegate excavation', *Interim: the Archaeology of York,* Vol 15(1), pp. 2-10

Peddie, J., 1998, *Conquest: Roman Invasion of Britain*, Surrey

Percival, J., 1976, *The Roman Villa – An Historical Introduction*, London

Phang, S. E., 2001, *The Marriage of Roman Soldiers (13 BC–AD 235): Law and Family in the Imperial Army*, Leiden

Phillips, A. D.; Heywood B., 1995, *Excavations at York Minster, Vol. I: Roman to Norman, The Headquarters of the Roman Legionary Fortress at York and Its Exploitation in the Early Middle Ages (71–1070 AD)*, London

Philpott, R. A., 1991, *Burial Practices in Roman Britain: A Survey of Grave Treatment and Furnishing*, Oxford

Pohlsander, H. A., 1995, *Helena: Empress and Saint*, Chicago

Pohlsander, H. A., 2004, *The Emperor Constantine*, London

Potter, D. S., 2005, *The Roman Empire at Bay: AD 180–395*, New York

Potter, D. S., 2013, *Constantine the Emperor*, Oxford

Price, J., 2002, .Broken Bottles and Quartz-Sand: Glass Production in Yorkshire and the North in the Roman Period' in Wilson, P. R., (Ed) *Aspects of Industry in Roman Yorkshire and the North*, pp. 81-93, Oxford

Radley, J.,1966, 'A section of the Roman fortress wall at Barclay's Bank, St Helen's Square, York', *Yorkshire Archaeological Journal*, Vol 41, pp. 581-4

Radley, J., 1970, 'Two interval towers and new sections of the fortress wall, York', *Yorkshire Archaeological Journal*, Vol 42, pp. 399-402

Radley, J., 1972, 'Excavations on the defences of the city of York in an early medieval stone tower and the successive earth ramparts', *Yorkshire Archaeological Journal*, Vol 44, pp. 38-64

Raistrick, A. 1972, *The Romans in Yorkshire*, London

Ramm, H. G., 1956, 'Roman York: excavations of 1955', *Journal of Roman Studies*, Vol 46, pp. 76-90

Ramm, H. G., 1971, 'The End of Roman York', in Butler *Soldier and Civilian,* pp. 179-200

Reed, N., 1978, 'Pattern and Purpose in the Antonine Itinerary', *The American Journal of Philology*, Vol 99(2), pp. 228-254.

Rees, Roger, 2004, *Diocletian and the Tetrarchy*, Edinburgh

Rice Holmes, T., (1907) 'The Cassiterides, Ictis, and the British Trade in Tin' in *Ancient Britain and the Invasions of Julius Caesar*, Oxford, pp. 483-498

Richardson, A., 2004, *Theoretical Aspects of Roman Camp and Fort Design*, Michigan

Richmond, I. A., 1949, 'The British Section of the Ravenna Cosmography', *Archaeologia*, Vol 93, pp. 1-50

Rivet, A. L. F., 1964, *Town and Country in Roman Britain*, London

Rivet, A. L. F., 1970, 'The British Section of the Antonine Itinerary', *Britannia*, Vol 1, pp. 34-82, London

Rivet, A. L. F.; Smith, A., 1979, *The Place Names of Roman Britain*, London

Rodgers, B. S., 1989, 'The Metamorphosis of Constantine', *The Classical Quarterly*, Vol 39, pp. 233-246

Rollason, D. W., 1998, *Sources for York History to AD 1100*, York 'Chronology of York and the Empire', 1962, in *An Inventory of the Historical Monuments in City of York, Volume 1, Eboracum, Roman York*, London, p. 44. British History Online www.british-history.ac.uk/rchme/york/vol1/p44

'Roman York: Military Sites', 1962, in *An Inventory of the Historical Monuments in City of York*

Rose, M., 1997, 'Ashkelon's Dead Babies', *Archaeology*, Vol 50

Roskams, S, et al, 2013, 'A late Roman well at Heslington East, York: Ritual or Routine Practices?, *Internet Archaeology*, Vol 34

Roskams, S; Neal, C., 2020, *Landscape and Settlement in the Vale of York*, London

Rothe, U., 2020, *The Toga and Roman Identity*, London

Rowland, T. H., 1970, *The Romans in North Britain*, Newcastle

Rowland, T. H, 1976, *Roman Transport in the North of England*, Newcastle

Royal Commission on Historical Monuments, 1995, Welfare, H.; Swan, V. G., *Roman Camps in England – The Field Archaeology*, London

Royal Commission on Historical Monuments, 1962, *An Inventory of the Historical Monuments in the City of York, 1: Eboracum, Roman York* (1962); 5: *The Central Area* (1981)

Russell, M., 2010, *Bloodline: The Celtic Kings of Roman Britain*, Amberley

Russell, M., 2019, *UnRoman Britain: Exposing the Great Myth of Britannia*, Cheltenham

Sage, M., 2020, *Septimius Severus and the Roman Army*, Barnsley

Salway, P., 1985, *Roman Britain*, Oxford

Salway, P., 2009, *The Frontier People of Roman Britain*, Cambridge

Sampson, G., 2019, *Rome: Blood and Power*, Barnsley

Sampson, G., 2020, *The Collapse of Rome*, Barnsley

Scheidel, W., 2005, 'Marriage, Families and Survival in the Roman Imperial Army: Demographic Aspects' (PDF). *Princeton/Stanford Working Papers in Classics*, Princeton University

Shaw, C., 2021, *Women of York*, Darlington

Shotter, D. C. A., 1996, *The Roman Frontier in Britain*, Preston

Shotter, D. C. A., 1999, 'Cerialis, Agricola and the Conquest of Northern Britain', *Contrebis*, Vol 24

Shotter, D. C. A., 2000, 'Roman Coins from north-west England', Second Supplement, Centre for North-West Regional Studies, Lancaster

Sitch, B., 1992, *Roman Humberside* (Second Edition), Humberside County Council Archaeology Unit

Smith, D. J., 1976, *The Roman Mosaics from Rudston, Brantingham and Horkstow*, Hull

Smith, D. J., 2005, *Roman Mosaics at Hull*, (Third Edition), Hull

Smith, L., 16 May 2018, 'The Honest Truth: How the Romans came close but ultimately failed to conquer Scotland under Septimius Severus', *The Sunday Post*

Smith, P., 1992, 'Identification of Infanticide in Archaeological Sites', *Journal of Archaeological Science,* Vol 19, pp. 667-675

Smith, R. A., 1927, 'The Roman Pavement from Horkstow', *The British Museum Quarterly*, Vol 2, No 2, pp. 44-46

Snyder, C. A., 1996, *An Age of Tyrants*, Philadelphia

Snyder, C. A., 1998, *An Age of Tyrants: Britain and the Britons AD 400–600*, Pennsylvania

Sordi, M., 1994, *The Christians and the Roman Empire*, Oklahoma

Soren, D., 1995, 'What Killed the Babies of Lugnano?' *Archaeology*, Vol 48 No 5, pp. 43-48

Soren, D.; Soren N., 1999, *A Roman Villa and a Late Roman Infant Cemetery*, Rome

Southern, P., 1980, 'Signals versus Illumination on Roman Frontiers', *Britannia*, Vol 21, pp. 233-42

Southern, P., 2001, *The Roman Empire From Severus to Constantine*, London

Speed, G., 2014, *Towns in the dark? Urban Transformations from Late Roman Britain to Anglo-Saxon England*, Oxford

Spratt, D. A., 1990 'Prehistoric and Roman Archaeology of North-East Yorkshire', *Council for British Archaeology (CBA) Research Report No 87*, York

Spring, P., 2015, *Great Walls and Linear Barriers*, Barnsley

Stead, I. M., 1958, 'Excavations at the south corner of the Roman fortress at York, 1956', *Yorkshire Archaeological Journal*, Vol 39, pp. 515-38

Stead, I. M., 1968, 'An excavation at King's Square, York, 1957', *Yorkshire Archaeological Journal*, Vol 42, pp. 151-64

Stead, I. M., 1971, 'Yorkshire Before the Romans: Some Recent Discoveries', in Butler, *Soldier and Civilian*, pp. 21-44

Stephenson, P., 2011, *Constantine, Unconquered Emperor, Christian Victor*, London

Stevens, C. E., 1951, 'Britain between the Invasions in Grimes, W. F., (Ed), *Aspects of Archaeology in Britain and Beyond*

Stevens, C. E., 1957, 'Marcus, Gratian, Constantine', *Athenaeum*, Vol 35, pp. 316-47

Stiles J., M., 2012, 'Excavations of a Roman camp at Huntington South Moor', *York Historian*, Vol 29, York

Stockwell, M., 1990, 'Sorry about the smell but...', *Interim: the Archaeology of York*, Vol 15(1), pp. 20-5

Summerton, N., 2007, *Medicine and Health Care in Roman Britain*, Aylesbury

Swan, V. G., 1992, 'Legio VI and its men: African legionaries in Britain', *Journal of Roman Pottery Studies*, Vol 5, pp. 1-33

Swan, V. G. 2002, 'A Rhineland potter at the legionary fortress of York', in Aldhouse Green, M., *Artefacts and Archaeology. Aspects of the Celtic and Roman World*, Cardiff, pp. 190-234

Symonds, M., 2021, *Hadrian's Wall: Creating Division*, London

Syvanne, I., 2020, *Military History of Late Rome*, Barnsley

Taylor, J., 2007, 'An Atlas of Roman Rural Settlement in England', *Council for British Archaeology Report* No 151, York

Taylor, J. W., 1998, *Tacitus and the Boudican Revolt*, Dublin

Terry, J. E. H., 1909, *The Book of the York Pageant*, York

Thompson, E., 1982, 'Zosimus 6. 10. 2 and the Letters of Honorius' *The Classical Quarterly*, Vol 32 Issue 2, pp. 445-462

Thompson, E. A., 1977, 'Britain, AD 406–410', *Britannia*, Vol 8, pp. 303-318

Thompson, E. A., 1984, *St Germanus of Auxerre and the End of Roman Britain*, Woodbridge

Tilley, E., 2018, *Old Collections, New Questions: Researching the Roman Collections of the Yorkshire Museum*, York

Tillott, P. M., (Ed), 1961, 'A History of Yorkshire: The City of York', *Victoria County History*, York

Todd, M., 1973, *The Coritani*, Stroud

Todd, M., 1985, *Roman Britain*, London

Todd, M., 2004. 'The Claudian Conquest and its Consequences' In Todd, M., *A Companion to Roman Britain*, Oxford

Tomlin, R. S. O., 2014, '"Drive away the cloud of plague": a Greek amulet from Roman London'. In Collins, R., *Life in the Limes: Studies of the people and objects of the Roman frontiers*, Oxford, pp. 197-205

Treggiari, S., 2002, *Roman Social History*, London

Van Dam, R., 2007, *The Roman Revolution of Constantine*, Cambridge

Verboven, K., 2007, 'Good for Business. The Roman Army and the Emergence of a "Business Class" in the Northwestern Provinces of the Roman Empire (1st century BCE–3rd century CE)' in n De Blois, L., (Ed), *The Impact of the Roman Army (200 BC–AD 476). Economic, Social, Political, Religious and Cultural Aspects*, Leiden, pp. 295-314

Wace. H, 1886–1900, *Nicene and Post-Nicene Fathers*, New York pp. 499-500

Wacher, J. S., 1971, 'Yorkshire Towns in the Fourth Century', in Butler, *Soldier and Civilian*, pp. 165-178

Wacher, J. S., 1974, *The Towns of Roman Britain*, London

Ward, J., 1973, 'The British Sections of the "Notitia Dignitatum": An Alternative Interpretation', *Britannia*, Vol 4, pp. 253-263

Webster, G. A., 1965, *The Roman Conquest of Britain*, London

Webster, G. A., 1971, 'A Hoard of Roman Military Equipment from Fremington Hagg in Butler, *Soldier and Civilian*, pp. 107-126

Webster, G. A., 1985, *Rome Against Caratacus: the Roman Campaigns in Britain AD 48–58*, Abingdon

Webster, G. A., 1991, *The Cornovii*, Stroud

Webster, J, 1999, 'At the End of the World: Druidic and Other Revitalization Movements in Post-conquest Gaul and Britain', *Britannia,* Vol 30, pp. 1-20

Wenham, L. P., 1961: 'Excavations and discoveries adjoining the south-west wall of the Roman legionary fortress in Feasgate, York, 1955–57', *Yorkshire Archaeological Journal*, Vol 40, pp. 329-50

Wenham, L. P., 26 May 1962, 'Roman and Viking Discoveries in York', *Illustrated London News*

Wenham, L. P., 1962: 'Excavations and discoveries within the legionary fortress in Davygate, York, 1955–58', *Yorkshire Archaeological Journal*, Vol 40, pp. 507-87

Wenham, L. P., 1968, 'Discoveries in King's Square, York, 1963', *Yorkshire Archaeological Journal,* Vol 42, pp. 165-8

Wenham, L. P., 1971, 'The Beginnings of Roman York' in Butler *Soldier and Civilian*, pp. 45-54

Wenham, L. P., 1972, 'Excavations in Low Petergate, York, 1957–8', *Yorkshire Archaeological Journal*, Vol 44, pp. 65-113

Wenham, L. P., 1978, *Eboracum*, London

Whitwell, J. B., 1976, The Church Street Sewer and an Adjacent Building, *The Archaeology of York*, Vol 3 Fasc 1, York

Wilmott, T., 2008, *The Roman Amphitheatre in Britain*, Stroud

Wilmott, T., (Ed), 2009, *Roman Amphitheatres and Spectacula; A 21st-Century Perspective* Papers from an International Conference held at Chester, 16-18 February 2007, Oxford

Wilson, B., 2005, *The City Walls and Castles of York: The Pictorial Evidence*, Archaeology of York Supplementary, York

Wilson, P., 2003, *Aspects of Industry in Roman Yorkshire and the North*, Oxford

Winterbottom, M., (Ed), 1978, *Gildas, The Ruin of Britain and Other Works*, Chichester

Witts, P., 2005, *Mosaics in Roman Britain*, Stroud

Wood, I., 1987, 'The Fall of the Western Empire and the End of Roman Britain', *Britannia,* Vol 18, pp. 251-262

Wood, I., 1995: 'Turning a fortress into a cathedral', *British Archaeology*, Vol 7, Issue 7

Woods, A., 17 October 2018, *Constantine the Great and the Wold Newton Hoard*. Lecture given at the York Architectural and York Archaeological Society Meeting

Wright, D. H., 1987, 'The True Face of Constantine the Great' *Dumbarton Oaks Papers*, Vol 41, pp. 493-507

Wright, T., 1902, *The Celt, the Roman, and the Saxon: A History of the Early Inhabitants of Britain, Down to the Conversion of the Anglo-Saxons to Christianity; Illustrated by the Ancient Remains Brought to Light by Recent Research*, London

Wright, R. P., 1976, 'Tile stamps of the sixth legion found in Britain', *Britannia*, Vol 7, pp. 224-35

Wright, R. P., 1978, 'Tile stamps of the ninth legion found in Britain', *Britannia*, Vol 9, pp. 379-82

Websites

www.british-history.ac.uk/rchme/york/vol1/ – An inventory of Roman monuments in York and the access roads to the city.

www.digforeboracum.co.uk/ – York's forthcoming Roman Quarter attraction.

https://digyork.com/ – DIG is a hands-on archaeological adventure giving children the chance to become trainee 'diggers' and discover the most exciting artefacts from 2,000 years of York's history. Tours last one hour.

www.finds.org.uk/ – Portable Antiquities Scheme (PAS) database run by the British Museum and National Museum Wales to encourage the recording of archaeological objects found by members of the public in England and Wales. So far the scheme's network has recorded over one million objects, all of which are accessible via the PAS database.

www.historicalpageants.ac.uk/pageants/ – Bartie, A., et al, *The Redress of the Past: Historical Pageants in Britain*, 1905–2016 (published online 2016).

www.northofthetyne.co.uk/HWC1.html – Hadrian's Wall east to west.

www.paulchrystal.com

www.pastscape.org.uk/

www.penelope.uchicago.edu/Thayer/E/Gazetteer/Periods/Roman/Topics/Engineering/roads/Britain/_Texts/CODROM/4*.html#9 – Reproduction from *Roman Roads in Britain* by Thomas Codrington, published by the Society for Promoting Christian Knowledge, London, 1903.

www.romaninscriptionsofbritain.org – Hosts Volume One of *The Roman Inscriptions of Britain*, R. G. Collingwood's and R. P. Wright's magisterial edition of 2,401 monumental inscriptions from Britain found prior to 1955. It also incorporates all Addenda and Corrigenda published in the 1995 reprint of *RIB* (edited by R. S. O. Tomlin) and the annual survey of inscriptions published in Britannia since.

www.romanroads.org/historicalbackground.html – Roman Roads Research Association

www.romanroads.org/rrragazetteer/rr72b/rr72b.html

www.thesebonesofmine.wordpress.com/category/york-osteoarchaeology/

www.vindolanda.csad.ox.ac.uk/exhibition/history-3_to.shtml – Vindolanda tablets online.

www.web.archive.org/web/20061231090447/http://www.roman-britain.org/tribes/brigantes.htm

www.en.wikipedia.org/wiki/Roman_sites_in_Great_Britain – By modern county.

www.en.wikipedia.org/wiki/List_of_Roman_place_names_in_Britain

www.en.wikipedia.org/wiki/List_of_Latin_place_names_in_Britain

www.en.wikipedia.org/wiki/ Roman roads in Britannia

www.yayas.org.uk – Yorkshire Architectural and York Archaeological Society

www.yorkarchaeology.co.uk – York Archaeological Trust

www.yorkarchaeology.co.uk/case-studies/newington-hotel/-

www.yorkarchaeology.co.uk/case-studies-blog/2019/6/3/excavating-eboracums-common-people

www.yorkarchaeology.co.uk/wp-content/uploads/2017/08/Selected-Roman-Small-Finds-from-the-Cemetery-at-nos.-3-and-6-Driffield-Terrace-York-1.pdf)

www.yorkosteoarch.co.uk/ – York Osteoarchaeology

General Index

Acheron, plate 13

Acta Diurna, 51

Administration and bureaucracy, 98, 107, 113, 115, 142, 144

Adminius, 37, 52

Aelia Aeliana, 125, 204-205, 211

Aelia Severa, 189, 204

Aelius Spartianus, 121, 220

Agricola, plate 4, xvii, 46, 51, 75ff, 76, 80, 81ff, 93, 105, 195, 250-251

Alaric, 160, 162, 164, 165, 166-167

Albinus, Clodius, 111-112, 113-114, 119, 130

Albion, 3, 5, 7

Aldborough, 62, 63, 64, 77, 107, 108, 109-110, 131

Alexander the Great, 18

Allectus, 104, 137, 138, 145

Amphitheatre, Aldborough, 110

Amphitheatre, York? 220-221

Ancient Britons, plate 1

Anglian Tower, 97

annona militaris, 240

Antonine Itinerary, xix, 89, 239-240, 241

Antonine Plague, 109, 112, 187-188; Appendix 12

Antonine Wall, plate 6; 50, 99, 104, 107-108, 111, 188

Antoninus Pius, 10

Arbeia (South Shields), 115-116

Archaeology of Roman York, 172ff

Arciacon, 196

Arimanius, 176-177

Aristotle, 5, 209

Army, of the Britons, 60

Army, Roman in Britain, 20, 21-23, 44, 59, 93, 101-102, 135, 163, 214-215

Asclepiodotus, 138, 145

Atrebates, 38

Attis, 179

Augustus, 20, 21, 34, 35-39, 47-50, 55, 57, 59, 61, 69, 103, 132, 140-142, 167, 190, 216

Aulus Didius Gallus, 65

Aulus Platorius Nepos, 103

Aulus Plautius, 39, 52, 56, 60

Aurelius Super, 189

Auxiliaries, 102, Appendix 3

basilica, 93, 97

BAME, 123, 185

Barbarian Conspiracy, The, 158

Bath house, 92, 94, 173, 187, 198

Belgae, 11, 12-13, 24, 57

Bellona, 121

Blakey, David, 200

Booty, 18, 29, 37, 48, 58, 84, 94, 137, 164

Index of Places in York and Nearby